The Liar's Ball

The Liar's Ball

The Extraordinary Saga of How One Building Broke the World's Toughest Tycoons

Vicky Ward

WILEY

Published by John Wiley & Sons, Inc., Hoboken, New Jersey.
Published simultaneously in Canada.

For general information on our other products and services or for technical support, please contact our Customer Care Department within the United States at (800) 762-2974, outside the United States at (317) 572-3993 or fax (317) 572-4002.

Wiley publishes in a variety of print and electronic formats and by print-on-demand. Some material included with standard print versions of this book may not be included in e-books or in print-on-demand. If this book refers to media such as a CD or DVD that is not included in the version you purchased, you may download this material at http://booksupport.wiley.com. For more information about Wiley products, visit www.wiley.com.

Library of Congress Cataloging-in-Publication Data:

ISBN 978-1-118-29531-1 (Cloth)
ISBN 978-1-118-41987-8 (ebk)
ISBN 978-1-118-42151-2 (ebk)

Printed in the United States of America
10 9 8 7 6 5 4 3 2 1

For Richard

Contents

Preface

Every year, toward the end of January, around 2,000 members of the New York real estate industry gather in the Hilton Hotel to celebrate the Real Estate Board of New York's annual gala: an event affectionately known by its attendees as "the Liar's Ball."

The dress code is black tie, but that's the only nod to decorum.

The senior U.S. senator for New York, Charles Schumer, is a regular, as are the presiding mayor and New York's archbishop, John Cardinal O'Connor. The dignitaries sit on the dais and, during dinner, one by one, they rise to make speeches, but they don't expect to be heard by an openly disdainful audience that is busily clinking glasses and shouting over and at each other, boasting about last year's profits and deals.

The public figures are glad, for once, that there are no national TV crews on hand to record this ritualistic humiliation. Senator Schumer grins while he talks, trying to appear as if he is in on the joke. But there is no joke. The diners talk over him and the rest simply because they've got other priorities.

Every year, for just one night, these wheelers-and-dealers come to make nice with competitors they cheerfully deride the rest of the year. They come to pick up a deal or maybe five. And although they often wish they could exist without their peers—their fellow pirates—this is an incestuous club, where connections to the right partners, lawyers, bankers, and brokers are key for deal flow.

So they come to the Hilton to schmooze, to pretend, to shout. "It almost doesn't matter who the speakers are, because I've never seen—as much as I love my colleagues—a ruder group of people than at this banquet," Peter Hauspurg, the chairman and CEO of Eastern Consolidated, told the *New York Observer* in 2012.

To an outsider, the behavior seems bizarre. To witness a mob in tuxedos and tulle yelling over a U.S. senator? To hear someone whisper, "I can't stand this guy; I fired him a year ago," before turning to monopolize his prey with a serpentine charm? To the cognoscenti at the Liar's Ball, dissembling is as natural and necessary as breathing.

This party celebrates characteristics most of us condemn: brashness, mendacity, greed. . . . On this one night the industry revels in who and what it really is and it does not care who sees.

Welcome to the Liar's Ball. It's rough, it's vulgar, and it's a riveting show.

Cast of Characters

The Early Years
Principal: William Magear "Boss" Tweed
Principal: Judge P. Henry Dugro
Principal: Harry S. Black
Principal: Conrad Hilton
Principal: William Zeckendorf

The Rayne/Benattar Years
Principal: Max Rayne
Principal: Cecilia Benattar
Principals' lawyers: Jesse Wolff, Martin Ginsberg
Principals' spouses: Jack Benattar, Michael Schwartz (Benattar),
    Lady Jane Vane-Tempest-Stewart (Rayne)
Principals' children: The Honorable Robert "Robbie" Rayne;
    Naomi, Simon, Jessica, and Judith Benattar
Principals' tenants: Mary Wells Lawrence, Estée and Leonard Lauder,
    Ira Millstein, Harvey Miller, General Motors
Principals' broker: Harry Macklowe
Principals' architect: Edward Durrell Stone
Principals' supporting cast: James Nagy, Geoffrey Wharton

The Disque Deane Years
Principal: Disque Deane
Principal's wives: Anne Delafield, Marjorie Schlesinger, Carol Gram
Principal's acknowledged children: Marjorie Deane, Kathryn Deane,
   Disque Deane Jr., Walter Deane, Anne Deane, and Carl Deane
Principal's unacknowledged child: Hare Deane
Principal's mentor: André Meyer
Principal's senior executives: Hans Mautner, Jerry O'Connor,
   G. Martin Fell, Warren Hamer, Thomas Zacharias
Principal's mistress; Barbara Koz
Seller to Principal: Harry Macklowe
Principal's supporting cast: Roderick Johnson
Principal's business partners: Fred and Donald J. Trump

The Simon / Trump / Hilbert Years
Principal: Donald J. Trump
Principal: Stephen Hilbert
Principal: David Simon
Principals' leading ladies: Melania Trump, Tomisue Hilbert,
   Louann Hilbert
Principal's supporting cast: Rhona Graff (Trump)
Principals' senior executives: Abraham Wallach (Trump),
   George Ross (Trump), Ngaire Cuneo (Hilbert), Rollin Dick
   (Hilbert), James Adams (Hilbert)
Principal's advisor: Robert B. Horowitz (Trump)
Principal's would-be broker: Rita Jenrette
Principal's lenders: Lehman Brothers (Mark Walsh, Charles Schoenherr)
Principals' opponents: Charles Cremens, Reed Oslan,
   JB Carlson (Hilbert), John Menard (Hilbert)
Principals' competitors: Michael Fascitelli, Steven Roth,
   Samuel Zell (Trump)
Principal's friend-turned-nemesis: Benjamin V. Lambert (Trump)

The Macklowe Years
Principal: Harry B. Macklowe
Principal's leading lady: Linda Macklowe
Principal's family members: William S. Macklowe (spouse Julie),
   Elizabeth Macklowe (Kent Swig)

Principal's supporting cast: Liliana Coriasco

Principal's lawyers: Robert Sorin, Joseph Forstadt, Jonathan L. Mechanic

Principal's financial broker: Robert Horowitz

General Motors Building sales brokers: Wayne Maggin, Benjamin Lambert, Roy March, Douglas Harmon

Principal's lenders: Eric Schwartz, Robert Verrone, Andrew Bednar, Peter J. Briger, Steve Stuart, Roger Cozzi, Steven Mnuchin

Principal's design team: Daniel Shannon

Principal's chief rivals: Michael Fascitelli, Steven Roth, Sheldon Solow, and representing Solow: David Boies, Andrew Hayes, Steven M. Cherniak

Principal's art dealer: Andrew Fabricant

Principal's partners at Apple: Steve Jobs, George Blankenship; Peter Bohlin and Karl Backus (architects)

Some of Principal's tenants: Joseph Perella, Leonard Lauder, Sanford Weill, Carl Icahn, Weil, Gotshal & Manges

Sellers of Equity Office Properties (EOP) to Principal: Jonathan D. Gray, Anthony Myers

Former owner of EOP: Samuel F. Zell

The Zuckerman Years
Principal: Mortimer Zuckerman
Principal: The Safra family
Principal: Zhang Xin

Introduction

Many people have asked me over the past three years what this book is about. For months I hesitated and stumbled when answering. I knew it was about a group of flamboyant real estate tycoons whose rise-and-fall stories spanned 150 years and whose connections to one another were entwined in their desire for a plot of land upon which stands a gleaming white marble tower, the most expensive office building in the United States: the General Motors (GM) Building.

I knew that the first of the overreachers was Tammany Hall scoundrel William Magear "Boss" Tweed, whose lust for lucre meant he wound up bankrupt in jail. After him came Harry S. Black, America's most prolific builder in 1900. Black committed suicide in the house he used to own with his first wife, a woman he had foolishly betrayed and lost. Then there was the towering, talented William Zeckendorf, a man who expanded the importance of the job description *developer*, but who also died alone and bankrupt. There followed the urbane British Lord Max Rayne and his colorful, indefatigable female chief executive, Cecilia Benattar, the so-called "housewife tycoon" who brazenly battled New York's social and business elite, then disappeared as suddenly as she'd arrived. There was

Disque D. Deane, a brutal man who, it was whispered, as good as killed his wife with cruelty. Next came David Simon, the mall heir; he was quickly followed by Stephen "Steve" C. Hilbert, the one-time insurance salesman from Indianapolis who helicoptered five miles to work each day—and married a woman who jumped, practically naked, out of a cake. His partner was Donald J. Trump, who needs no introduction. And then came Harry Macklowe, the most charismatic of these characters and perhaps the most tragic.

Why do their stories matter? Why should anyone care about a group of rich guys competing for a very expensive building? What became both bewildering and absorbing as I researched this book were the extraordinary lengths to which these men went to achieve their goals.

Dream chasing, it turns out, in the world of global real estate is a sordid pursuit.

In these pages, lying, cheating, stealing, suing, and tax evasion are just humdrum ways of business. Friendships and alliances get made to be broken; a man's word is never his bond; partners routinely sue one another; wives are discarded and cheated on; but so too are bankers, colleagues, and brokers.

The boorish behavior at the Liar's Ball, the party that the Real Estate Board of New York throws itself each year, had intrigued me when I attended the event. It also paled in comparison to the roughness I would unearth. And yet . . . .

Tempering the grotesque intemperance was the humanity, the vulnerability that these characters—for the most part—revealed.

I realized as I combed through more than 200 interviews with my crowd of "rough riders" (as the New York real estate deal makers were once called—there was even a room in the Roosevelt Hotel where they negotiated over lunch) that my fascination with them lay as much in their insecurities as in their ambitions. And that one explained the other.

And whatever faults these people share, these leaders of the dance at the Liar's Ball have at least danced.

A friend of Harry Macklowe's long-suffering wife, Linda, put it this way: "This is not a normal world. . . . None of these people are fuckin' normal. And, again, what is normal? They're all gifted in such a way that they are unique, disturbed individuals. . . . And the level of disturbance is oftentimes about how successful they are."

Chapter 1

Stealing the Spotlight

I think that I've been able to lead and have a high enough profile where people say, "Hmmm, how would Harry Macklowe do this? He's my hero."

—Harry Macklowe

He spotted his chance the night the letters vanished.

They were there, as usual, one dusky summer's evening in Manhattan, but the next morning they were gone. All of them. Their disappearance immediately spurred frantic, gossipy phone calls between the major real estate offices in New York City. Everyone knew the significance, but very few knew what had happened. There was speculative chatter about a "midnight raid," even a "robbery."

Bizarrely, some of the garish letters began to show up on office walls around New York, where they still remain. Their proud owners were coy about how they had acquired their trophies. Was Donald J. Trump, the flame-haired, flamboyant developer, furious? No one dared ask him. All they knew was that the letters' disappearance marked the end of his most cherished dream.

For Harry Macklowe, it was the beginning of a metamorphosis.

■ ■ ■

June 2003. As the sun rose over Manhattan, passers-by, commuters, tourists, and members of the audience assembled for CBS's morning show noticed that something was dramatically different about the 50-story, white marble edifice soaring above midtown known as the General Motors (GM) Building.

In almost every other detail, the legendary and much-coveted trophy building looked as it had for years: the white, minimalistic tower with the small inset windows that gave tenants spectacular views of Central Park; there was the glass box of FAO Schwarz, the iconic toy store, on the southwest corner of the building's first floor. There was the plaza—that "problematic plaza," as industry insiders and architects had always called it because no one had found a sensible, or profitable, use for it—stretching out to Fifth Avenue.

But the building's most jarring detail: brass letters, each four feet tall, spelling out TRUMP—the ultimate vanity plate—was gone.

For five years, Donald Trump's name had been bolted onto the base of the otherwise spartan façade designed by the late Edward Durrell Stone. The brass letters ran around the creamy wall like a golden ticker tape, a constant reminder of the building's co-owner and manager. The sunlight had reflected off those letters so brightly that senior executives at CBS, whose morning show was shot in the building's ground-floor studios, successfully negotiated with Trump to tone them down. The glare was "blinding," they said, and they were not in the business of "advertising Trump."

When he heard about the negotiations, Ira M. Millstein, a white-haired lawyer who works on the 32nd floor of the GM Building—at Weil Gotshal & Manges, the building's oldest extant tenant—had chuckled gently with his colleague, the well-known bankruptcy lawyer Harvey R. Miller. The two of them had tangled with Trump on other matters. They suspected the issue would irk him.

Some of the GM tenants felt that Trump's initials marred not just the aesthetics but the spirit of their tower. The building wasn't just another ho-hum high-rise. No, this was the GM Building, a symbol of America at its finest.

She had been commissioned in 1964 by General Motors, then the biggest company in the United States—and, therefore, in the world. GM had occupied 26 floors of the building, which took up an entire city block between Fifth and Madison Avenues and 58th and 59th Streets. Her location—where Central Park meets the heart of both commercial and residential New York—was, like her name, unbeatable. Unsurprisingly, the world's alpha dogs rented office space there. The blue-chip brands included Estée Lauder, Carl Icahn, the hedge fund Perry Capital, the talent-management firm IMG, and the Wall Street legend Sanford "Sandy" I. Weill.

Trump didn't usually buy office buildings—but he viewed the GM Building as an exception; she was the fitting monument to his ambition. In 1998 he had finally found a way to buy her by partnering with the Indianapolis-based insurance giant Conseco, run by a friend of his, Stephen "Steve" C. Hilbert.

Conseco put up most of the money, but Trump became the face of the building. He took out an ad in the *New York Times* that read "$700,000,000 . . . THE GM BUILDING . . . A 50-story 2 million square foot office building . . . Developer Donald J. Trump." The ad ran two days in a row because initially someone forgot to insert Trump's middle initial, J., a detail he is most particular about.

He instantly set to work "Trumpifying" the tower. The building's white lobby interior was replaced with a deep green marble. There were plaques on the wall that read "The General Motors Building at Trump International Plaza." He tried to evict Houlihan's, the chain restaurant in the basement, because, it was said, he hated the smell of greasy food. He raised the sunken plaza to street level, and made it pristine and pleasant to sit in for the first time in 40 years.

But he got stopped just as he was accelerating. In 2000, Hilbert left Conseco; he had made a disastrous bet on Green Tree Financial, which provided financing for low-income housing. Conseco went bankrupt. Trump negotiated to buy the building from his partner, but in the fall of 2001 those talks stalled; the partnership grew distinctly less friendly, and

Trump entered into two years of intense legal battles. In the summer of 2003, Conseco won the building. An Illinois bankruptcy court awarded the insurance firm the right to retain a broker, Eastdil Realty, to sell her on the open market. To make the best deal possible, Conseco knew it was imperative that the world would know Trump was out. His name *had* to come off the building.

The man tasked with making this happen was Charles "Chuck" H. Cremens, a plainspoken Bostonian.

Cremens told Trump directly that the letters he'd put up now belonged to Conseco, and that as a courtesy, Trump could remove them himself, or Cremens would do it for him. The negotiations were described by a lawyer for Conseco, Reed S. Oslan, from the Chicago firm of Kirkland & Ellis, as resembling a "tennis match." "Chuck's one of the best negotiators ever. So [Trump's side] made some offer. Chuck would say no. [This went on] for about four or five hours."

Cremens would later admit he underestimated the significance of those letters for Trump. Before the two sides reached a formal agreement, Trump had sent a team out into the darkness to remove them. "I wanted them to come off in a dignified way," Trump said in an interview. "It was the right thing to do. I no longer owned the building."

Trump's team put up "big sheets" to obscure the dismantling—and then the letters were given to Cremens, who dispersed them; and it was this that, people speculated, must have angered him—though Trump says not so. "I was sad to lose the building, but not angry about the letters."

Over at Eastdil, Wayne Maggin, the executive in charge of the sales process, has the "M." Reed Oslan has an "R." Mary Anne Tighe, the CEO of CBRE, Inc., has the "T."

Cremens was baffled as to why it had been so easy to get the letters removed—why "we had accomplished so much."

A month later, that mystery was solved. Something new had come into Trump's life that he loved as much as—or even more than—the GM Building. He was shooting the first season of NBC's *The Apprentice*, the reality show in which contestants vie for a position in Trump's organization. The show would set Trump up as an international figurehead businessman who repeatedly got to say, "You're fired."

And just like that, Donald Trump was extricated, and the GM Building was once again on the auction block. Eastdil prepared to send out its offering book. They all felt this was going to be the priciest commercial real estate bidding war ever. Cremens noted that someone would undoubtedly pay an extraordinary price for something he called the ultimate bauble of "ego gratification."

■ ■ ■

When Harry Macklowe heard that Donald Trump was out of the GM Building, he pounced. If this small, soft-spoken, slightly shambolic-looking, moon-faced man permanently attached to a Starbucks cup was ever going to vault himself out of the shallows of the New York real estate pool and into the spotlight, now was the time. He had waited 40 years for this moment. "I thought [the GM Building] was the best building in the world," he'd say later. "I knew exactly what to do with it."

On June 6, 2003, he tried to muscle his way to the front of the line. He phoned Cremens and asked him what it would take to "pre-empt" the bidding on the building. Cremens brusquely shot him down; he told Macklowe that "we don't do pre-empt." Eastdil would be running a sealed bid process. Macklowe would have to play by the same rules as everyone else.

Macklowe had anticipated this. He had also anticipated that no one considered him a serious candidate to buy the most expensive and prestigious office building in the world. A deal for over $1 billion would require an enormous amount of leverage. Macklowe didn't have much money (in real estate terms), and, to make matters worse, he had limited options with most real estate lenders. Maggin knew there were "certain bankers, including Lehman Brothers, who were not prepared to do business with Harry."

Ben Lambert, Eastdil's tall founder and chairman, liked Macklowe but saw through his charm and affectations. Each time Macklowe pulled out his little black sketchbook filled with his riffs on architectural drawings, Lambert studied it politely, but remained skeptical. "I've often thought that there must be another book in which [Harry] wrote down what he really thought," Lambert says. He would not be gulled into selling the building to anyone who couldn't come up with the right money and terms.

■ ■ ■

Macklowe knew his reputation, but he also knew that some people—quite a few even—thought his charm and taste redeemed him. "He can be elegantly articulate in the way he draws out his vision on a napkin or talks about a building," says Douglas "Doug" Harmon, Eastdil's most prolific broker.

Macklowe has always deployed his charisma as skillfully as a wartime general deploying his artillery, treating laughter, tears, gentility, vulnerability, and jokes as different parts of his arsenal. "He is quite capable of bursting into tears if he thinks that will help him get what he wants," says Harmon, smiling.

An afternoon with Harry Macklowe is like spending time with the personification of *Vanity Fair* magazine: at one moment highbrow, the next low, always, always intriguing. Among the numerous topics he talks about: He'd love to buy the American rights to the Smart car. He imported a few for six months and lobbied hard, but Mercedes stopped him, "and then I thought I should get back to my day job." He'd like to own a hotel. He did once—Hotel Macklowe in Times Square on West 44th Street. He liked getting to know the staff, and hearing them say, "Good morning, Mr. Macklowe, how are you?" "How could I not like it?" asks Macklowe. "It was a show every day."

He loves to tell stories—about buildings, about himself, about his friends. He enjoys being with writers, artists, and performers. He collects them much in the way Andy Warhol assembled his Factory crew.

He gets lost in reveries on Mies van der Rohe; the precision of a Henri Matisse drawing ("his lines . . . the pencil seems to never leave the page"); the modernist influence of Hungarian-born architect Marcel Breuer; the details of Paris's Place Vendôme and Place de La Concorde. In moments of tension or if he wants to change the subject, he breaks into songs—funny, nostalgic show tunes, often by Cole Porter. He talks about art; he and his wife Linda (whom he describes as "very clever") have accumulated a "massive" contemporary art collection that includes works by Alberto Giacometti, Mark Rothko, and Willem de Kooning.

Then there are his endless off-color jokes delivered with the panache of a stand-up comic. Macklowe slips into an Irish accent while delivering them, as if distancing himself from the filth of his utterances. The accent and the sparkle in his eyes disguise, temporarily, the sordid, mostly sexist nature of what he is saying.

"There are layers of darkness to Harry," says Doug Harmon. "There's a complexity that's difficult to explain."

■ ■ ■

That dark side was first exposed in what is commonly called the "SRO debacle." As Macklowe and his wife moaned to close friends, for more than 20 years it wasn't possible to read a news item about Macklowe without finding a mention of the incident.

SRO stands for single-room occupancy—or, according to Joseph "Joe" L. Forstadt, one of Macklowe's lawyers, an apartment building full of "rooms without a bathroom."

In 1984 Macklowe put a $1 million down payment on two Manhattan SROs from a developer named Sol Goldman—with the intention of demolishing them along with two neighboring structures and erecting a 38-story hotel, the Hotel Macklowe.

Then the city government under the administration of the mayor, Edward "Ed" Koch, imposed a moratorium on such destruction, since most SRO inhabitants had nowhere else to live.

Macklowe needed to move quickly—before the ban took effect. He recalled, "We had instructed our construction department to get their demolition permits and move forward. For some reason, they dropped the ball. They promised me that they had all the papers in hand."

On January 7, 1985, with only hours left before the law changed, a cold winter's night darkness fell—as did the four large buildings at 145, 147, and 149–151 West 44th Street. A crane was moved into the street and one by one the buildings were pulled down. Their destruction created so much debris that one onlooker said the air "looked like fog."

Not only had the permits not been "in hand," but the gas had been left on. It was a miracle no one was killed.

There was an immediate outcry. The Real Estate Board of New York held an emergency meeting. Macklowe waived immunity and appeared before a grand jury. Reports of his testimony stated that he categorically knew—as opposed to what he now says—that his team did *not* have a permit. Still, he maintained he absolutely thought the gas was off. "Whether I had a demolition permit or not, I relied on and presumed that my demolition man would do a proper job," he told the grand jury.

His vice president for construction, John Tassi, would admit he had given the go-ahead to the owner of the construction company, Edward "Eddie" Garofolo, *knowing* that the permits weren't in place and that the gas wasn't turned off. Both Tassi and Garofolo were charged with reckless endangerment. (Garofolo would later be killed in a mob hit.) Tassi, who now lives in North Carolina, refused to discuss the incident for this book.

Macklowe was not indicted.

The foreman of the grand jury told the court that "our concern is that the man who initiated the whole thing hasn't been charged." District Attorney Robert Morgenthau told a reporter for the *New York Times* there hadn't been sufficient evidence to indict Macklowe.

The city sued Macklowe, who settled and paid a fine of $2 million; he was banned from building on the site for four years.

"We have sent a loud and clear message to real-estate developers," Mayor Koch said. "You cannot shield yourself from the consequences of your misconduct by having others do your dirty work."

Just two years later, the Hotel Macklowe was under construction.

How? Why? Editorials in the *New York Times* criticized the government and called the saga "the Macklowe Mess."

Harry Macklowe had beaten the system with the help of a "very, very brilliant attorney" named Joe Forstadt of Stroock, Stroock & Lavan, who argued the case all the way to the United States Supreme Court.

In a rather garbled way, the city now stated there had been a muddle. It had been "unconstitutional" to ban Macklowe from building on the site.

Macklowe moved on blithely. "What a privilege it is to go to Washington and argue before a seven-judge panel," he said in the summer of 2013, about his visit to the Supreme Court.

■ ■ ■

The SROs left a stench about him. Subsequent headlines almost always conjured up a ruthless, sinister profiteer. The story lines were variations on a theme: He bought buildings; he lost them. He fought with tenants, with everyone. He defaulted on loans. He played hardball. Some of the headlines: In 1995 he was embroiled in a long-running border dispute in East Hampton with neighbor Martha Stewart over a row of trees he put up—and she took down. In 1997, as he was clearing a building site at Second Avenue and 53rd Street, he evicted 13 rent-controlled tenants, including an 82-year-old blind man, Carl Steindler, who compared the eviction to a death sentence. Later that year, bricks fell onto the sidewalk from a building Macklowe had bought on Madison Avenue. And, again, he was lucky no one got killed.

It seemed he couldn't outrun his origins. Macklowe was an outsider, a hustling striver in a world of very rich men. The son of a textile converter, he used leverage—borrowed money—to buy properties, while many of those around him—the children or grandchildren of rich families with names like Rudin, Durst, and LeFrak—"viewed leverage, at least on a grand scale, as a last resort." But what was Macklowe, a college dropout from upstate New York, to do? He wasn't rich and he was in a hurry. "I was impatient," he says of his early days in the business. Leverage was the only way he could play in New York City's rocketing real estate market.

By the late 1990s, his net worth was around $100 million. But he wanted much more. "I just . . . love it; it's a challenge, and I love being the designer. I love being the architect. I love being able to execute my vision, and I think my vision—this is obnoxious—I just think my level of taste is better than most architects'. I think I have my finger on what it is that I want to do, and the actor in me, that little bit of bravado, all of that shit which just bubbles up, gives me a lot of gratification, and kinda drives me to it. So I could talk passionately about how this [building at 610 Broadway] was a car wash, and I bought it from a Russian Jew. I did this, and I did that. But what I'm most proud of is the graceful lines of that building, the glass elevator there. Nobody has a glass elevator to the street. This is hot shit," he said.

A friend of the Macklowe's put it this way: "There's a German expression, *Profilneurose*; it means literally 'fear of invisibility.' That's what Harry had. He wanted to be recognized for the attributes he saw so clearly in himself."

■ ■ ■

In June 2003, Harry the scrapper wasn't about to give up the idea of owning the GM Building just because he might have been the poorest man in the bidding. He had said he was going to buy the GM Building, and he would. He believed he had a plan—a vision—for how to make the building more profitable.

"A very clever entrepreneur who sees something there that somebody else doesn't see . . . has the advantage," he says. "I perceived that to be the best piece of real estate in the city; . . . it was being sorely neglected, there was room to grow the rent, there was room to change the building."

In a spin that only the very bold or very delusional can manage, Macklowe saw his lack of funding as another advantage: "I didn't have to sit with a loan committee. I didn't have to sit with an investment committee. . . . I could be much more nimble than a larger company. . . . I could feint, weave, adapt."

"Why do I do what I do?" he asked rhetorically one sunny afternoon in his office. "I do it for the money, the drama. And the satisfaction of being right."

Chapter 2

Alpha Males

You need people who are loyal to you if you are an entrepreneur.

—Eric Schwartz

I t was time for Harry Macklowe to call the *consiglieri*—the two advisers he had relied on more than anyone else since the mid-1990s. Both men were called "Rob."

Robert "Rob" Sorin was a partner at the Fried, Frank, Harris, Shriver & Jacobson law firm. He was dark-haired, bespectacled, and polished. He and Macklowe had begun working together when Sorin was a lawyer at the real estate law firm of Robinson, Silverman, Pearce, Aronsohn, and Berman. Macklowe followed him to the broader, more international firm of Fried Frank in 1997. That was a typical Macklowe move. He was fiercely loyal to people, not institutions.

And it was easy to be loyal to someone so talented and useful: Sorin was a rising star. A graduate of Georgetown University, he had made his mark on the New York City market by executing the sale of the Metropolitan Transportation Authority (MTA)'s New York Coliseum— a 3.43-acre site to the southwest of Central Park—for $337 million. He had accomplished this after a decade of volatile negotiations among the city, the MTA, and Mortimer "Mort" Zuckerman—whose $455 million proposal to develop the site collapsed in 1994.

Macklowe appreciated Sorin's quiet, careful style. Other lawyers, bankers, and brokers knew him, trusted him, and liked dealing with him. He diplomatically described the extreme peaks and troughs of Macklowe's professional life as, simply "interesting." It also helped that Sorin, aged 45 (in 2003) was younger than Harry but older than his son, William "Billy," then 35, who had started working for his father soon after graduating from New York University.

When Macklowe told Sorin he was planning to buy the GM Building, Sorin wasn't surprised. He'd have been surprised by anything less audacious. "When he latches his jaws onto something, it's very hard for him to let go. When [the GM Building] became a real opportunity . . . he was very, very focused on it," Sorin recalled.

■ ■ ■

Sorin sensed Macklowe had been plotting his move on the tower for months. Earlier in the year, Macklowe had asked Sorin to represent him on a deal that had seemed unusual. Macklowe said he would buy the land under the old St. Moritz Hotel on Central Park South (now the Ritz-Carlton). It was a small deal—$125 million—with no opportunity for development. "It wasn't a typical Harry acquisition," Sorin recalls. "There wasn't a lot of creative opportunity to it."

Macklowe told Sorin he knew the deal was "flawed . . . but"—and this was a crucial "but"—Eastdil was the selling agent. Eastdil, it was known, would, most likely, be the selling agent for the GM Building. Eastdil would want to see a track record from Macklowe before it would take him seriously as a buyer of something as monumental as the GM Building.

"I don't give a shit—let's just close the deal," Macklowe told Sorin. He explained, "I wanted to have a reputation of being a closer, being honorable, and having done a deal with these guys."

Sorin understood. He drafted the paperwork and negotiated the deal.

■ ■ ■

The counterpoint to Sorin's white-shoe persona was a broker named Robert "Rob" Horowitz. The "other Rob" in Harry's stable had played a vital role in every one of Macklowe's deals since 1997, amounting to over $15 billion in transactions.

"Rob," Macklowe said to the broker, a slight man with shoulder-length dark hair that curls at the ends, "we're buying the GM Building." There was a brief pause as Horowitz leaned back in his chair. "We need some money."

Cooper-Horowitz, the brokerage started by Horowitz's father, Barry, did not believe in wasting its fees on office rent. The firm had occupied smoke-filled rooms with aging black vinyl sofas in the Grand Central Terminal station area for 50 years. "We don't bring our clients to meetings here ever," Rob Horowitz chirps through the gloom and stench. "I don't want to spend a nickel I don't have to."

"Nobody thought that Harry was going to be the winning bidder—nobody," says Horowitz. "Because most people thought that the amount of equity that would be required would be too large for just an individual to buy. That's why everybody thought the building was going to be traded to Vornado [a vast public real estate investment trust (REIT)] or to Equity Office Properties [EOP, the largest commercial space owner in the country]."

But when Macklowe said he was going after the GM Building, Horowitz knew immediately whom to call. He began with the bank he was closest to: Deutsche Bank. "Harry very rarely, if ever, spoke to a lender. It was always through me," he says.

■ ■ ■

Harry Macklowe and Rob Horowitz did everything together. They golfed most Fridays, they drank, they dined, and they went away on trips, including to Las Vegas. They kept each other's secrets. On December 18, 2002, Macklowe wrote Horowitz a letter, telling him, "You are a great friend, a great supporter, and I love you."

What really bonded the two men was money. As Macklowe got richer, so did Horowitz. By 2002, Horowitz had made $50 million in fees. "Harry was extraordinarily loyal to me," he says. "We trusted each other emphatically. We never questioned anything either one of us did. We looked out for each other's interests.

"He once said to me, 'Rob, don't tell me what you think I want to hear. Tell me what you think.' Harry and I had disagreements over a number of financings, a number of strategies, but he wants [an honest opinion]."

The way the duo worked was very efficient. Horowitz would visit Macklowe in his office. Macklowe talked; sometimes his son, Billy, would be there, sometimes not. Horowitz scribbled notes with a ballpoint pen on A4 paper. These sheets were usually all that were needed for Horowitz to call the banks and lawyers to draw up the paperwork for deals worth hundreds of millions of dollars.

◾ ◾ ◾

Macklowe also trusted Horowitz because he knew Horowitz had served other real estate titans well, especially Donald Trump, with whom Harry occasionally golfed and lunched.

Horowitz had started working for Trump in 1996. Trump always let Horowitz breeze into his office without checking in with his vice president and assistant, Rhona Graff. (Macklowe didn't want quite such a loose arrangement. Before walking into Macklowe's office, Horowitz needed to check in with Harry's petite vice president and assistant, Liliana Coriasco, a doppelganger for Audrey Hepburn. Horowitz sometimes joked that this was because no one ever quite knew "what might be going on in Harry's office.")

Trump was very open with Horowitz. Horowitz knew, for example, that Trump kept his office the way it had been for years—cluttered with piles of papers and photographs and magazine covers of himself on the walls—because he was superstitious and didn't think he should move anything.

If Trump received a letter that amused him, or read an article he found particularly interesting, he often took out a black marker pen and scrawled, editor-like, "ROB H," and popped the document in the mail for his broker to peruse.

When Trump's daughter Ivanka told her father she intended to convert to Judaism and marry real estate scion Jared Kushner, Trump turned to Horowitz. "How rich is he?"

Horowitz replied, "He's very successful and a good guy. Don't worry about it, Donald."

To which Trump replied, "Then he has my blessing."

■ ■ ■

Horowitz liked Trump immensely but he loved Macklowe. He loved his humor, his elegance, his generosity. It was also extremely "helpful" and not coincidental that Macklowe had the loyalty and trust of Rob Horowitz's closest friend—and client—Eric Schwartz, the U.S. head of real estate at Deutsche Bank, one of the biggest lenders in the world. It didn't hurt that Schwartz and Sorin were longtime friends. Schwartz, Macklowe, and the two Robs often played golf together. Horowitz sometimes jokingly describes the foursome as a truncated version of *Ocean's Eleven*.

But the friendship was complicated, hierarchical. Sorin explains the way it worked as follows: "Rob Horowitz is very good at what he does. He is Harry's confidant and he is Deutsche Bank's confidant. . . . Everybody knows that Rob's playing both these roles, but . . . it's often easier to negotiate through someone [that way]. Both sides can use Rob as a conduit to negotiate without having to face each other directly. When you're in a relationship as a lender and a borrower, everybody wants to be buddy-buddy."

Schwartz, a former lawyer and Moody's Investors Service analyst, liked working with Macklowe and the Robs. He believed he always understood where they were coming from and where they were aiming. He liked that Macklowe developed only in a market the bank felt he truly understood: New York City.

But most important from Schwartz's perspective, Macklowe always offered his business to Deutsche Bank first. "Harry is a serial entrepreneur," Schwartz says. "He needs a lot of people around him who are loyal—that's how entrepreneurs work."

For Macklowe, earning Schwartz's trust was crucial. He was the conduit to the rest of the bank's real estate team: they included Jon Vaccaro, Deutsche Bank's Global Head of Commercial Real Estate; Justin Kennedy, a Stanford University graduate and son of U.S. Supreme Court Associate Justice Anthony M. Kennedy; and Tobin "Toby" Cobb, the son of an ambassador.

But when Horowitz called Schwartz about the GM Building, he was surprised to learn that his friends at Deutsche Bank had a conflict and couldn't back Macklowe. They were backing Vornado Realty Trust, the massive public REIT founded and run by Macklowe's friend, helicopter co-owner—and nemesis—Steven "Steve" Roth.

■ ■ ■

In some ways this was understandable.

Vornado was a public company with a market capitalization of more than $5 billion. Given the amount of debt that would need to be raised for this deal, Vornado was a far more credible bidder than a solo developer like Macklowe. But there was also another, more human factor. Vornado held a card that, for Deutsche Bank, would always trump Macklowe. His name was Michael "Mike" D. Fascitelli.

Fascitelli was a good-looking, fit Italian-American who had grown up in a "rough" neighborhood in Rhode Island. He was irreverent and irrepressible. Until 1996 he'd run the real estate department at Goldman Sachs, where he had trained, among others, Justin Kennedy and Toby Cobb. They adored him. He still used the vernacular of his youth and computed complex figures faster than most people can make a call on their iPhone. He had few pretensions. He called things exactly—and hilariously—as he saw them.

In 1996, Steve Roth realized he needed a second in command, someone with credibility, leadership, and charisma—and he had seen these qualities in Fascitelli. Roth paid Fascitelli $50 million to run Vornado as its president.

Since then, it was no secret that Fascitelli kept trying—and trying—to buy the GM Building. The files of paperwork representing the countless hours he spent on the structure took up the most shelf space in his office. "She's like the girl you keep asking to the prom but says no," he joked. "And each time you ask, she gets more expensive."

Her price was what worried him in 2003. He told Eric Schwartz he wanted Deutsche Bank to finance Vornado's bid—but he wouldn't pay "stupid money." If Harry Macklowe was prepared to "blow us all out of the water," let him—and Fascitelli would try to come at the building through a back door. That's how this game worked.

Meanwhile, Harry Macklowe needed to figure out how to claim his prize with a lender other than Deutsche Bank.

■ ■ ■

Robert "Rob" Verrone was in Harry Macklowe's office with Rob Horowitz in the summer of 2003 when Macklowe said: "I'm going to bid for the GM Building. Will you lend us the money?"

This was the moment Verrone had been angling for since being promoted, in 2001, to run Wachovia's loans department. His eagerness to establish Wachovia as a major lender in real estate circles had earned him the sobriquet "Large Loan" Verrone.

Verrone was not a member of the Fascitelli-trained club that filled the desks at Deutsche Bank. He had a big smile and a shaved head. He'd grown up in a large, blue-collar Catholic family in New Jersey. He was direct and ambitious, yet not overbearing. He'd learned the business in Bear Stearns's gumshoe, commercial real estate securitization department before joining Wachovia in 1995 (which, at the time, was called First Union Bank). He, with his wife and four children, had lived in Charlotte, North Carolina, until 2001, when, thanks to his promotion, they moved to Chappaqua, New York.

They were still unpacking boxes when Harry Macklowe summoned him to his office. "My wife had to unpack the whole house," Verrone later said. "Maybe this is the reason we're [now] divorced."

■ ■ ■

The two men had met at the annual Cooper-Horowitz party in 2001, where Verrone had introduced himself to Macklowe. Macklowe told him, "Show up early at my office tomorrow morning."

Verrone had stayed sober. He drove home in the small hours to shower and change and immediately headed back to the city to meet Macklowe and Horowitz. "Maybe that impressed [Macklowe]. I don't know. Or maybe I am just good-looking and charming," Verrone jests.

Wachovia lent Macklowe $125 million for a building at 125 West 55th Street.

Soon after, Macklowe chose Verrone as the banker for the tactical deal on Central Park that was intended to show Eastdil he was a "closer." As negotiations on that purchase wound down, Macklowe told Verrone about the GM Building.

Macklowe (and everyone else) knew Wachovia desperately wanted the prestige and fees that would come with taking part in the biggest real estate deal ever. Verrone also had some personal motivation to beat Deutsche Bank—he and Eric Schwartz were considered keen rivals. Verrone offered to lend Macklowe *more* than the announced $1.2 billion price. Verrone warned Macklowe that Wachovia would need to sell the so-called junior piece of the loan, but that looked doable. He'd already lined up the hedge fund and investment house Fortress, whose senior executives Macklowe knew well. Steve Stuart, the tall, blond managing director of Fortress's investment group, was viewed as "one of us": in other words, he played golf well—and often—with Eric Schwartz and Rob Horowitz.

Verrone felt comfortable making such a remarkably aggressive loan chiefly, he would say, because of Macklowe's compelling vision for the building, which Macklowe, in his typical fashion, drew for Verrone on a napkin. (This was part of Macklowe's shtick: He seduced people by sketching, apparently impulsively. He knew the gesture made them feel like they were part of the creative process, as if they were present at the birth of a lofty cultural idea.)

Macklowe sketched out three very big ideas: an Apple store with a glass entrance on what he called the "terrible, terrible" plaza; the construction of a skirt with "triple A" retail around the base, currently just sitting there, without throwing off much income. There was FAO Schwarz (in bankruptcy), a Bally shoe store, and the studio for CBS's *The Early Show*. Finally, he drew a sky deck with an elevator to the top of the building.

■ ■ ■

Over at Eastdil's offices on West 57th Street, the task of running the GM Building bidding process belonged to a 19-year veteran at the firm named Wayne L. Maggin, chiefly because Maggin had known Chuck Cremens for many years. They had worked together several times.

Cremens trusted Maggin implicitly; he liked Maggin's directness and also that he wasn't impressed by flashiness.

During the summer of 2003, Maggin and Cremens spent several hours discussing Donald Trump over cocktails. "[Cremens] has some great stories about his confrontations with Trump," Maggin later said. It was clear Cremens was not a member of the Donald Trump fan club.

Maggin made a chart of all 121 potential bidders to whom the GM Building prospectus had been sent on July 18. Beside the name of each was written the source of the bidder's potential funding and how much due diligence, if any, it was doing on the building. He and his colleagues were also busy canvassing the banks to see how much they were willing to invest and with whom.

First bids were due by August 11. The second and final bid would be due two weeks later. Maggin gave a "pricing guidance" in the area of $1.2 billion.

On August 1, Maggin e-mailed Cremens that he thought there would be around 26 bidders in the first round. The group included major real estate players, such as Beacon/Equity Office, Boston Properties, Brookfield, Davis Companies, Ideal Ventures, SL Green, Sheldon Solow, Tishman-Speyer, and Vornado. Harry Macklowe was also on the list.

It looked like an impressive collection, but Maggin and his colleagues at Eastdil were concerned that it wasn't "real." Their fear was that bidders would overpromise and then not deliver, that lenders just couldn't get there. Maggin explains: "You have to realize the pricing was thought to be very aggressive because the building's cash flow didn't support it."

■ ■ ■

On August 11, the first bids came in. Like any good poker player, Maggin now raised the stakes. He issued a more refined pricing guide north of $1.25 billion for the second round. Oh, and Maggin told the second-round bidders that Conseco had some other very specific requirements.

Those were: hard evidence that all the financing was in place; hard evidence that the bidder could close in 30 days; and, third, as proof of sincerity Conseco wanted a cash deposit of $50 million.

The cash deposit had the immediately sobering effect Maggin intended.

"Most of the real [as in big] players . . . dropped out at once," he says. This was too aggressive for their blood. It was unheard-of to ask for so much hard money down upon signing, and to some degree it was also "crazy"—but Eastdil couldn't afford to strike a deal with someone who ultimately couldn't close. Only someone desperate—and certain—to close would drop an unrefundable $50 million.

"One of the things that laypeople don't understand," Maggin explains, "is that when you have very large deals like this, in the middle of a dicey market—because you're not sure where it's going to go, where interest rates are going to go—if someone ties up a deal and doesn't perform, you've done a lot of damage to your client and to the property."

Vornado—just as Fascitelli had declared—wouldn't bid over $1.2 billion, nor would Boston Properties. Fascitelli went to plan B. If Macklowe won, he'd try to insert himself into Harry's financing so that if—and when—Macklowe lost the building because he had overpaid and couldn't hold on, Vornado, as a lender, would be waiting like an open-mouthed crocodile to snap up the prize on the cheap; real estate, especially in New York, is a blood sport.

Maggin looked over the remaining bidders, and realized Harry Macklowe suddenly looked like a real possibility. "We were left with less qualified people like Brener International Group and Wells Fargo and a guy called Leslie Dick whom we had never heard of," recalls Maggin. "And none of those guys had done huge New York real estate transactions." There was one exception: Sheldon Solow, the septuagenarian billionaire. He checked every box; his money was certainly real. But he was both capricious and notoriously litigious.

This was the largest single transaction Eastdil had ever handled; the fees would be enormous, and Wayne Maggin wasn't going to mess it up. Nor was Ben Lambert, who was socially friendly with Solow. But friendships were expendable with the "street fighters," as Lambert called the developers he represented. Unlike them, he was a deal guy who "didn't want to see my name all over the place." He had a wall of photographs capturing his "trophy" moments: There was a picture of Leona Helmsley, whose estate was probably the most difficult of many "difficult prizes" he had won over the years. He was determined to hang a picture of the GM Building, too.

Chapter 3

The Rigged Bid

The whole thing was a charade from start to finish. Even the opening of the sealed envelopes was pure theater. It was ridiculous. There was nothing fair about it.

—David Boies

Wayne Maggin and Ben Lambert watched Sheldon Solow carefully—which they could do almost literally, since their offices are directly across the street from his on West 57th Street. Maggin noticed that most of Solow's initial correspondence regarding the auction for the GM Building came through his lawyers. This bothered Maggin. He wanted to "get a clearer sense of" how much the building mattered to the developer. Maggin was also concerned about Solow's apparent lack of due diligence on the building. His team had examined the books, sure, but where were the visits from bankers, surveyors, and architects? Who knew what problems he might suddenly find after contracts were signed—and before the all-important closing?

"Sheldon had done virtually no work—we didn't know if Sheldon was dependable. We knew that there was a great potential for Sheldon to create some sort of legal uproar at some point in the process, and we were very concerned about that," Maggin said in an interview.

Solow, obliviously, thought he was the front-runner.

They didn't know this over at Eastdil, but he liked to stand in his office and look at the condition of the marble, which he feared needed repair. That was on his list of things to fix when he bought her; he believed that, provided he bid the highest price, he had the building in the bag. After all, he had a net worth of $3.5 billion; they'd know he had the capability to close.

Still, he also knew from experience that auctions could get tilted toward a favorite. Eastdil's offering letter had a disclaimer that stated, "The owner reserves the right, in its sole and absolute discretion, to accept or reject any offer for any reason." So he wanted to double-check the process with his good friend Ben Lambert. On August 26, the day before the final bids were due, Solow asked to meet with Lambert and Maggin in the presence of an attorney, Chris Smith, and Solow Realty's chief executive officer, Steve Cherniak.

"I said to Ben . . . 'Is this going to be a straight game?'" Solow recalled. "'Is this going to be a fair game?'"

"You have my word," Lambert replied, according to Solow.

Maggin's version of that meeting is very different. In a memo to file dated August 26, he wrote:

> We informed Solow that we had not definitely defined our process and that it depended on how the proposals came in. We made it extremely clear that they should not rely on our offering materials and that they and all investors needed to do complete independent due diligence on all legal, financial, economic, market and physical issues. We informed them that the important variables that Conseco would consider in its selection were price, hard money amount, due diligence timing, closing timing and control and availability of capital. Solow, et al., was

specifically told that some investors were considering submissions of proposal without any due diligence period.

■ ■ ■

Sheldon Solow had wanted the GM Building since her inception. Back in the 1960s, he'd negotiated with her first owner, Max Rayne (later Lord Rayne), and his CEO, a British petite pit bull of an executive named Cecilia Benattar.

Solow had grown up in Brooklyn, the son of a bricklayer who went bust in the Great Depression. The experience molded him, and taught him both ambition and caution. Solow dropped out of college and, to help his father, began working in construction. He discovered he loved it.

Andrew "Andy" Hayes, one of his attorneys, says that when Solow talks about the minutiae of a building he is "like a child . . . any detail, anything, even a glass curtain wall," will hook his attention.

The young Solow filled in marshland in the Rockaways and built multifamily units there. He started to develop around Manhattan in the "suburban boom" of the 1950s and then decided to "shoot the moon." He put together the financing for a 50-story glass tower designed by the architect Gordon Bunshaft of Skidmore, Owings and Merrill. Located at 9 West 57th Street, the building would be called "9 West."

Like the GM Building, 9 West is an entire block deep (it has entrances on 57th and 58th Streets); for four decades it has been the only other tower to command the same height and views of Central Park. The two buildings quickly became complements—and competitors; 9 West also attracted a glittering tenant roster: Some of the biggest hedge funds and private equity firms, including Apollo Global Management, Silver Lake Partners, Kohlberg Kravis Roberts (KKR), and Natixis, trickled in. In 2000, construction was completed on a $10 million design for the offices of plastics firm Tyco International; the company paid $100 a square foot for rent—a record.

In 2001 Tyco's facility manager sought out Andy Hayes, who had acted for Solow in a number of his legal cases. (Solow has filed over 350 lawsuits over the years.) He was by now infamous for his gloves-off attitude with tenants and with anyone else. "I wanted to meet you," the manager told Hayes, "because I've just got to tell you . . . I manage 148 properties in 19 countries . . . that guy Solow is the toughest landlord I deal with."

Hayes responded, "He'd take that as a compliment."

■ ■ ■

Yet beneath the battle-hardened exterior, Solow was vulnerable and eccentric. Hayes was surprised to find that his client sometimes wore rose-tinted spectacles to court, an apt metaphor for Solow's unexpected sentimental streak.

Over the years the trial lawyer David Boies both represented and befriended Solow and warned him "to be careful" of Marc Stuart Dreier, a Yale-and Harvard-educated lawyer Solow knew well. Boies had reason to believe Dreier was mixed up in business deals with a client, which is "not what lawyers are supposed to do." But Solow ignored Boies's advice—at great personal cost. Dreier would go on to forge Solow's promissory notes to embezzle more than $380 million—for which, in 2009, he was sentenced to prison for 20 years.

But even after Dreier's conviction, Solow maintained a soft spot for the fraudster. Solow told Boies he "felt sorry" for Dreier, "sad" for him.

Solow would say, when it was too late, that it was his trust for his "friend" Ben Lambert that screwed him on the GM Building deal. He didn't see in time that over at Eastdil they thought he was too litigious to be the ideal purchaser. They weren't sure he would close.

The day after meeting with Lambert and Maggin, Solow sent Steve Cherniak across the street to Eastdil to submit his bid. Cherniak's envelope contained an offer of $1.4 billion and asked for a 10-day period for due diligence. He didn't offer hard money down. He thought he didn't need to. Hard money, in his view, was for people without his depth of reserves.

■ ■ ■

Harry Macklowe, meanwhile, was dividing his time between shaping his bid and planning how to monetize the property.

He sketched away in his little black book and conferred with his "design team," led by Daniel "Dan" Shannon, the architect he had worked with on the Metropolitan Tower. He drew a big glass pyramid rising out of the ground, just like I. M. Pei's at the Louvre in Paris. He asked Pei, a friend, for his opinion. "Harry, it's *too big*," the architect said.

So Macklowe scaled back his drawings.

"Harry knew that reviving the [GM Building] plaza [was] the first order of business," says Shannon. "He wanted that clean, pristine, modern plaza—a monumental plaza—and in the midst of it, he wanted a glass pavilion, so a retailer could access the 20,000 square feet of retail space below. So, simply, we wanted to take the [idea of the] Seagram plaza and the Pei pyramid and bring it to the plaza at the GM Building.

"He had spoken with Sir Norman Foster. He had spoken with [the architect] Santiago Calatrava. And he had spoken with [the architect Henry "Harry" N.] Cobb. That's how Harry works. He gathers information and inspiration and concepts from other people, looking at how all this could come together."

In perhaps his most inspired move, Macklowe called George Blankenship, then the vice president of real estate at Apple. Macklowe had limited knowledge of the company and its technology—he still dictates his letters—and had barely heard of Steve Jobs.

Blankenship told Macklowe, "If you have anything interesting on Fifth Avenue, we're looking to open a store; it has to be different." Macklowe replied, "Well, I'm bidding to buy the General Motors Building. I want you to look at this. I mean it's sensational; it's got everything you want. And this is what I'm doing with the plaza."

Mackowe says, "He had no confidence [in my plan], I subsequently found out."

■ ■ ■

In the midst of chasing the biggest deal of his career, Macklowe did what he always does in July—he went on holiday. According to Rob Horowitz, "Harry works harder on holiday than most people do during usual hours. He doesn't sleep."

This holiday would have an unexpectedly crucial role in Macklowe's professional life. It is a bizarre story, one that he tells often, with relish.

The Macklowes always traveled to Europe via the Concorde. Macklowe had a close relationship with Air France, his tenant at 122 West 55th Street, and considered the Concorde to be a bit like a "traveling nightclub." Everyone knew everyone.

So he got a shock when he turned up at the Air France first class lounge at New York's John F. Kennedy International Airport in July 2003 and spied a stranger carrying a tote bag branded with "Eastdil."

Macklowe looked at the guy long and hard. He looked like "a freak," he recalls. "He had long hair down to his shoulders. He had leather braces—and on his feet were pointy crocodile cowboy boots."

He recalls nudging his wife, Linda. "I said to her, 'Look at that freak,' because not only does he have long hair—like he's Robin Hood—he's got shit-kicker boots, with these pointy toes, like he's going to kill a cockroach in the corner. And he's carrying a canvas bag that says 'Eastdil.' I wonder what he's doing here, but I say nothing."

After exiting the Concorde at Charles de Gaulle Airport, Macklowe and his wife boarded the shuttle for their plane to Naples, where they would board their 112-foot yacht, *Unfurled*. To Macklowe's astonishment, getting on the same shuttle was the freak with the Eastdil tote.

Macklowe couldn't contain himself any longer. "Do you by any chance know anyone who works for Eastdil?" he asked the man, pointing at his tote bag.

"Yeah," he replied. "Me. I've only been there for 25 years." He introduced himself. "Roy March."

Macklowe gasped. Roy Hilton March was the chief executive officer of Eastdil. He was Ben Lambert's right-hand man, and, although March was based in Los Angeles, Macklowe knew he'd be hugely influential in the sale of the GM Building.

Macklowe grinned and said, "I'm Harry Macklowe."

■ ■ ■

It was a small miracle March and Macklowe hadn't met before. In addition to their common interest in the impending sale of the GM Building, Macklowe quickly discovered that March was exactly what he liked in a guy—unusual, laconic, and gossipy.

March told the Macklowes he was spending the summer in Italy, trying to sell the exclusive group of Ciga Hotels. (Among them was the Cala di Volpe hotel in Sardinia, where the disgraced former Tyco chief executive Dennis Kozlowski infamously held a 40th birthday party for his wife with money pilfered from his company—the party that showcased a towering ice statue of Michelangelo's *David* with vodka pouring out of its penis.)

Like Macklowe, March was very comfortable in Italy. His wife Barbara was partly raised there; a brunette, she was a former model turned singer whose nude portraits were positioned in March's offices in New York and Los Angeles so his clients could see them. She had grown up singing in a Roman nightclub, Malindi, owned by her family.

Two nights after their introduction, March and Macklowe ran into each other at Aurora, one of Capri's finest restaurants. Macklowe was with Linda and his brother Lloyd, an antiques dealer. March was accompanied by Barbara and the Colavitas, the couple who own the eponymous olive oil label.

The next day, they all sailed on *Unfurled* to Li Galli, the cluster of private islands that were once the home of the late dancer Rudolf Nureyev. Italian hotelier Giovanni Russo, who now owns the islands, invited them over for lunch.

Macklowe remembered it as one of the most romantic afternoons he'd enjoyed in years. "So we go off sailing, and we have an afternoon at Li Galli with Russo entertaining us and a guns dealer from Lichtenstein and a gambling operator from somewhere else. There's 25 people and Giovanni is saying, 'Pasta waits for no man! So eat quickly.'

"We have this most wonderful afternoon, you know—swimming, eating, wine. It's just fabulous . . . and, you know, there's Barbara, swimming topless in the pool."

■ ■ ■

There wasn't much Linda Macklowe hadn't seen in her long marriage, a relationship often compared to an Edward Albee play. Both Macklowes have been heard to disparage each other and their marriage, forcibly and publicly. "She has said, 'I could have had a different life. . . . I should have divorced him.'" He has also complained bitterly.

Yet they were inseparable. "They drive each other crazy and they can't live without each other," says a close friend, adding: "She hates the country but they go out to [East Hampton] because Harry wants to play golf. So she's out there in this big house by herself not playing golf. But she has to be out there because Harry's out there."

Tiny (under five feet) and dark-haired, Linda Burg grew up in the Bronx in considerably grander social circles than those frequented by the man she would marry. In interviews, Harry always referred to his wife as better than him. "She's brilliant. She's just fantastic. I don't know why she married me, but she's extraordinary."

When she met Harry she was "stunning," according to her confidant, the art dealer Andrew Fabricant. "She's extremely funny," he says, "a feminine version of Woody Allen . . . but really, really sped up. She's hypercritical of everything and everybody."

Linda and Harry married in 1959. He'd dropped out of the University of Alabama, dabbled in advertising at the Kudner Agency on Madison Avenue, and fallen into real estate almost by accident, the result of a conversation with the owner of a Brooklyn brownstone in which he and Linda rented an apartment. He signed on as a broker with Julian Studley before co-founding Wolf and Macklowe with realtor Mel Wolf.

He and Linda had two children, Elizabeth (Liz) and William (Billy).

But all the while there was Linda's other child: her art collection. The Macklowes began collecting quietly. Fabricant recalls that Linda would wander around galleries on Saturdays. "In those days, if she liked something, she would make a commitment, and then she'd bring Harry by later to see it. And then a decision would be made," he says.

Over 55 years she built a collection said to be worth around $1 billion. It has works by Mark Rothko, Franz Kline, Andy Warhol, Gerhard Richter, and Jackson Pollock. . . . It is considered to be almost on the same level as the top contemporary art collections in the United States, which belong to David Geffen, Samuel Irving "Si" Newhouse, and Leonard Lauder. What started as a quiet pastime turned into what one friend describes as an "obsession for all the right reasons. . . . It truly began to be the dominant, driving force in her life."

Harry Macklowe liked it for different reasons, according to an art adviser. "Harry loves [bidding at auction] for the theater, for the social aspects, 'cause everybody's there. And he likes to be seen out."

He also liked that he could show off his wife's work and intellect. In 1972 he built 2 Dag Hammarskjold Plaza in the Turtle Bay neighborhood of New York City, and Linda curated several sculpture shows in the gardens.

An assistant helps her hang the artwork in their homes, schemed so minimalistically that the decor has been described by one regular visitor as "the bible by Florence Knoll. . . . You could have ophthalmological surgery on any given surface."

Liz, their daughter, has been heard to joke that the kitchens in the Macklowe homes serve but one peculiar purpose: "My mother goes in there to open her mail."

■ ■ ■

Every summer the Macklowes go sailing. "Their first boat was built so they could actually sail it themselves, just the two of them," says a friend on the condition of speaking anonymously. To her friend's surprise, Linda loves being on the boat with Harry. The couple also enjoys the theater, film, and dinners in polite society, with emphasis on "polite."

When Linda Macklowe fixed her eyes on the Marches—the nude swimming and all the shenanigans—it's easy to imagine her seeing the scene as a tawdry business schmoozefest. Her friends have not heard her eagerly repeat the narrative of the vacation the way her husband and Roy March have. "She doesn't like these kinds of stories," Harry explained later. Anything that reminded Linda Macklowe of the under-lying seediness and ruthlessness of her husband's business was not some-thing she wanted to talk about.

■ ■ ■

Once they got back from Italy, Harry Macklowe and Roy March stayed in frequent contact. "We had struck up a nice little friendship," says March. "Harry was charming beyond all measure."

March and Macklowe held a surreptitious meeting at the Starbucks near the GM Building. March recalled Macklowe buzzing around him like a bee. "[He asked me] what kind of bid was he supposed to come up with. I remember writing down a number, some blanks, and then another number. He said, 'Well, you haven't filled in the numbers.' And I said, 'That's what *you* have to do. It starts with a one, and we know it's gonna have this number in it as well, but the two middle numbers are the most important.'"

Macklowe reported all of these details to the three Robs. They all agreed it was crucial to learn, if possible, precisely what Conseco wanted. This was the secret to winning any bid. "There are other considerations besides being the highest bid," Rob Horowitz explains. "If someone says to you, 'I'll give $500 for your used car, and I want to do some due diligence and I want to take the car for a test drive,' and then someone says, 'I'll give you $490 and I'll take it today,' you might take the $490 today."

Macklowe knew Eastdil was worried that his financing might be shaky. By his name in Eastdil's files were written the phrases "too litigious" and "not shown ability to close." He suggested to Wayne Maggin that to shore up their confidence he could bring Rob Verrone in to Eastdil's office on August 26th—the same day Lambert and Maggin were meeting with an anxious Sheldon Solow.

"The meeting wasn't binding on Wachovia," Rob Sorin later said. "But the point was to show how serious they were."

Verrone's presence had a calming impact on the jittery brokers. Maggin later testified, "Macklowe had gone to the effort to introduce to Eastdil his lender and potential equity partner Wachovia. At the meeting Wachovia confirmed they were fully prepared to back Mr. Macklowe's proposal and finance the acquisition."

Macklowe returned to his office to noodle on the most tricky question of all: how to separate himself from the other bidders. It had become obvious to him that what Conseco and Eastdil really wanted was something that was completely unheard of: an unmarked contract. Certainty was the crucial ingredient here.

He picked up the phone and—with some difficulty—reached Rob Sorin, who was away on holiday on a houseboat on Lake Powell, a reservoir on the Colorado River. Sorin needed a satellite phone and sat on the boat's roof to hear him. Macklowe told his lawyer he wanted to make an offer of $1.38 billion, which would be delivered in two parts—a bid of $1.365 billion, with a letter adding $15 million if his offer was not the highest.

But he was also going to sign a contract with no markups—and hand over a nonrefundable deposit of $50 million.

Sorin says he gulped when he heard this. "I'm sitting in the middle of nowhere on the top of this houseboat that we had rented with my kids, and I'm talking with Harry and these guys on this deal that's the deal of his life. But one of the brilliant things about Harry is that he knows how to get what he wants and to typically do it in a way where other people may create issues and stumbling blocks that in the end probably will never matter.

"And after a lot of back-and-forth, Harry said, 'I want to sign the contract with my name on the bottom, and I'm not going to change a letter. That's it. We're just gonna sign it the way they presented it.'

"Most people wouldn't do that," Sorin says.

As Macklowe talked with his team about including the $50 million in his bid, one person there queried his strategy. "Are you sure you want to do that?" his son, Billy, asked.

"Shut the fuck up, Billy," Harry replied. "It's my money."

Billy Macklowe didn't say anything, but soon after that harsh conversation—and on the eve of potentially the company's biggest real estate deal ever—he left for a rock-climbing vacation.

■ ■ ■

At around five o'clock on the evening of August 27, 2003, Harry Macklowe personally delivered the bid to Eastdil's offices at 40 West 57th Street. He entered the first floor lobby and asked for Wayne Maggin. Maggin's assistant, Susan, took him up to the 22nd floor, where Maggin met him in the Eastdil foyer. Maggin took his envelope but told Macklowe he couldn't talk, as that would undermine the spirit of the sealed bids. Macklowe went back down.

"I had advised my assistant to not let Mr. Macklowe up to our office, as it was inappropriate for me to talk with him (or any other investor) at that time," Maggin recalls. "I was then very surprised when I learned that Mr. Macklowe had arrived unannounced [to me] at Eastdil's reception area. Having no alternative, I met Mr. Macklowe at the elevator and advised him that I did not wish to speak with him. He then said he only wanted to deliver his offer personally to me. He did so in a sealed envelope, which I did not open at that time. He left after less than a minute."

Macklowe now watched the clock. He knew that around 6:00 P.M. Maggin and Conseco's lawyers would open the sealed bids. Around 7:30 P.M., unable to contain himself, he called Ben Lambert and asked how things stood. Lambert laughed. "I am going out to dinner, Harry."

Maggin, Cremens, and the others did not go to dinner with Lambert. They remained in the office strategizing until 1:00 A.M. They all agreed that one proposal "stood out."

It was Harry Macklowe's because he had "gone hard"—he'd accepted their terms and offered an unrefundable deposit on the contract—*but* they would try to squeeze him further.

At 9:00 the next morning Maggin called Macklowe. Maggin told him that he needed to get to $1.4 billion. If he did that—and Maggin needed to know right away whether he could—they had a deal. Macklowe was thrilled. Of course he'd get to $1.4 billion. But first, there was a glitch.

"I said, 'Hey, that's terrific. But I want to check with Billy. You know, he's kind of my partner. He's my son. I'll get right back to you. He's rock-climbing.'" Macklowe dialed Billy. "I said, 'Billy, come here. We've got to sign the contract. We've got a couple of hours. I'll stall,'" Macklowe recalls. "And he drove back quickly, and put on a suit and tie."

By lunchtime, father and son walked with Rob Horowitz to the New York offices of law firm Kirkland and Ellis, and signed the paperwork. The $50 million deposit was wired from Macklowe's North Fork Bank. Billy, according to his father, was very happy.

As was Harry Macklowe. "I didn't want to know who the underbidder was. I didn't care. As long as I won and I could afford to pay the billion-four, I was happy. As long as I got the award, I felt terrific. And I think that they were really very happy to sell it to me. I think they really wanted me to buy it. And they kind of instinctively knew that I was gonna do a good job."

The biggest real estate transaction in U.S. history was going into contract. All they had to do now was close in 30 days. If not, Harry would lose $50 million—and his reputation.

■ ■ ■

Sheldon Solow felt wronged. Wayne Maggin had the gall to say to one of his attorneys, Chris Smith, that Solow "should have used the same approach" as Macklowe if he'd really wanted the building. He began to feel duped. "The whole process really smelled," he said.

The billionaire phoned Richard LeFrak, Eastdil's landlord at 40 West 57th Street. He asked LeFrak for the building's security tapes. LeFrak handed them over.

Solow took the tapes to his home in Greenwich, Connecticut. He asked Steve Cherniak and Andy Hayes to come over.

On Sunday afternoon the three men gathered around Solow's television and watched Cherniak enter the first floor lobby at 40 West 57th Street and ask the receptionist if he could go up to Eastdil's reception area. He was told politely that he could not. He remained standing there and phoned Solow.

A few minutes after the clock had struck 5:00 P.M. Macklowe strode into the building, clutching an envelope. A woman soon appeared. Together, they went upstairs. A few minutes later Macklowe emerged from the elevators—without his envelope—and left the building.

The three men watched the tape over and over—scenes of betrayal on a loop.

Solow was "outraged," according to Hayes. David Boies would add the adjectives "hurt," "offended," and "angry."

"It's a fix," Solow told Hayes and Cherniak. "Stop that sale."

■ ■ ■

Andy Hayes hunkered down to try to find a credible suit since there'd been no contract that was broken and no proof of fraud. Late one night, at 1:30 A.M., Hayes found a legitimate claim: "I found a line of cases from the 1800s, about a duty to have a fair auction . . . any frustrated bidder has standing to sue you for not holding a fair auction."

On September 23, the Honorable William B. Chandler III heard the case in the court of chancery of the State of Delaware—and watched the video produced by Solow's attorneys three times. He denied the injunction to stop the sale. The disclaimer language in the contract stood. Conseco could sell the building to whomever it wanted.

But it wasn't over for Solow. He believed he should own the building. He would, years later, sue Conseco in New York. David Boies would help him prepare his testimony and would say in an interview that he believed Eastdil had duped the developer. All along, it was their belief, Eastdil wanted to sell the building to Harry Macklowe.

"Sheldon is litigious, okay?" Boies said. "There's no question about that. But just because you're litigious doesn't mean that sometimes you're not right. . . . Sheldon has a very strong sense of justice."

■ ■ ■

The 30-day closing period between August 27 and September 27 would turn into a cloak-and-dagger narrative so suspenseful that even now the participants tell the story in the manner of a John le Carré thriller, each wanting a share of the intrigue, and the glory. What happened is hailed generally as one of the most dramatic industry coups of all time.

Herewith snippets of their narratives:

Rob Sorin: "Less than two weeks before the closing I get a voice mail from the lawyer at Cadwalader, Wickersham & Taft [Wachovia's attorneys] basically saying, 'You need to get an extension. I can't give you an assurance that we're gonna be there to close. We're working hard to get there, but. . . .' It just left a really uncomfortable feeling. So I hit save on this voice mail, and I called Harry and I said, 'Harry, we've got a problem. You know, I don't think they are gonna be there.'

"Rob [Horowitz] calls Eric Schwartz, who's playing golf in Ireland with Steve Stuart [of Fortress].

"So they literally get off the course, get on a plane, and fly back. Now, I'm not telling Wachovia [anything]. . . . I'm still trying to get Wachovia to close this loan. Then we've got Deutsche Bank going. And Deutsche Bank literally starts this process maybe 10 days before we have to close.

"A couple of days before the closing . . . I stopped returning Wachovia's calls because I just didn't want to put myself in an uncomfortable position. I certainly wasn't going to betray the confidence that we were working with Deutsche Bank.

"Skadden [Arps] represented Deutsche Bank, and we go to Skadden's offices to close the deal on the last day of the 30-day period. There's all these conference rooms going, and people are walking around . . . , it's like a zoo. And it's 2:00 and it's 3:00 and it's 4:00, and the title companies are still fighting over who's gonna get what share of the deal and there are all these other issues. . . . There's all this last-minute stuff that we're trying to put together. So at some point, I said we've got to wire the money now or it's not gonna make it. Literally at five [minutes] to 6:00 on the last day the money was wired.

"At about 6:20 I walked into a conference room by myself and called [Rob Verrone, who had not been told what was going on]. He asked, 'You closed, right?' I said, 'Yeah, we closed.'"

Rob Horowitz: "We all thought Wachovia was going to be there to fund the deal, but they were having a hard time selling off junior classes of the debt.

"Wachovia said to me, 'Can Harry get some more time to close the loan, to close the purchase?' Time was what we didn't have. I went over to see Harry. I said, 'Harry, . . . they're not here to close the loan. We've got a problem.' I said, 'Let me call Eric.'

"I called Eric. He was playing golf in Ireland. I said, 'Eric, do you want to come into this financing? I need a billion-four.' And he said, 'Sure, we'll do it.' He flew back. Their team got together. And then we started running dual tracks about 10 days before the escrow was closing.

"Deutsche Bank brought in [Steven] Mnuchin. At that time Mnuchin was working for George Soros's real estate fund. So Deutsche Bank brought Soros into the deal, to take down $250 million.

"Mnuchin put up $250 million, which Harry guaranteed. Now, of the $250 million, Deutsche Bank lent Mnuchin half of it, so in reality Mnuchin put up $125 million and Deutsche Bank lent him $125 million.

"No one knew what was happening. We kept it completely secret. That was the amazing thing. Normally in this city everybody knows what everybody's doing. I mean, everybody knows if someone else is going to the bathroom in this city."

Eric Schwartz: "That whole closing . . . my financing of that acquisition . . . the way we did it and the time pressures we had . . . that's a great real estate story in which everybody looks good, frankly—[except] probably not Wachovia."

Harry Macklowe: "Just before [the closing date], Wachovia said, 'We've thought about it, and we feel that we can't get there. . . . We want more guarantees. We want different terms than we had agreed to.' It was then that I went back to Deutsche Bank and said, 'Listen, I need you guys for a billion 150. I got 50 million up. I expect you to support me.' They looked at it, they looked at my business plan, and they said, 'You got it.'"

Mike Fascitelli: "Deutsche Bank made Harry an incredibly aggressive loan. But [it was] contingent on us having the mezzanine piece [of the loan] through Steve Mnuchin, who came to us while the bidding was going on. We loaned him some money.

"We didn't really want the mezz. We wanted the building. . . . Steve [Roth] is very jealous of Harry. He certainly didn't [make the loan] to help Harry get richer . . . he wanted the building."

Rob Verrone: "We had 30 days to close. The loan was involving a bunch of Harry's other buildings, too. And as we got closer to the closing, Harry stopped returning my phone calls and he did the loan with Deutsche Bank: better terms, more certainty. We were a little shaky on whether we were going to get there. Not everything checked out exactly like we thought it would check out.

"The building was fine but not the other collateral [Harry] was giving us. Let's say you wanted to borrow a million bucks from me. You say, 'I'll give you my house and my jewelry.' So the house was fine, but the jewelry wasn't worth what we thought it was worth. So we were starting to ask Harry some questions. I guess he got nervous and did it with Deutsche Bank. No one told us directly while it was happening. And no one had any hard feelings. I was pissed for about a day, but then it was probably the smart business move for him.

"We met right after—like two minutes after the closing he met me at The Four Seasons restaurant and we had a quick drink. And I was kind of pissed at him, but I got over it very quickly and I wished him luck and we moved on. We made some money on the deal. He paid us.

"If we'd done the GM deal we'd probably have done [the Equity Office Properties (EOP) deal] with Harry, too. So we always say that in the end not doing the GM Building saved us a lot of money."

Chapter 4

Harry's Hero

If you go through all the great dealers, who is the greatest real estate guy in history? Zeckendorf. . . . But he went broke.

—Samuel Zell

Harry Macklowe's love affair with the southeastern corner of Central Park had begun in the 1950s. He arrived in New York hungry, and wide-eyed at the possibility he saw all about him.

The place to live was "Park Avenue and 46th Street," he recalled.

"People actually rode and traveled by train. There were porters . . . on the trains, 'Here to serve you, yes, ma'am.' They had long baggage carts they used to pull by hand. . . . Oh, it was my youth—my youth of 1959.

"[The developer] Erwin [S.] Wolfson was the sponsor of [the] Grand Central [City Building] (which would become the Pan Am Building). He bought from the New Haven/New Hartford Railroad the baggage handling [in the] back of Grand Central Terminal. So he was a visionary. Because here was a building, and it was straddling Park Avenue. So think about this. Before the building was built, you would drive down Park Avenue and . . . you saw sky.

"Railroad tracks went right into Grand Central Terminal. And the buildings that were on Park Avenue were grand; there were exposition buildings; there were apartment houses. You drove into what is now the Union Carbide, Chase building on 47th Street. Joe Kennedy lived there."

Kennedy also had trysts with movie star Gloria Swanson in one of Macklowe's favorite spots, the Savoy-Plaza Hotel, a McKim, Mead and White–designed 1,000-room hotel situated where the GM Building is now. She had 33 floors, a steep green roof, and a pretty pair of chimneys.

Macklowe loved the glamour of the place so much that he held his wedding dinner there. "There was the Madison Hotel next door and then there was Longchamp's on Madison Avenue. There was a great clothing store. They sold English clothing. I always felt like Cary Grant walking into that store in *North by Northwest*. It was so fashionable."

The Savoy-Plaza was one of those rare places that both pulsated with the vitality of the city and yet was delightfully, refreshingly re-moved from it. It inspired fondness and loyalty rather than the awe of the bigger, grander Plaza Hotel opposite. Gossip columnists felt they were bound to see "everyone" at the daily English-style tea dances held in the downstairs restaurant "Columns" (so-called because of the ornate red-veined black marble columns spaced throughout the room). Mayors Jimmy Walker and Fiorello La Guardia, Greta Garbo, Lana Turner, Tyrone Power, and Clark Gable were all said to have had liaisons there.

Many people chose to make it their home in the post-Prohibition era, because, according to Yale Dean of Architecture Robert A.M. Stern, they did not want the expense and hassle of living in a townhouse.

In 1965 Gloria Steinem wrote that guests and residents included the King of Nepal, Groucho Marx, Prince Bernhard of the Nether-lands, Joseph P. Kennedy, Mr. and Mrs. John Daly, Frank Sinatra, Prince Michael Evlanoff, Martin and Joseph Revson of Revlon, and seven U.S.

presents. The actress Zsa Zsa Gabor moved in in the late 1950s when her second husband, Conrad Hilton, owned the joint. She had three bedrooms—one blue, one pink, and one green. One of her beds stood only 18 inches high—prompting some to joke, "She must have liked to sleep on the floor."

In the late 1920s, Adolph Zukor, the founder of Paramount Pictures, built a duplex called Le Chateau on the 22nd floor where he lived for 10 years. It had a banquet room that could seat 26, bathrooms with gold fixtures, four bedrooms, and a sweeping, red-carpeted circular staircase. It had an English-style library filled with leather-bound books with names on the spines like Dante, Homer, and Longfellow. These books were the ultimate Hollywood illusion—they were all hollow! The only real book, it would be observed by the *New York World-Telegram and Sun* on June 30, 1965, was the telephone directory.

Part of the hotel's appeal lay in its checkered history. It had been built in 1927 by the country's largest development firm, U.S. Realty, whose chairman, Harry Black, was a hustler. Black had come from "nothing" in Canada, but had wound up in Chicago, then New York, and caught the eye of an ailing George Fuller, then CEO and founder of a construction firm, the Fuller Company, which most famously built New York's Flatiron Building (originally called the Fuller Building). By 1896 Fuller, looking to safeguard his multimillion-dollar estate, had not only appointed Black the vice president of his company, but had married him off to his stunning 17-year-old dark-haired daughter Allon. Black was 15 years his bride's senior.

After Fuller's death in 1900, Black took over as president and merged the Fuller Company with Central Realty Bond and Trust Company and New York Realty to form U.S. Realty and Construction Company, the first development firm with branches all over the United States. As his success grew, so did his ego. He thought his wallet could manipulate anyone and anything. His young wife didn't agree. She confronted him over an affair with a pretty nurse, Lucy Kennard, and—amid considerable scandal—divorced him. She then married Tyler Morse, who came from a far more suitable family, but she died, quite suddenly, when she was just 37. Fourteen years after her death Harry Black, aged 65, shot himself at their former marital home, Allondale, named after her, in Westbury, Long Island. His suicide was described by a "friend" as "scarcely surprising." He had no life outside of work and had "betrayed" all his friends. He was left with just money and buildings. "What else could he do but kill himself?"

He was not, in fact, the first owner of the site to suffer the consequences of an outsized appetite. In fact, 767 Fifth Avenue, the title of the plot of land, might be said to be a magnet for men like Harry Black, so overcome by ambition for building as to lose all perspective. (Black once said, "Once [a man] owns a piece of real estate, an affiliation—it may not be actual affection but something very near it—grows and fastens into his consciousness which comes close to making him feel that it is somehow part of himself. . . . I know I own pieces of property that I couldn't let go any more than I would for a profit dismiss a near dear relative.")

His most famous predecessor was William Magear "Boss" Tweed, the political leader of the democratic workingman's group Tammany Hall. Tweed, possibly the most corrupt politician ever to rule New York, loved collecting real estate, especially lots that he purchased right before city improvements were announced on those very parcels. And 767 Fifth Avenue was no exception. In 1870 Tweed announced he'd pay $1.5 million to build the eight-story Knickerbocker Hotel on Fifth Avenue between 58th and 59th Streets. Construction began. Suddenly, it emerged that the southeastern boundary for Central Park would lie right where Boss Tweed's new hotel was.

Within eight years justice caught up with Tweed. He was charged with stealing a reported $200 million from New York City taxpayers ($4 billion today)—and he was slung in jail, where he died in 1878. The Knickerbocker Hotel lay derelict, a pile of concrete rubble, for 20 years.

The next "Icarus" to come at the plot of land was, ironically perhaps, the son of one of the erstwhile Tweed ring, who had no need to work for a living. In 1890 Judge P. Henry Dugro built a 12-story Savoy Hotel on the site. The *New York Times* reported that the judge could be found hammering in nails and then took on the role of superintendent. Dugro died—naturally—in an apartment there in 1920; the hotel changed hands briefly before being redesigned by McKim, Mead and White under the direction of Harry Black. And in

1957 she was sold to Hilton hotels—then run by the self-made hotel tycoon Conrad Hilton, who swiftly deposited his ex-wife Zsa Zsa Gabor there, exclaiming that his whirlwind marriage to the actress had been a terrible mistake. ("If I had waited one more hour I would never have married Zsa Zsa," he told a friend.) Gabor went on to have seven more husbands.

The hotel's popularity was seemingly entrenched in as much as anything is ever intrinsic in the city of perpetual motion.

To the south, some of the city's jewels were being demolished fecklessly. In 1961 the *New York Times* reported that authorities had green-lit the demolition of Pennsylvania Station, widely considered an architectural masterpiece. Protests sprang up; they were surprisingly spirited but also powerless. The official Landmarks Preservation Commission protecting New York buildings would not be formed until 1965 when Grand Central Terminal was under threat.

Fifth Avenue above 57th Street seemed safe. It had only recently become a fashionable place to live: In her best-selling 1920 novel *The Age of Innocence,* the literary society chronicler Edith Wharton had quite deliberately placed the character of the fat outsider, Mrs. Manson (based on Wharton's aunt Mary Mason Jones) in a house on Fifth Avenue between 57th and 58th Streets; the address was an indication of where she stood in society: on the outskirts.

But this was changing with the evolution of Central Park; Rockefellers, Whitneys, and Kennedys had moved north on Fifth Avenue so they could live facing the trees and in 1962 a lightbulb went on for one desperate—but brilliant—man. What if he built an office tower near the Upper East Side, to which the nouveau riche could walk to work?

The man's name was William Zeckendorf, and he was Harry Macklowe's icon. Heck, he was everyone's icon. He wasn't just a developer; he was a visionary, an actor, a leader. Samuel F. Zell, the Chicago financier, would say in 2013, nearly 40 years after Zeckendorf's death in 1974, that he was the greatest developer who ever lived.

■ ■ ■

Zeckendorf sometimes hung out in a room named the Rough Rider Room at the back of the Roosevelt Hotel on 45th Street; a very young Harry Macklowe nicknamed it the "real estate club." There, he says, he met "the end of the generation—the old kind of immigrant or the struggling Jews—who were the real estate players in the city."

Macklowe notes, "All these old codgers would sit around and have lunch and trade buildings and sell back and forth to each other. Each of them would buy a deal at the first table and go around the room trying to sell it by the end of lunch."

Zeckendorf dazzled Macklowe. "I had occasion to talk to him about some ideas. He was the first guy to have a mobile phone in a car [a Cadillac]. It must have been powered by a generator.

"I was a kid, in my early 20s, so of course I revered him, and how could you not if you were sensitive to developments and design and architecture?

"Zeckendorf was bolder than anybody else. He was just perilously financed."

■ ■ ■

William Zeckendorf was at the start of his financial decline when Macklowe met him in the Rough Rider Room. But he never behaved like a man with many worries. According to a 1965 profile by Christopher Welles in *Life* magazine, there were only mild, superficial signs that anything was amiss. The flowers at Webb and Knapp, his real estate firm, were suddenly plastic rather than fresh. Yet the food, Welles noted drily, had improved!

Zeckendorf curtailed his social life and retired to bed by 10 P.M. in order to rise by 5:30 A.M. He also limited his alcohol intake to one or two highballs after dinner. That was as far as the restrictions went. He'd gotten where he was through smarts and overwhelming charm, and he'd go down the same way. "It's not dishonorable to get knocked down," he told Welles when asked if he'd consider allowing Webb and Knapp to file for voluntary bankruptcy to avoid harassment from creditors and lawyers. "But to quit when you still have strength left is immoral."

A hulk of a man at six feet and 235 pounds, Zeckendorf, the son of a shoe manufacturer, had amassed the biggest real estate firm in the world. In 1942 Webb and Knapp was worth minus $127,000; by 1954 it was worth over $75 million, with control of more than $250 million worth of property. Unlike Harry Black, who had built a company through wheeling and dealing, Zeckendorf's empire was mostly the product of his ability to see an opportunity where other men saw wastelands.

His specialty was the global transformation of derelict slum areas into gleaming residential or commercial metropolises; urban heartbeats with futuristic designs, sometimes by the Swiss-French architect Le Corbusier but mostly by a Chinese-American architect fresh out of Harvard named Ieoh Ming "I. M." Pei, who designed Zeckendorf's own office "in the sky," a round penthouse on the 12th floor of 383 Madison Avenue. The lighting would change to reflect Zeckendorf's mood.

Among Zeckendorf's more famous developments were the Roosevelt Field shopping mall on Long Island, Kips Bay Towers in New York, the Mile High Center in Denver, L'Enfant Plaza in Washington, D.C., Place Ville Marie in Montreal, Century City in Los Angeles, as well as the redesign of Denver's Courthouse Square.

He flew by private jet and was feted like royalty—sometimes by royalty—wherever he landed. Tycoons and governments everywhere competed for him and his transformations.

He had a startlingly unusual—and prescient—attitude toward debt. "He understood that if you borrow most of the money needed to buy a property, you get a lot more for your small share of the investment," reported Welles. Debt in his mind meant possibility and room for imagination; and as long as the market went up, this was true. There was a legendary joke about his attitude toward money. "Oh, look," he'd say to an associate, "we can buy that building for $50 million," and the associate would reply, "So we first we need to find $5,000."

In 1953, while bone-fishing in Hawaii, he invented the "Hawaiian technique," a methodology by which you could sell the various components of a building separately for more than its total value. For example, you could sell a building's naming rights, its individual leases, its land, and the stocks and bonds that financed it, and still make a profit holding the title deed. "He even made money through mortgaging elevators," says Robert "Robbie" Rayne, a British developer who collaborated with Zeckendorf.

From 1949 to 1960 his bag of tricks worked better than any magician could have hoped. Zeckendorf sold, brokered, and implemented headline-grabbing deal after deal. "He could sell snow to the Eskimos, such was his charm," recalls Lester Crown, the billionaire son of the Chicago financier Colonel Henry Crown. "He could have been a billionaire—though no one talked about billionaires in those days—if he had only sold his ideas to someone who was willing to buy them and execute them." The problem, according to Crown, was that Zeckendorf executed too many transactions. "He got into the same dilemma as an artist with a half-finished portrait: you don't get the money until you've completed the job," wrote Welles. "Zeckendorf was in constant need of money *now*. The waiting killed him."

Slowly the debts mounted. He fired hundreds of people on his staff. On weekends, he took to marching around his garden on Long Island Sound with his Weimaraner, Cheer. It was reported that he much preferred the company of the dog—and his wife Marion—to that of his son, William Jr., who was struggling to establish himself in his father's shadow.

Right to the end he was talking on the phone from dawn to dusk, at times charming, at others bombastic; he remained mentally nimble, always finding some rabbit hole to shimmy down and provide a makeshift safety zone where he could temporarily stave off creditors.

■ ■ ■

In 1962 Zeckendorf thought he'd finally hit the jackpot. He knew General Motors, then the biggest U.S. company, with a market capitalization of $1.6 billion, was looking for a vast New York headquarters. GM was based in Detroit, but all big businesses—Exxon, Union Carbide—were moving their headquarters to New York City, partly to be closer to their bankers, J.P. Morgan, and partly because of the allure of the World's Fair, held in New York in 1964.

GM was planning to consolidate its New York offices into a new building. This would mean giving up the offices it leased in the 25-story edifice at 1775 Broadway between 57th and 58th Streets, where most of the 3,300 local GM employees worked.

Zeckendorf wrote in his memoir, *Zeckendorf*, that he planned to develop a double block around Times Square; he offered GM a tower in the new development. It would have been the coup he was searching for to save Webb and Knapp. It was, he wrote, the firm's "last great real estate effort."

He thought he had everything drawn up; the leases were ready, and the terms were agreed, verbally, with Colonel Henry Crown, who would finance the project.

Zeckendorf then went on vacation to Mexico.

On the final page of his memoir he writes that while he was away Crown backed out—something Crown's son, Lester, categorically disputes, saying that of the two men the one to "bait and switch" was Zeckendorf. "Bill was all over the place," Crown says. "He needed a CFO, which he did not have." He had run out of money and time.

Zeckendorf now had the biggest, richest tenant in the United States and nowhere to put them.

But then he had an idea. Among the many people to whom he owed millions was a handsome British industrialist and developer named Max Rayne, who was competing with a handful of other postwar British developers for trophy properties in New York.

Zeckendorf figured that if he introduced Rayne to General Motors, showed them the block of land between 58th and 59th Streets and Fifth and Madison Avenues—the current site of the Savoy Hilton and the Madison Hotel—and recommended buying and razing both buildings, then Rayne could build a gleaming trophy like no other. And Zeckendorf would, he hoped, get all the credit—and a hefty commission.

■ ■ ■

In 1962, Webb and Knapp (financed, quietly, by Rayne) bought the Savoy Hilton from Conrad Hilton. Speculators idly wondered what Zeckendorf was doing. The deal made little sense. The hotel lost money.

Zeckendorf was playing front-man. "In 1963, his group bought the Madison Hotel next door. He actually assembled the full site," recalls Harry Macklowe. "He bought the Madison Hotel. He bought the Emmett Arcade. He got the whole block."

■ ■ ■

The way Zeckendorf would tell the story of the origin of the GM building—and he often told it in his usual booming tones on his car phone (he even gave the *Wall Street Journal* a four-page press release)—

he contacted Frederic "Fred" Donner, GM's chairman and CEO in June 1963 and "negotiated the broad principles of the deal" with Donner, GM's executive vice president, George Russell, and Max Rayne. Webb and Knapp would realize $2 million to $2.5 million in commissions.

He didn't quite go so far as to take the credit for the building that would replace the Savoy-Plaza Hotel, of which GM would lease over half.

"I have the fullest confidence that [Rayne] in association with General Motors, who in the industrial world have done more to advance beauty in utilitarian design than any other company in history, will produce a building of which New York will certainly be proud," he would say to the *Wall Street Journal*.

It was too late for the protesters—of whom there would be many—to have any meaningful impact. The deal was done, the permits were secured, and the Savoy-Plaza Hotel was as good as dead.

So too were the fortunes of Webb and Knapp. Zeckendorf staggered on, but in 1965 the company declared bankruptcy. In 1968 so did he—and something even worse happened. He went to Guadeloupe and waited for Marion, his beloved wife. His memoirs open with the scene of him, clutching her dog, Mimi, a miniature pinscher, just waiting . . . and waiting.

Her plane never came. It had hit a mountain peak.

Just as he had made peace with his financial losses and found a "welcome stillness," he lost the love of his life. He would suffer a series of strokes. He died in 1976, under indictment for not paying his taxes. Obituaries captured not just his brilliance but his largesse, his charisma, his indomitable will—and his tragedies.

■ ■ ■

"He was a genius. I am not a genius," Harry Macklowe said in 2013, retelling the story of that plane crash with a wistful look. Macklowe said that in later years he had given money to Zeckendorf's son, the late William Zeckendorf Jr., just for the hell of it.

"William Jr. built a ton of buildings all at one time," said Macklowe. "He spent 10 years building a lot of buildings. He made a lot of money. And he lost a lot of money. I bought a piece of land from him, and I knew he owned it in partnership, and I had a feeling that he probably—I don't know if I was right or not—wasn't getting any money from the deal because probably the investors were getting the money first. So after the deal was done, I gave him the check.

"I felt that he was an important man in the world today, he was the son of a *very* important man, and I felt that the money that I was giving him would be more meaningful to him than to me."

William Zeckendorf Jr. died in February 2014; his surviving children, William and Arthur Zeckendorf, built 15 Central Park West, an apartment building designed by Robert Stern, which contains the most expensive and highest-profile residences in all of New York City as of 2014.

Chapter 5

The Odd Couple:
The English Lord and
the Housewife Tycoon

My father was brought up in the East End. He was incredibly determined. It was why he and Cecilia got on— they came from similar backgrounds in a way . . . Cecilia was a bully; a hardworking, total perfectionist.

—Robert A. Rayne

In 1960, Max Rayne told his eldest son that William Zeckendorf owed him a great deal of money. "Webb and Knapp was collapsing," recalls the Honorable Robert "Robbie" A. Rayne, a dark-haired, slim man who is a dead ringer for his late father. "He was in real trouble."

In 1962, Zeckendorf sold a third of his interest in the Savoy-Plaza Hotel to Max Rayne. "Then [Zeckendorf] got further into trouble and we bought the other two-thirds," says Rayne. No one knew anything about the transfer, conducted in total secrecy.

During that period, Zeckendorf introduced General Motors to Rayne as a potential tenant for a new building spanning the whole block.

In late summer of 1964 the press got wind of what was termed "the deal of the year." The name Max Rayne entered the U.S. lexicon for the first time; he was hailed as an "English real estate wizard," but there was also suspicion of the foreigner. The timing was terrible from a preservationists' standpoint. Penn Station had been felled by the wrecker's ball in 1963. Protesters led a "funeral procession" outside the Savoy-Plaza Hotel.

Typically—and sensibly—given the controversy, Max Rayne didn't conduct interviews; he was content to remain an enigma—albeit a quietly glamorous one. He was just 46. He was always photographed dressed in immaculately tailored suits accessorized by a trim pocket handkerchief that matched his shirt; he usually held a long, slim cigarette in his right hand. He holidayed in the South of France; he had an important contemporary art collection; his second wife was Lady Jane Vane-Tempest-Stewart, the daughter of the 8th Marquess of Queensbury; she'd held the Queen's train at her coronation, and was later called "the Pippa Middleton of her day."

He was the son of a tailor, a Polish immigrant. The young Rayne returned from the war and upon discovering his father owned not just his store but an entire building in London's West End, he leased it out. Then he expanded. His most significant and lucrative deal was with Britain's Church Commissioners, which owned swaths of bombed-out land around London's Marble Arch. He persuaded them not to sell it but to develop it with him, 50/50. He was so successful that the famous Portman Estates entrusted him with its property—a huge chunk of London's West End. He became one of a small group who developed most of the postwar English capital. (The others were Sir Charles Clore, Jack Cotton, and Sir Howard Samuel.) In 1957 he formed a holding company, London Merchant Securities (LMS), that would branch into distilleries, pharmaceuticals, cosmetics, and printing; LMS's real estate portfolio would one day be worth more than $500 million.

In 1969 he was knighted Sir Max and in 1976 was given a life peerage, Lord Rayne of Prince's Meadow—and as quietly as he'd made his fortune, he dispensed with it for the greater good; his charities included those in the arts, education, hospitals, and Jewish causes. "If you've got it, it's very easy to give it away," he once said. "It costs me more to give my time and I'm prouder of giving that."

So it was no surprise that when he bought the site for the new GM Building, he remained in the shadows. The press reports initially suggested that something hideous, corporate, and brash would replace something dignified, distinguished, and dainty—and this was not an association the refined Rayne wanted. As his eldest son, Robbie Rayne, recalls, "It wasn't so much the building that caused the controversy— as rude remarks about the demolishing of a landmark hotel." Anyway, Max Rayne had two very capable representatives in New York who were more than happy to do the proverbial dirty work for him.

■ ■ ■

Rayne, like all developers, knew that no deal is possible without the help of a very experienced and knowledgeable lawyer. He turned to a cerebral, gentle-mannered "truly remarkable" man, Jesse "Jess" D. Wolff. Wolff was a partner at a small law firm, Weil, Gotshal & Manges; he was a standout of the old school. He addressed his assistant as "Mrs. O'Hearn," and when others got excited he remained calm, quietly smoking his pipe.

"He was a very, *very* good lawyer and a good negotiator and a nice man," says Ira Millstein, the former co-senior partner of Weil Gotshal.

Wolff was considered the go-to lawyer in an important circle in New York: the immigrant European-born Jewish businessmen who had lost art to the Nazis in World War II. Among his prominent clients were Parke-Bernet, the New York art dealership that was later purchased by Sotheby's in 1967, and two collectors, Jacob Goldschmidt and Walter Bareiss, the latter a German-American art collector who was connected to a huge restitution art effort in Europe. Bareiss was the conduit between Wolff and Rayne.

"[Recovering the art] was a long process. There were lawsuits, and through Jesse's relationship with Bareiss, we met Max," recalls Millstein.

It was to be a meeting of immense import—not just to Rayne, but to the firm of Weil, Gotshal & Manges. Recalls Millstein, "We were maybe 40 or 50 lawyers; you know, a nice little law firm, but not very big and not very famous, and certainly not worldly connected. So this presented for Jess a big opportunity."

■ ■ ■

Ultimately, Wolff and Rayne became lead actors in someone else's script. That person was a British-born woman who didn't even know where, precisely, Times Square was and was relatively inexperienced in the field of real estate. But she didn't let that worry her. Rayne had told her to see if she could execute upon Zeckendorf's idea and introductions; this was her "brass ring," as she put it; and she wasn't going to fail.

Her name was Cecilia Benattar. She was a petite (5 feet 2 inches) chain-smoking, dark-haired, ferociously ambitious woman from Manchester. She was the daughter of a homeopathist, and she spoke with a thick northern accent that she would forever try to rid herself of by reciting poetry. She had won a scholarship to the London School of Economics; she met Rayne in the 1950s while she was in her twenties and working for a shelving company, Dexion. She immediately pitched him a real estate deal—and then asked to work for him. She would later say she saw in Rayne a largeness of spirit. It was essential, she would say, for women to find that rare male mentor who wasn't threatened by an ambitious woman.

Rayne wasn't threatened; he liked her feistiness, her brains, her audacity—and her hunger. In many ways he saw a reflection of himself: They were both proudly Jewish, and proud of their hard work and what it could achieve. "She was a remarkable person," says Robbie Rayne. "They got on extremely well because in some ways they were the same."

But only in some ways. While Max Rayne was soft-spoken and cerebral, she was a "hugger and screamer," says his son. "She was an interesting mixture—loyal, warm, unbelievably difficult."

Max Rayne suspected Cecilia could achieve anything she put her mind to, but he didn't want to be too close to the action. It was bound to be bumpy, full of inelegant friction. He wanted the results—not the process.

"He said, 'You can work for me—overseas,'" Robbie Rayne recalled.

In 1957, Benattar moved to Toronto with her architect husband, Jack. Benattar put together a couple of successful developments for Rayne, "out of a broom closet of an office," she later joked.

She was working in Toronto when Max Rayne introduced her to Wolff and Zeckendorf and laid out Zeckendorf's proposal for buying the entire block at 767 Fifth Avenue; it would be her job to convince General Motors that they wanted to partner with London Merchant Securities, and to negotiate all other contracts required to get it built and make it a success. Oh, and she also had to evict current tenants in the block—and knock down the beloved Savoy-Plaza Hotel.

She wasted no time. As Harvey Miller, a lawyer specializing in bankruptcy at Weil Gotshal, recalls, she said, "'I'm going to outwit these guys!' She was very smart. She just outnegotiated everyone."

Benattar's first priority was to buy up the entire block on which the building would stand. Wolff's expertise became indispensable during this extended, complicated period. "It took a long time," says Ira Millstein. (Jesse Wolff died in 2011.) And there was also the pesky business of evicting the hotel tenants. "The big problem was the hotel—there [were] a lot of stabilized and rent-controlled people."

Millstein says, "I know that Jess and she worked together for years, putting the block together, buying out this and buying out that, dealing with The Mayflower [coffee shop] and all the other ticky-tackies that were all over this [site]. . . . I wasn't familiar with what exactly they did, but I knew Jess was spending half his time if not more with her."

The two became inseparable. Cecilia would even name her second daughter Jessica after the lawyer. She knew she couldn't have managed without his graceful ways, which were sometimes much more effective than her open aggression.

Next she had to sell General Motors on the location—which, to use her language, was a "desert." "It wasn't obvious," says Robbie Rayne of the location. "It was going to be the most uptown office building at the time."

She also had a credibility issue. Benattar was a 32-year-old unknown, a foreigner, and a woman operating in a man's world. The GM executives had barely heard of Max Rayne—and certainly not her. They were taking this meeting because of Zeckendorf. No one would be impressed if she told them the truth—that she worked out of a "broom closet of an office" in Toronto, and was staying in a room in the Savoy-Plaza.

"She went to Bill Zeckendorf, and asked to borrow his senior management team," recalls Geoffrey Wharton, a former colleague of Jess Wolff. "This way she could pretend they were hers." Zeckendorf—perhaps knowing he'd met his match, and also perhaps thinking he'd enjoy the performance—acquiesced.

"She met his team for the first time the night before meeting GM," recalls Wharton. "She remembered all their names and then the next day [she] introduced each one to GM's senior executives as her employees. In other words, she pretended his COO was her COO, his secretary was her secretary, his head of acquisitions was her head of acquisitions. GM fell for it. They were sold."

When asked if she'd been frightened that her bluff might have been discovered, her reply was characteristically blunt. "I had nothing to lose," she said. "I had grown up desperate to work. This was my one chance. I didn't have any fear. . . . I needed an organization. I borrowed one."

■ ■ ■

With GM locked down, Benattar was able to get the deal for the GM Building financed at terms that made even Rayne, notoriously conservative with financing, happy.

Recalls Robbie Rayne, "GM's lease was 30 years at $7 a foot. So when we financed the building, which we did with Metropolitan Life, we did it on the back of General Motors' lease. They provided $90 million at an interest rate of 4¾ percent fixed. So the build cost of the building was $110 million, thereabouts, just under that, but the $90 million, 4¾ percent fixed mortgage was, extraordinarily, guaranteed by General Motors."

General Motors would take up over half the building. In August 1964 the deal was announced.

There was a stunned reaction—and not just because of the proposed building or the presence of a British aristocrat. That a diminutive

32-year-old British mother from a working-class background had pulled off the most audacious development coup in the world was a shock.

David English, who would become Sir David English and the venerated editor of England's *Daily Mail* before his death in 1998, was then the New York correspondent for the *Daily Express*. In August 1964 he wrote a long article about Cecilia Benattar, the "housewife tycoon," who had pulled off the "business shock of the year."

"When the last signature dried on the contract," he wrote, "she emerged as cool and crisp as if she had just been to the hairdressers." Benattar told English that while she considered her salary to be "phenomenal" by English standards, it was merely "substantial" in the United States.

■ ■ ■

In September 1964, a practical question remained—what would the new building look like? Benattar shrewdly established a "committee" of three leading architects, the sole purpose of which was, she said, to check that the new building conformed with the "character and dignity" of the area.

In December 1964 the committee—and the press—was informed that Benattar had, behind their backs, already selected an architect. Benattar, according to her son Simon, had never had any intention of dealing with an architect she couldn't handle.

But she could work with Edward Durrell Stone, who would, in due course, build her a house in Rye, New York. Stone was very much in vogue; he had recently designed the British Embassy in India and the Kennedy Center in Washington, D.C. In December 1964 he gave interviews in which he promised that the new white marble 50-story tower he envisaged for the GM Building would pay tribute to the past, as well as to the future. Critics weren't sure they believed him. Ada Louise Huxtable, the *New York Times'* architecture critic, wrote that the new building, as far as she could tell, would be a "delicate juggling act between esthetics and economies."

Stone promised the following: The new building would be white marble, 50 floors, with a great plaza from which pedestrians could see the GM showroom. GM would take the first 26 floors. The whole building would be set back from the street 100 feet. There would be shops and a car park on the subterranean level. His vision was that people would walk off the street to shop below ground—an idea John D. Rockefeller Jr. had tried down on 48th Street with Rockefeller Center.

The concept was lampooned by some as the unwelcome footprint of capitalism; in early 1965 a group of New York socialites led by the writer Fannie Hurst protested along Fifth Avenue and declared that the city was losing its historic landmarks to the ugly clang of the wrecker's ball. Famed economist John Kenneth Galbraith was quoted saying, "Americans spend $5 billion a year visiting the historic shrines of Europe and then spend the same amount tearing down their own."

Cecilia Benattar was ready for the protesters. She had lined up her public relations strategy. "I said I was willing to meet with them," she told the press. "But I never heard from them."

Partly this was because, with typical foresight, Benattar changed the conversation: she gave the media another story to chew on.

■ ■ ■

The contents of the Savoy-Plaza Hotel needed to be sold before the building could come down. When told the estimated price she would likely get for them at public auction, Cecilia decided upon a path that, she hoped, was both newsworthy and would bring in twice the dollars.

She decided to hold a "discreet" private sale that, she figured, would get the "cognoscenti" excited. She hired an auctioneer from Florida, Bob Johnstone, and told him to get a New York telephone directory and mail out invitations to everyone with the initials "S.P." When he'd finished with them, he could invite anyone with the initials S.H. (The hotel was called the Savoy Hilton after 1957.)

The result? Would-be purchasers of monogrammed silver descended upon the place in such numbers that the sales had to be moved to a bigger hall.

It was the most written up, successful private sale New York had ever seen. Benattar earned more than twice what she was originally offered by job-lot auctioneers and was hailed as a marketing genius. "It took a woman to think of this piecemeal disposal," remarked the feminist author Gloria Steinem in the *Ladies' Home Journal*.

Steinem added: "The Marquise Gerini bought part of the grand staircase for her villa near Rome; a marble statue was shipped off to composer Frederick Loewe's house in Palm Springs; a millionaire named Jack Fink put the entire contents of rooms 2211 through 2213 aboard his yacht and sent them to his summer home in the Bahamas; Arlene Francis, the television personality, bought a chandelier for her bathroom in the Ritz Towers and regretted being 'a little too late for the Baccarat glasses.'"And there was also the "race" for Zsa Zsa Gabor's three beds. One bed was purchased by the actress Esta Mann, who commented that it was very low. "This has got to be the most chic secondhand business in the history of Manhattan," one antique dealer said.

■ ■ ■

Benattar's next order of business was to secure tenants for all the floors not occupied by General Motors. She was asking $7 to $7.50 a square foot—double the usual midtown rents—in an untested area from people who were wary of what she was selling them.

Estée Lauder, the cosmetics maven, was just becoming a worldwide name. Cecilia befriended her young son Leonard, who was Estée's right hand. Wouldn't Estée like an office where she could walk to work from her home on the Upper East Side? An office where she would have a giant floor and terrific views and be associated with the most successful company in the world?

Leonard thought it was a great idea. He and Cecilia became fast friends. Estée, however, was more cautious. She wasn't familiar with electronic elevators and was nervous initially about going higher than the second floor. She also didn't like the hand-painted Chinese wallpaper that had been selected. "Remove it," she said when she walked in one morning. And they did. They also expanded the reception area when she took a look at it and said it was "too small." She told her son she didn't think she needed the new offices and that she'd never go there— "but then she went every day," says Leonard. "She loved it." The offices have remained Estée Lauder's flagship.

Estée Lauder wasn't the only tenant afraid of new technology. Charles Revson, the founder and CEO of Revlon, had rented arguably the best floor—top of the building—yet he wanted to move once he realized the air-conditioning units were above him on the roof. He was afraid they might be too noisy. (His successor, Ronald Perelman, didn't like the high floor for another reason: He hated the long wait for the elevator, so he had an assistant hold the doors open with a garbage can shortly before he was due to leave.)

In 1968 Helena Rubinstein signed a lease and the building acquired a nickname, remembers Leonard Lauder: "the General Odors Building!" People like to joke that the three resident cosmetic companies asked to be in separate elevator banks to avoid corporate espionage.

Benattar quickly became known as a ruthless negotiator; she didn't rely on lawyers to draft her leases. She and Jesse Wolff created originals—often staying up late—and once done, she wouldn't brook argument with potential signatories. She explained her thinking to Geoffrey Wharton: "Look, it was really simple. I had the General Motors Building. I had a lease. Either you signed it or you didn't. I allowed you the discretion of the color of the ink. Beyond that, I wasn't interested in your comments."

A young broker named Harry Macklowe hoped to forge a lease for a hot new advertising firm named Wells Rich and Greene. Macklowe thought they would make an ideal tenant in the building: the cofounder— a young, chic blonde named Mary Wells—was already renowned in the industry and rumored to be dating Harding L. Lawrence, the president of Braniff Airlines. These were the sort of cutting-edge connections and branding Benattar wanted for her new building.

Macklowe introduced the two women with some trepidation, thinking, "Wells is very WASPy, . . . and Cecilia is not." He wasn't sure they'd get on.

They did. "She was very funny," Wells recalls. "She was very cute. She didn't really think that I could afford [the lease]. She told me that she told the people at General Motors that it was ideal because, by the time I went bankrupt, they would need an extra floor." Wells Rich and Greene went on to become so successful that Mary Wells took two more floors.

■ ■ ■

There was a tenant Cecilia badly wanted: Weil, Gotshal & Manges. Partly this was for altruistic reasons: She wanted to thank Jesse Wolff, and she firmly believed that if Weil Gotshal was the only law firm she allowed into the building it would be the making of the small partnership.

She told Wolff he could take as much space as the firm wanted. The only catch: The rent, at around $7 a square foot, would be double what the lawyers currently paid.

Well, that was not the only catch. The location also gave them pause. "It was not a place that law firms would want to be," says Ira Millstein, explaining that all other big firms were downtown. "There was a big debate among us as to whether we should take the chance and move. I remember coming up here with Jess and riding the elevators. We stood at the top of building while it was still steelwork. We looked out and said, "Wow! This is really terrific!"

At one point, Benattar even mentioned to the firm's senior partner, Sylvan Gotshal, that she could build a cable car line between the Sherry Netherland hotel (where he lived) and the building so he could have a particularly easy commute.

"Sylvan, you can just go over—you'd never have to hit the street," Millstein recalls teasing him.

"Cecilia said, 'Take as much space as you want—you're never going to lose any money on this.' And so we convened and decided that the most we could take was a half floor."

Benattar was right. Weil Gotshal would come to wish they'd taken more space. "Moving into the building was a game changer for us not only because of the location, but because it got us to meet and be liked by the biggest company in the world," says Millstein. "And that relationship developed over the years and we eventually became one of GM's major law firms, which was fine. I mean, that was great. But Jess was the one who broke the ice on that. . . . At GM, they loved Jess."

Partly they loved Jess because he was so much easier to deal with than Cecilia Benattar.

"I think they always had trouble with Cecilia because she was tough," says Millstein. "So Jess worked out most of the wrinkles in dealing with General Motors. . . . He was her rock of Gibraltar."

■ ■ ■

As more and more blue-chip tenants came in, Benattar worked day and night with outfitters, personnel, and construction workers. She interviewed every employee in the place and kept cash in the office in case of any crisis. Her son Simon recalls that she liked to hire ex-convicts from minority backgrounds, if possible. She wanted to give them a second chance. She believed that they were a far more worthy cause than the mobsters who staffed many other buildings in New York.

The mob, which controlled garbage collection, noticed her snub. In 1969, Robbie Rayne recalls, garbage costs escalated dramatically— "they went from something like six to 16." Benattar, typically, refused to pay the bill. A standoff began, and the building was closed down due to overflowing garbage. The vice chairman of the board of GM, George Russell, intervened and told her to surrender. She did, but reluctantly. Benattar did not like to compromise on anything.

■ ■ ■

Robbie Rayne had joined Benattar in New York as his father's eyes and ears in 1967. He was impressed by the hive of activity and remembered, "We were particularly busy one Friday in 1969, when Cecilia had a baby daughter."

Benattar returned to work as usual on Monday and "since we remained busy with leasing for six months," the baby went unnamed for that period. No one was much surprised.

Colleagues recall that Benattar liked to work in bursts. She'd go all out for a couple of weeks, then disappear for three days to be with her family—and then she would reemerge, armed with six packets of cigarettes, and put in three days and nights straight.

By 1969 she had four children: Naomi, Simon, Jessica, and Judith (who had gone unnamed for a while). She explained in media interviews that her mother, along with a housekeeper, helped her run the house and take care of the children and that most days she left the office to have dinner with her family—only to return. "I strive to make people forget me as a woman and see me just as someone who knows her job," she said.

The men around her—almost everyone she dealt with *was* a man— were charmed, bewildered, and, very often, beaten by her. They'd never seen anyone—least of all a woman—like her.

"She always looked for an edge," recalls James "Jim" Nagy, who was the first building manager appointed by General Motors.

She loved doing crossword puzzles, and sometimes entered national puzzle competitions. Geoffrey Wharton recalls that once she made it to the final round and was so competitive that she shut down the offices for a couple of weeks so she could focus. "Everyone else had to focus on winning it, too!"

She also asked Wharton, then a young lawyer in his twenties, to work directly for her. Jess Wolff told him not to do it. "She is too strong for you; she'll eat you up," he said. "Be her friend instead."

As her friend, Wharton had a blast. She provided him with an inexhaustible supply of stories. There was the time in Westchester, New York, when she went to buy a Cadillac; she was dressed down. When she asked the salesman how many miles to the gallon it got, he retorted that if she had to ask about the cost of gas, the car was probably too expensive for her. She asked him who he would like to be fired by—the branch manager or the head of GM himself?

■ ■ ■

Once the building was leased, Benattar needed a new project. She eyed a building known as the Claridge House on Sixth Avenue at 55th Street. It was a residential building that, she told Max Rayne, would make a great office building once it was rezoned and the 400 tenants were evicted. She was given permission to build 400,000 square feet above the current property.

Wolff smelled trouble. He told her he didn't think that many tenants would easily be evicted; he also foresaw problems with the zoning laws under a very ambitious mayor, John Lindsay. So she hired an outside lawyer to represent her, Michael Schwartz, "a nice man completely dominated by Cecilia," according to Robbie Rayne. Benattar and Schwartz subsequently married.

Jack Benattar, the father of her four kids, who had been working for her as an architect on the building, was easily dispatched. "She fired him without any problem," said Robbie Rayne. He moved to Israel.

Schwartz did his best to maneuver for her on the Claridge House, but things started to go wrong. Lindsay was running for U.S. president in 1972. He was introduced to Benattar and asked her for a donation of $100,000 to his presidential campaign. According to several people, she was outraged and refused. "She felt he was so brazen," says Wharton. But she paid for her recalcitrance. Suddenly, she found that the Claridge House was no longer approved for commercial use.

Max Rayne had already spent a lot of money on the project. He was not amused. "It was a disaster," recalls Robbie Rayne. "We lost a lot of money on that."

Max and Cecilia had always argued, but until now they'd easily gotten over their differences. She even had a 10-by-8-inch photograph of him on her desk. The pair usually communicated daily by telex. He signed his missives "love Max." In a sign of just how close they were, she was the only person allowed to mock his growing stature in the world. She addressed him with ever-inflated titles: "your holiness, your greatest excellence, your hugeness." But in public she always deferred to him as "Sir Max."

But in the 1970s something in their relationship changed. Simon Benattar says his mother felt there was "jealousy" of her "success and power" in Rayne's London office. Of course the Londoners didn't see the hard work she put in; what they did see was that to many people she, not Rayne, was the face, the brand, of the GM Building. Max Rayne was scarcely in town. And that was the problem. He didn't want to be in New York. He wanted to be in London. He wanted to sell the GM Building.

"Cecilia was very much looking to create a bigger empire here, and there was discussion about the basis on which she was continuing to be involved. We got her message. She wanted to expand—and he [Max] wanted to get out," says Robbie Rayne.

"They didn't have a falling-out," he says. "They just had different objectives at that point. And the amount of time and distraction that we had was becoming too much."

■ ■ ■

In 1971, Benattar executed the sale of the building to General Motors, and made a profit of about $30 million for her boss. "Of course had we kept it, it is now worth more than our entire portfolio," says Robbie Rayne. But Max Rayne remained conservative. "When you come from nothing and you make something, you'd like to capitalize," his son explains.

And Benattar? She got a stake in one floor and 5 percent of the profits. Letters from her in 1975 show a new company logo: PBU, which stood for "Pro Bono US."

"She had," says Robbie Rayne, "a very good sense of humor."

She relocated to Toronto, where Rayne had a new site for her to work on—and there were tax advantages. According to Harvey Miller, Benattar was openly opposed to paying U.S. income tax. "She felt, 'It's my money. My money supporting all these people on relief and so forth!'" Weil Gotshal's tax lawyer, Martin "Marty" D. Ginsberg, whose wife, Ruth Bader Ginsberg, would go on to be a U.S. Supreme Court Justice, helped her set up PBU to make sure "there was no extended tax liability," recalls Harvey Miller.

She was also growing disenchanted with the rising crime in New York, which almost went bankrupt in the 1970s.

In 1978 she liquidated PBU and set up a new real estate holding company called NIOT: Now It's Our Turn. Across the Atlantic, Max Rayne chuckled at the acronym. But Cecilia Benattar slowly faded out of the limelight. In 1991, her son Simon bought her out of NIOT and she spent her time investing in stocks. She was busy writing a book to be called *Structures*, but had not completed it before her death in 2003 on a plane traveling from Florida to California. Max Rayne also died that year in London; he was hailed as an "outstanding philanthropist," an "extraordinary patron of the arts," and a developer who "left a great mark . . . in renovating a damaged London." His recognition far exceeded that of Cecilia Benattar—except in the minds of the few who knew the truth and who had watched the housewife tycoon with awe.

"Most people thought she was the owner of the building; they didn't realize it was Max," Harry Macklowe would recall. Jerry I. Speyer, founding partner of Tishman Speyer, never forgot her impact. "Right after I met her, I said to my colleagues: 'We have got to hire a senior woman executive' . . . and we did. We had no women in the business until that moment. She changed the way we thought."

"The toughest woman in real estate" is what the headline on her 1965 *Life* magazine profile had read.

Chapter 6

The Age of the Wolf

*He was beyond mean. He was crazy. He made Leona
Helmsley look like one of the sweetest young women
on earth. That's how bad he was. . . . I've never known
anybody meaner than Disque Deane.*

—Donald Trump

G eneral Motors looked impregnable in its gleaming white fortress. There was a popular saying, "What's good for General
Motors is good for the country." It was derived from a slight misquote from the Senate confirmation hearings of Charles Erwin Wilson,
the former GM president and CEO who was appointed Secretary of
Defense in 1953. He was asked if he could conceive of making a decision
as Defense Secretary that would be adverse to the company. He said he
could but he could not conceive that such a situation should arise. "For
years I thought what was good for the country was good for General
Motors and vice versa."

He might have added that what was bad for the United States was very bad for GM. When the Arab oil crisis of 1974 hit, GM was plagued with product issues. In 1980 the great recession struck; there were standoffs with the unions, and slowly the behemoth's fortunes began to slide—and with them the building's polish. It became "dirty, shabby" and asbestos was discovered, according to Ira Millstein and Harvey Miller. They knew things were amiss when GM's Frigidaire division on the first floor disappeared. The next thing they knew, GM employees were eating in Weil Gotshal's cafeteria. This was a real turnabout. For years, everyone had eaten in the subsidized GM cafeteria.

GM turned to Weil Gotshal, in particular an attorney named Martin "Marty" J. Rabinowitz, for ideas on how to raise money—without paying taxes. Rabinowitz came up with the idea of using the building as a cash machine; they'd purchase a loan—with the building as collateral. This way they'd avoid $150 million in sales tax.

On January 5, 1982, it was announced that Corporate Property Investors (CPI)—a real estate investment trust (REIT) few had heard of since it was primarily invested in unglamorous suburban shopping malls—was "buying" a convertible note on the GM Building.

A report in the *New York Times* stated that the deal, the largest mortgage ever, was so unusual that it didn't even have a name. Essentially, CPI had loaned GM $500 million. GM had to pay CPI back 10 percent a year for 10 years—at a remarkably low interest rate, since Treasury bonds were at 14 percent—at the end of which GM could either pay off the debt or sell the building to CPI. Neither side was hit with a tax liability.

Once again the building had been at the heart of stealthy negotiations with a bidder on one side who appeared to come out of nowhere.

This was exactly what Disque D. Deane, the sandy-haired financier who had founded CPI in 1971, wanted. He thought all press was bad press. He was so low-key that he didn't bother to move his offices to the GM Building, because he thought the rents were too expensive—and, anyway, his headquarters at 305 East 47th Street housed a few secrets.

Roderick "Rod" Johnson, the GM Building's manager, was relieved to hear that Deane wasn't moving. Johnson had heard Deane was someone to be feared, that he had a terrible temper; that he was a screamer, unpredictable; that he had once hit a man over the head with a bottle of wine; that he kept a stuffed Alaskan timberland wolf in his office as a reminder both to himself and others that it was a dog-eat-dog world. The wolf was also the logo on CPI stationery.

■ ■ ■

Disque Deane had always believed that a person's value was defined entirely by money. His father was a seminarian turned landscape architect who found little work in the 1930s, but young Disque's aptitude for figures and science won him a place at Stuyvesant High School in New York City, and from there he won a scholarship to Duke University.

He was neither rich nor "connected," he would later write in his unpublished diaries. He felt he had no choice but to become what he called "an innovator" on Wall Street. He started out as a bond trader at Eastman Dillon Securities, where he created the sale-leaseback: he and his investors bought real estate from companies like Safeway and Loblaw and gas stations, firms that would rather monetize their buildings than own them, and then Deane and his investors would profit from the building's tax loss or shelter.

He was so successful—with annual returns of 17 percent—that a team sprang up under him at Eastman Dillon. He hired a Harvard Business School graduate named Hans C. Mautner, who had an offer from a management consulting firm; Deane persuaded Mautner he wouldn't regret coming to him for a smaller salary. Business was booming.

Or was it? There was a hiccup within months; Deane and Eastman Dillon had a falling-out. (Colleagues recalled that Deane had awarded himself some warrants that his partner disputed.) Mautner was worried. Had he given up a much higher-paying job, only to be fired?

But Deane took Mautner, an executive named Jerry O'Connor, and two others with him to work for the person who would be key to Deane's long-term success: the senior partner and chairman of Lazard Freres, the legendary financier André Meyer.

■ ■ ■

Most of Wall Street at the time was interested in mergers and acquisitions. Real estate and tax shelters were frowned upon by blue-chip firms—but not by the wily, cutthroat Frenchman at the top of Lazard. "Mr. Meyer had an open mind about things, and he also had a great belief in the ultimate value of hard assets, so real estate appealed to him," recalls Hans Mautner. "He had done some transactions with Bill Zeckendorf and done relatively well as a consequence of that." Meyer, with Deane's help, had invested in Zeckendorf's giant Long Island mall, Roosevelt Field.

He loved Deane's facility for cutting corners, and encouraged it. According to Deane's notes, when he first got to Lazard he encouraged Meyer to sell nondomestic interest in a Texas lease to an offshore entity to avoid paying 40 percent tax. Meyer sold the interest to all his foreign friends, men such as Pierre David-Weill, Gianni Agnelli, Charles W. Englehart, and others in London. What Deane didn't realize, he wrote, was that all of them had "a voluntary obligation" to give "Mr. Meyer reciprocity for any profit they might make."

When the property was sold for a profit of $18 million, the Internal Revenue Service started making inquiries. Around the world affidavits were given while the partner promised that the "new foreign entity was independently owned." At that point, Deane writes blandly, "there was no mention of potential reciprocity, as it was voluntary!"

■ ■ ■

Meyer also saw the advantages to being the principal in real estate—not just the middleman. Deane formed Peerage Properties, in which Meyer and his wealthy friends, such as the Agnellis, were the chief investors. Meyer soon realized, according to Mautner, that "it wasn't a night-and-weekend proposition."

Meyer suggested it be run outside of Lazard, with Deane at the helm. Meyer took aside Mautner, widely considered "more elegant" than Deane. "He phrased it, like, 'You can stay, but I'd like you to go and become a full-time employee of Peerage.'

"He had given me a choice, but it was no choice at all," Mautner says. "I either had to do it or I'm sure that I would've had a circumscribed career at Lazard."

Peerage would shortly become the private REIT known as CPI. Deane was happy to have an umbrella of his own. A former senior officer of CPI, Thomas "Tom" E. Zacharias, says Deane had found it difficult to deal with the constant fighting and backstabbing at Lazard. For a while he'd thought that since he made the most money, he should be considered Meyer's natural heir. But, much to his frustration, he would find that this bank was run like a mercurial French court and nothing worked according to rules. Felix Rohatyn, whom Deane considered an enemy, was Meyer's favorite.

G. Martin Fell, an Englishman who went to work for CPI as an accountant, would recall that when Meyer died in 1979, Deane and the other partners at Lazard went to the funeral "to check he was really dead." He remembers that "Felix took a separate plane."

■ ■ ■

In 1972, Meyer and Deane set up the most famous of all their tax shelters: a vast housing complex in New York with its own power plant, post office, and shopping center. Despite the fact that Starrett City was set up to provide subsidized housing for poor people, its main purpose was to shelter income for its rich investors.

One of Deane's partners in Starrett was the son of a Queens builder, Fred Trump, whom he knew and respected. Donald Trump came into the Starrett deal at the very last moment. Trump would recall that he had just hours to close. "I didn't have time to hire law firms, so I said, 'Listen, I will take it, but I want the exact same deal Disque Deane has and Pierre David-Weill has and André Meyer has.' I said, 'I want a certified statement, and if I have that certified statement guaranteed by an accounting firm, I will take the deal.' . . . It turned out to be one of the greatest tax deals ever made."

Deane, Trump would recall, was a terrific partner. He shouted and bullied to get exactly what he wanted. At a meeting with Henry Benach, the CEO of Starrett, Deane screamed at Benach, threatening him if the project fell behind: "'I will bankrupt you. I will destroy you.' You almost had to hold him back, he was so crazed," says Trump. "They ended up not being late, believe me.

"He was probably the meanest, angriest human being I've ever met, and one of the greatest partners, because he was *my* partner. So what he was fighting—he was fighting for me because I had the same deal that he had, okay?

"He was a great partner, but he was a horrible human being."

■ ■ ■

Deane's meanness wasn't confined to work. In 1991, when Trump was getting divorced from Ivana, wife number one, his attorney told him that ultimately most of his clients behaved reasonably, "except one."

Trump recalls, "He said, 'I have a client named Disque Deane, and he is the meanest client I've ever had. He doesn't want to give her nothing [*sic*]. He wants to destroy her, and he was married for 39 years.'"

Even those with fond professional memories of Deane struggle to explain the dissolution of his long marriage. "I think he started having a bit of a midlife crisis," says Zacharias.

Deane had also watched the "French" way of life at Lazard Freres; he'd seen André Meyer install his wife on one floor of the Carlyle Hotel and his mistress on another. "Disque started having these very public affairs," says Zacharias.

No one would have paid much notice to Disque Deane's personal life except for two facts. The first was that his wife of 39 years, Marjorie, was loyal, beautiful, and hardworking; and for reasons that some found unfathomable, she really loved her husband. The second was that Deane's treatment of her and their children was breathtakingly brutal. Deane had married Marjorie Schlesinger in his early thirties. They had four children: Marjorie Gregg (known as Gregg), Kathryn Morgan (Kathy), Disque Jr. (D.D.), and Walter. According to Walter and Zacharias, their father neglected to tell either Marjorie or his children that he'd been married before. His first marriage was to Anne Shepard Delafield, a woman with family roots in high society. They'd had a son, Hare, who emerged in the 1990s—toothless and a complete surprise. Walter Deane would remember a young man who looked very like his father suddenly appearing—and his father shouting at him to go away. Despite the fact that Disque Deane would make a billion dollars—as he'd brag to the journalist and author William "Bill" D. Cohan—Marjorie Schlesinger Deane paid for her children's private schooling out of her salary as the first woman senior vice president at Macy's department store.

Both Kathy and Walter say it was also their mother's earnings that paid for their day-to-day expenses, including household staff. Their father was an emotionally remote man who grilled his children about "compound interest" at the breakfast table and sporadically beat them with his belt.

Though he would appear robotically for dinner with Marjorie every night, he would always disappear afterward, "to walk the dog"—a euphemism for "catting around."

Part of him wanted to belong; another part really didn't. His daughter Kathy recalls that he loved jogging shirtless around Southampton on weekends—right past signs stating clearly that one should keep one's shirt on.

He was thrown out of the Southampton Bathing Corporation for getting into a fight with Charlie Magowan (a member of the family that founded Merrill Lynch) and smashing a bottle of wine over his head.

He could be desperately cheap, often driving miles to avoid paying bridge tolls. He frowned on frills in his homes, which had grand bones, but spartan decor. Yet he spent a large amount of money on mistresses— of whom he had a few.

"He believed that he could buy women," explains Zacharias.

■ ■ ■

One of the reasons he didn't want to move his corporate headquarters to the GM Building in 1982 had to do with one of those women.

Deane had started a very public liaison with a dark-haired real estate broker named Barbara "Barbie" Koz around 1980. He once flew Koz in the company plane with both Zacharias and another colleague, Warren Hamer, to Novia Scotia to look at a yacht.

One memorable Christmas he flew with his wife and children to Montreal on his private plane, checked them into a hotel, and then abruptly left for New York. There he packed his bags, met Koz, and flew with her to Paris. Even the Deanes' doorman knew about it and hugged an embarrassed Marjorie Deane upon her return.

It was Koz who found the building on East 47th Street, then owned by one Harry Macklowe. Deane clearly viewed his new headquarters as a home away from home; he installed a wine cellar, a squash court, and lavish bathrooms there. "He thought it could achieve an attractive rehabilitation tax credit," said Tom Zacharias.

■ ■ ■

Finding tax exemptions and credits where no one else saw them was the true love of his life. "The guy slept with the tax code," joked one of his best friends, Warren G. Hamer. But in 1982 when he saw that GM wanted to monetize its building he leapt.

"It was not generally our business," recalls G. Martin Fell. "Our business was shopping centers. But this was an attractive proposition."

Deane believed firmly that GM would never be able to buy it back, and it would be his at the end of those 10 years. He was so delighted about his 1982 coup that, most atypically, the day after they signed the deal, he left the office early with his two senior partners, Hans Mautner and Jerry O'Connor, and the three of them posed for a photograph outside the building. Of course, he hadn't pledged all of that $500 million alone. Most of it was, as was Deane's modus operandi, other people's money.

■ ■ ■

"We bought the GM Building in two phone calls," says Zacharias. One call was to David Feldman, who ran the pension funds at AT&T. Feldman pledged $200 million or thereabouts. The other call was to Fuad Jaffar, then the general manager of the Kuwait Investment Authority (KIA).

The Kuwaitis had some questions before committing $200 million. Mautner got on a plane to Kuwait to meet with them. "I outlined the deal. I said, 'This is the rate of interest, and the building could be worth X in the future, and yada, yada, yada. What do you think?'"

Their answer floored him: "Well, it could be interesting, but do you think General Motors will be around to service their debt?"

Mautner says, "And I thought to myself, I mean, who are these guys? [GM] was an icon of American corporate industry and financial strength, and to have these guys ask a question like that—it almost seemed seditious.

"But, you know, given what happened in subsequent years, they weren't so stupid."

■ ■ ■

The KIA signed. They realized, like Deane, that the building would be worth at least $500 million at the end of 10 years, with its blue-chip tenants, long leases, and location. Deane kept a beady eye on his investment. While he didn't like spending money—and according to his son, he didn't care a jot about the "aesthetics" of the building—he also didn't want the building going to seed under GM's "ownership."

He turned his attention to the plaza. The only successful retailer there was hairdresser Vidal Sassoon. Everything else, including the themed restaurant, the Auto Pub, was a disaster. And the plaza was ugly. "It was like a wind tunnel on Fifth Avenue," recalls Walter Deane. "Trash flying everywhere."

Disque Deane held an architectural competition and even sent Mautner to see the architect Philip Johnson for advice. Mautner says Johnson was "very condescending" about Edward Durrell Stone's design. It was "fatuous," said Johnson, to have put a small plaza anywhere near the much larger Grand Army Plaza across the street.

Johnson suggested raising the plaza, but Deane never acted on the advice—partly because of the cost. He was a numbers man, not a developer.

■ ■ ■

In 1991, after sitting on his note for 10 years, Deane bought the building from GM, which ultimately relocated back to Detroit.

Deane was reasonably well-behaved while he ran the building. Rod Johnson, the manager, remembers him being "charming . . . never ranting and raving." His son Walter recalls that his father made sure he visited all the tenants on a regular basis. "My father, even though he didn't spend money on the building, cared greatly about it, cared about the tenants, knew the tenants, knew the building, walked up and down the halls, knew all the security guards, was very involved on a day-to-day basis."

But the tranquility didn't last long. That same year Deane was—to his astonishment—ousted from CPI. This was a company he had started with a $50 million investment and that was by then worth $5 billion. How, he railed, could he be kicked out?

Ironically, he had himself to blame. Months before, when he'd felt the board was getting too large, Deane had introduced a clause into CPI's corporate rubric that company officers must retire at 70. And he'd just turned 70. Apparently he thought the rules didn't apply to him.

But the board suggested it was time for him to go. At his last board meeting he thanked everyone.

Inside he was furious. "The firing just knocked him right out," says his son. "These were arrogant people who were not very smart, and were in positions that were quite extraordinary in terms of the money that they made only because of my father."

■ ■ ■

As part of his retirement package Disque Deane was given an office at the top of the GM Building for 10 years. "You could see the whole world from up there," Walter would say.

Deane watched from his 50th-floor perch as the building, from his perspective, fell apart. "The bathrooms were very dirty, and the urinals didn't work," remembers Walter, who took offices on a lower floor, where he set up a real estate brokerage firm, Longstreet Associates. He recalls he had a fax machine stolen from his office, which was broken into five times.

"No one was managing the building. There was nobody who cared about the building. What they cared about was the money. CPI declined rapidly after my father's retirement."

Actually, it wasn't quite fair to say CPI declined. In 1998 Hans Mautner decided to sell it—the shareholders' positions had gotten so large that liquidity was impaired. He hired the bankers Lazard Freres and J.P. Morgan to shop CPI.

A young Midwesterner by the name of David Simon learned of the impending sale. The shopping center group his father and uncle had begun, the Simon Property Group, had recently gone public. Simon didn't know anyone at CPI. He rang Joseph "Joe" R. Perella, an investment banker he'd worked for at First Boston and then Wasserstein Perella. Perella had joined the Simon board when it went public.

"David said, 'Hey, I'm trying to buy this,'" Perella recalls. "'These people don't know us. Can you talk to them about us?' So I called up Dennis Dammerman." Dammerman had been the CFO of General Electric, and was on the board of CPI.

■ ■ ■

Mike Fascitelli and Steve Roth were part of a rival bid by the Rouse Company, also a shopping center group, for one reason only: "We [believed] we were taking the GM Building over for $700 million."

It wasn't to be. CPI preferred Simon's bid of $5.8 billion. (Mautner would later say he smelled a "desperation" about the Rouse/Vornado bid he didn't like.)

After the deal was closed, Mautner recalled:"I got a note from Disque saying 'Hey, you shouldn't have sold this company. The GM Building is worth more than that.'"

■ ■ ■

David Simon never met Disque Deane. But he did meet Disque's wolf. He went over to the CPI lobby on East 47th Street to meet the team prior to the closing and saw the beast. He was first taken aback by its size, its daunting aura. "It was shot and killed and stuffed, I guess." After the closing, he noticed the wolf was gone. "I thought that wolf was mine 'cause I paid for it, but somehow Disque got the wolf and it disappeared, long gone," he said with a laugh.

■ ■ ■

Disque Deane did not slow down after his retirement. He had gotten remarried in his early seventies to Carol Gram, his daughter Gregg's best friend. It was a union that poisoned many of his relationships.

They had met through work. According to Tom Zacharias, around 1990 Marjorie and Gregg had asked Deane if he could find Carol a position at CPI. Carol worked for Marjorie's best friend, a woman named Roz Jacobs who consulted on merchandising for the malls.

Within days of being hired, Carol was frequently in Deane's office and they began an affair.

In 1991, she got pregnant. "Fat" was what she told Gregg—who had no clue about the affair with her father. And then she said she was leaving for Paris.

Right before Carol had his child, Disque Deane went to Bermuda, where he obtained a divorce from Marjorie—the cheapest way possible. After 39 years of marriage, he ended up paying her $2.4 million. This would not be enough to see her through her later years, during which she suffered from Alzheimer's disease. "What happened to my mother taught me that all women must have their own money," Kathy Deane said. "Basically my father killed her. She died of a broken heart.

"When he left her, he left all of us."

■ ■ ■

Disque and Carol had two children, Anne and Carl. Once his second set of children reached school age, he and Carol moved to Beacon Hill, in Boston. He realized, in a rare moment of social sensitivity, that it would be embarrassing for his young wife to put their kids into the same New York private schools his first four children—and his grandchildren—attended.

He and Carol also spent time in Bolivia, where he made a fortune in land and soybeans. He also bought Ecuadorian gold mines. He invested his fortune in trusts, partly for the children he had no personal relationship with. He was irked, according to his diaries—and to friends—that his children never pursued careers as lucrative as his. He donated $20 million to his alma mater, Duke University. But, in rather typical Disque Deane fashion, the gift came with strings. He wanted the university to consult him on new faculty hirings. There was a dispute before there was a settlement.

■ ■ ■

Deane suffered a stroke in 2004, but even this didn't deter him from coming to the office. Martin Fell remembers he was back at work the Monday after he'd collapsed, joking that it had been a mistake to eat fish every day at Paper Moon, a regular haunt; he should have had the steak.

In 2006 and 2007, he and Carol tried to sell Starrett City—firing up lawmakers, especially the U.S. senator from New York, Charles Schumer, who insisted it remain low-income housing. When they couldn't sell, they refinanced it. The owners earned $200 million. The Deanes were sued for allegedly shortchanging senior executives.

■ ■ ■

After their father's stroke, Kathy, Gregg, D.D., and Walter tried to spend time with him. They would call the house in Boston and ask if they could stay for Thanksgiving, and would be told no. The third Mrs. Deane wanted little, if anything, to do with her "stepchildren."

On November 8, 2010, Walter Deane heard that his father had died in Boston. He and his three siblings drove out to a funeral in East Hampton. To his horror he discovered, too late, that his father had been cremated. Walter burst into tears. His father had been terrified of being cremated, and had repeatedly asked to be buried. He'd even bought a plot in Bermuda. That the unthinkable had happened merely reinforced to his children that even at his death, they were all so far apart.

On November 19 a memorial service was held at the Fifth Avenue Presbyterian Church. Hare, his unrecognized son from his first marriage, attended. So did the four children from his second marriage. They couldn't understand why they were at a Presbyterian church; Deane was Episcopalian.

According to Tom Zacharias, at some point the four "Schlesinger" kids decided they'd had enough of being passive onlookers. D.D. stood up and gave a startling eulogy. "He talked about what it was like to grow up with Disque Deane. He said that if you didn't know the compound interest tables at breakfast, you would be punished. It was biting. He even talked about Disque starting another family and what that meant for his first family. He touched a lot of very interesting issues."

D.D. ended his eulogy by saying, "I am still mourning his loss, as I truly loved him, despite everything he did to us."

Chapter 7

Donald Trump's
Bag Man

I called it Alice in Wonderland because when you work in Donald's office, everything that's up is down. Everything that's black is white. I became absolutely insane.

—Abraham Wallach

David Simon knew that at $5.2 billion he'd paid a premium for Corporate Property Investors (CPI). "People thought we were nuts," he'd later say, but he anticipated a heated contest among the "New York sharpies" for the GM Building, for which he wanted $800 million. The "geniuses," as he sarcastically referred to the big New York real estate families (he's from Indianapolis), would surely line up for the prize and he'd get his money back and—crucially—avoid paying taxes, by flipping it as he bought it.

In February 1998 he hired Lazard and Morgan Stanley to shop the building. Both industrialist Marvin H. Davis and Vornado expressed interest; both asked to sign confidentiality agreements and enter the so-called war room—where they could view the building's data. This meant they were serious. But Simon was worried that neither would make a credible bid: He felt Davis looked at *everything* and Vornado would never get beyond a price in the mid-700s. "I begged them to get serious," says Simon. "Now, [Steve Roth] will deny this, but I begged him to get serious."

He soon realized that he was the victim of timing. The Internet was booming and real estate developers were worried that office space values would plummet. Another problem: The people at Vornado had no idea they had any competition. They believed there was no "cover bid."

They were wrong.

There was *one* person intent on making the $800 million price tag—but Simon was wary, initially, of this person: Donald Trump. Trump, Simon knew, had "not had a good run" in the early 1990s. His casino business had been massively overleveraged and had had to go through a restructuring.

■ ■ ■

Simon remembers that Trump was introduced to his representatives via an unexpected route—it was not Morgan Stanley or Lazard, his brokers; instead the conduit was a blonde, a broker who was "very aggressive," as he would recall. Her name was Rita Jenrette.

Jenrette was infamous—but not as a real estate broker. A Texan, she was the ex-wife of John Jenrette, the former Democratic congressman from South Carolina convicted of receiving a bribe from a fake Arabian sheik in the Abscam sting of 1980 (recently the inspiration for the movie *American Hustle*). After he was indicted, she turned over $25,000 in cash she claimed she had found in a shoe in her husband's closet. She later posed nude for *Playboy* and boasted in the magazine that she and her ex-husband had had sex on the Capitol steps, triggering an alarm and summoning the police and the FBI. She went on to pursue a career in acting, starring in both *Fantasy Island* and *Zombie Island Massacre* (in which she performed the obligatory nude shower scene). She then turned to journalism and appeared as an on-camera reporter for

Fox News' *A Current Affair*; in 1994 she became a real estate broker and cofounded a brokerage firm, Sullivan Jenrette. "I wanted to prove I wasn't a figure of scorn," she told people. "I wanted to be able to reclaim my life, show my intelligence." She saw a big chance when one of her colleagues, a salesperson named Janine Riccoboni, said her uncle, John Rulli, was an executive at Simon DeBartolo (as the Simon Group was then known). Rulli let her show the GM Building's offering book to prospective clients.

Jenrette humorously referred to the whole situation as rather like the movie *Working Girl*, given the Janine-Rulli connection. She set up a meeting with Abraham "Abe" Wallach, Trump's executive vice president for acquisitions and finance.

"Wouldn't you want to see the name Trump around the GM Building?" she asked Wallach, a slender man with an intense stare. He recalls telling her that Trump wasn't interested. He didn't generally buy office buildings, and the GM Building was expensive and fully leased.

Wallach also received the offering brochure in the mail. He opened it while sitting on a flight from Los Angeles to New York with Donald. They both agreed there was no room for development, so Wallach put it away. The flight droned on. Wallach pulled out the offering book again. What about the retail possibilities of the plaza and the enormous GM showroom that took up the first floor? If you added in the space from FAO Schwarz, then facing bankruptcy, that added up to more than 150,000 square feet of potential prime retail space.

Wallach spun out his ideas for Trump, who grew interested. But they would need a cash-rich equity partner. Who? Wallach remembers flipping through his Rolodex while on the plane. "I started to scroll through it. I threw out names. Apollo. He said no, he didn't think that Bill Mack would be interested. AIG was the next name I mentioned. Again he said no, he didn't think he could make a deal with Hank Greenberg. I continued to scroll down into the Bs. . . . I went into the Cs. I next mentioned the Carlyle Group in Washington, D.C.; he dismissed them without an explanation. Without really knowing who they were or what they did in real estate, I blurted out Conseco. His eyes lit up. He turned to me and said, 'Yes, Steve Hilbert will do this deal.'"

When Trump landed, he got on the phone to Hilbert, and said, "Do you know David Simon?"

Hilbert did.

Jenrette phoned and phoned Trump's offices; she'd claim she had flown to Charlotte, North Carolina, to put together financing for Trump—and she'd later sue Simon DeBartolo for nonpayment of broker's fees of $6 million (the case was dismissed, but Simon paid her a small amount). "We didn't need her," Wallach says. "We had Steve Hilbert."

■ ■ ■

As it happened, Steve Hilbert didn't just know the Simon family; "they were wonderful, wonderful friends." The Hilberts and the Simons were Indiana's two royal families. The Simons owned the National Basketball Association (NBA)'s Indiana Pacers, and Conseco was in the process of buying the naming rights of the team's arena, soon to be known as the Conseco Fieldhouse.

Hilbert loved the idea of buying the GM Building with Trump. He told Trump he wanted his people to go over the details with Trump—quickly—but if all looked good, sure, he'd approach the Simons and put up nearly all the equity.

Hilbert was the flashiest guy in all of Indiana—he would take a helicopter for the five-mile commute to his office—but he was still relatively unknown on the national stage. A man of enormous appetites, he wanted to expand his business from a plain-vanilla insurance company. He believed Trump was the ticket. There was a quick meeting to check the building's rent rolls and leases—and then Hilbert went to see the Simon family on Memorial Day weekend. He met with David, his father Mel, and his uncle Herb. He told them that he'd gotten a call from Trump, and that together he was confident they could put together a bid for $800 million. He said he would personally "stand behind it." He agreed to their terms of paying an additional $40 million nonrefundable deposit to CPI. He promised they would close on time so that Simon could flip the building the same day they merged with CPI and avoid hefty transfer taxes.

The Simons trusted Hilbert. "He was very successful at the time," remembers David. "Hilbert came over, gave me the bid. It was clean. In real estate, a lot of people try to play games with closing—this, that, and the other. He made this simple. They were paying all the taxes. They were giving us $800 million. There was no due diligence, no financing. I shook his hand, and he closed without changing one nickel of the deal."

■ ■ ■

Abe Wallach was, as usual, Trump's eyes and ears; he would joke, "I was the chief cook and bottle washer." His first job on this deal was to negotiate a partnership agreement with Hilbert's executive vice president of corporate development, a woman, a former General Electric senior executive named Ngaire E. Cuneo.

Cuneo was widely respected but not versed in real estate. Even so, Wallach, who felt that "worrying was my job specification," was worried. He knew Cuneo understood that Trump wanted to manage the building—that was fine—but Trump also insisted on being a 50 percent "co-owner" and yet he would put up only $20 million (a minuscule fraction) in equity. Cuneo, in return, insisted Trump pay a steep "preferred" interest payment on the balance between $20 million and Conseco's equity in the deal—which ended up at $230 million. Wallach calculated that over the next five years Trump would owe Conseco $175 million, and he didn't like this one bit. He felt that the GM Building, valuable as she was, wouldn't throw off that kind of income unless his vision for the retail component was implemented. "I knew that trouble lay ahead," he would say later.

Next Wallach raced through the due diligence on the building, which the Simons had stipulated would take no more than two weeks. "The volume of documentation that would have to be reviewed was staggering," he said later. "There were over 50 leases. There were more than 30 service agreements, real estate tax documents, and insurance policies that had to be read and understood. A total analysis of the building's physical condition would have to be undertaken. . . . Staff worked till 3:00 and 4:00 in the morning; everyone had a job. Lawyers from both firms and outside counsel had their top attorneys working through the night for weeks along with staff of the two organizations. Both Ngaire and I were there reading documents till all of our eyes started to tear." Wallach added that both "Trump and Hilbert slept well."

It was imperative for all this to happen in utter secrecy. But nothing in real estate is completely leakproof. Mike Fascitelli and Steve Roth showed up for breakfast in Trump's penthouse apartment on the top of Trump Tower, at 725 Fifth Avenue, and asked Trump point-blank: was he interested in buying the GM Building?

Fascitelli recalls the apparent astonishment on Trump's face as he pointed to the building, visible from his windows. "He said, 'It's a piece of shit building, the granite falling down, everything sucks.'"

Trump played like he had "no idea" it was for sale—and no, he wouldn't want it.

Trump had Fascitelli fooled—for the moment.

Wallach told Hilbert to wire the nonrefundable $40 million deposit to CPI's escrow account. He assured Hilbert he wouldn't lose the money. Once they had the deal secured, there'd be a race among the lenders. Wallach would insist that a nonrefundable deposit of $40 million was a lender's requirement—and thus would pay back Conseco if the deal fell through. Hilbert liked the plan, and wired the money.

Now the deal was in the public domain. Fascitelli didn't know whether to laugh or cry. He wasn't quitting—but for now he was out. "I said [to Trump], 'You fucking asshole,'" he recalls, adding with a laugh, "I'm good friends with Trump." He would, however, enjoy ribbing Trump about his new partner. "My impression of meeting with Steve Hilbert? He was a complete bullshit artist and a blowhard. He made an awful lot of money, and he was very much centered on Steve Hilbert. He was like the three most important things are Steve, Steve, Steve.

"I said to Donald: 'Did you ever see the movie with Bette Midler where she talks about herself for a day, and then she says: "We've talked enough about me. Let's talk about you. What do *you* think of *me*?"'"

"I said, 'You and Steve Hilbert must have a hell of a time together.'"

■ ■ ■

Enter Lehman Brothers, the biggest real estate lenders of the era. Their point person was a managing director, Charles "Charlie" Schoenherr, a former General Electric executive who had worked with Trump and Wallach previously. Rob Horowitz now entered the mix as well.

Schoenherr, Horowitz, and Wallach spent "hours and hours" during the next few weeks "crashing" the entire deal.

The final terms were as follows: Lehman would loan $700 million, and Conseco and Trump would put in the remainder, with Conseco putting in the lion's share.

Trump pushed them all to work "very, very quickly," according to Schoenherr. Even though Simon and CPI now had what they wanted—certainty and a price of $800 million—Trump was concerned that Vornado would try to find a way to outbid them. On the last weekend of July the deal was closed.

■ ■ ■

Once it was official and Trump was the GM Building's co-owner, Trump got to work renovating.

"I fixed up the building. I cleaned it up," Trump said later. "It was a real mess, all dirty and filthy. It hadn't been well run under Disque, and I made it great. I put in the most magnificent granite floor.

"It was called 'Verde marble.' It was the most beautiful stone, and I had the best masons in New York do it. I honed the white marble walls, and that lobby was gorgeous."

Steve Hilbert was thrilled with his new partner. He thought Trump was like an Energizer bunny on steroids. "I got calls at 8:00 at night. I got calls on Sunday at 7:00 in the morning. I got calls on holidays. He was there constantly," Hilbert recalls.

"The first thing [Trump] did was fix the parking situation. He told me before we ever did the deal that we were going to make a million and a half overnight because, he said, 'the parking garage people are stealing from us.'

"And boom, he told me he was going to get the [GM showroom] cars out of the lobby.

"Donald was the first to break the $100-a-square-foot rent barrier at the GM Building. He did little things . . . like the prior owner wasn't charging anyone for the common space. So, in essence, we bought a 900,000-square-foot building and ended up with a 1,400,000-square-foot building, because [Donald] started charging for the common space.

"I don't think anyone appreciates how hands-on Donald is.

"It was a Sunday morning. I get a call from Donald, and he says, 'Steve, I'm in front of the GM Building, and we were thinking about what we're going to do with these windows,' because they painted those windows, painted the trim, and he had one of his guys take some of the paint off, and it was brass underneath.

"He said, 'You know, you couldn't afford to do brass windows today. No one in their right mind could—only General Motors would've done that.' And he had all the paint taken off."

■ ■ ■

Trump also raised the subterranean plaza to street level. The new plaza was much prettier than its predecessor. It was creamy and clean, and it had greenery and lighting.

Then, in a very clever public relations move, he put CBS's morning show featuring Bryant Gumbel in at the base, so pedestrians could watch it at street level. Every morning CBS viewers would see the GM Building—with Trump's name on it.

Next, Trump drew up plans for a restaurant on the raised plaza. It would have a glass dome. "I came up with the idea of the dome in front. . . . It was going to be a glass pyramid. And it was going to have a Cheesecake Factory in it. I came up with this architectural plan, and I did these gorgeous renderings. . . . I'm so angry at the guy from the Cheesecake Factory. It would have been the most successful restaurant in the country, and he was all set to do the deal, but he backed out at the last moment because he was afraid of the unions in New York.

"Every time I see a Cheesecake Factory, I think what a mistake that guy made."

■ ■ ■

Abe Wallach worried that the changes—as numerous as they were—weren't throwing off enough money fast enough. CBS was a wonderful public relations asset, but it didn't pay competitive retail rent. He asked his boss to see if he could negotiate with Hilbert to reduce the preferred interest rate. Hilbert said that he would if, in exchange, Trump repaid the equity quickly. Conseco, it would soon emerge, was in trouble.

It was typical of Wallach to be five steps ahead, worried about things Trump himself wasn't concerned about.

Wallach was whip-smart and loyal to a fault, and therein lay the good and the bad. There was nothing Wallach wouldn't do to achieve success for Donald Trump.

When Trump had hired him in 1989, Wallach had had some brushes with the law, which Trump knew nothing about. Wallach was gay and at times felt isolated. He confided this to Trump, who was always quick to defend him, telling him he did not care what his sexuality was. But, regardless, Wallach was prone to deep anxiety that, at times, got the better of him.

He told this author a tale from his past that he says he was far too ashamed to ever share with Trump. It played out on a long-haul flight.

In his own words:

I called the airline prior to leaving New York and made sure that I would be seated next to [a competitor]. . . .

The flight groaned on and I was not getting anything out of him. What to do? All I wanted was information that was in the head and briefcase of the guy sitting next to me.

He and I ordered a round of drinks but when they arrived he excused himself saying he wanted to stretch his legs. This was my opportunity; it was enough time to slip two sleeping pills into his drink.

He returned; we toasted, and began to sip our drinks. I was extremely nervous. What I was doing was wrong, illegal. . . . What if I gave him too many pills and, combined with the alcohol, he died or went into a coma? I was flipping out.

We continued our conversation and he ordered another drink. Shit, I thought, one drink with sleeping pills was enough, but two drinks! In about 15 minutes, he was clearly drunk and said he was extremely sleepy. I got him some additional pillows, turned off his light, and asked the attendant to cover him with a blanket.

Within five minutes he was snoring away. . . .

For the first five minutes I kept putting the palm of my hand over his nostrils to make sure he was still breathing.

Slowly and quietly I reached for his attaché case. Should I open it and review the papers while he slept next to me? What if he woke? The alternative was to take the attaché case to the bathroom where I would have ample light and could take notes. I chose the latter.

With his attaché case in hand, I carefully walked around him, entered the bathroom, and locked the door. I was so nervous that I had trouble opening the

*case, thinking at first that it was locked. It was not locked. Once opened, I began
to read the documents and notes taken by him on yellow pads. . . .*

*I went back to see what condition he was in. He was fast asleep, still snoring.
I went back to the bathroom and took notes on those items that I thought were
important. . . .*

*I went back to my seat, placed his attaché case where it had been, and began
to monitor his condition. So long as he was snoring I knew he was alive, but what
if he was in a coma?*

*Purposefully I pushed my leg against his to see if he would wake; he did, I
apologized, and he fell back to sleep for another three hours.*

*I was a nervous wreck, tired, famished, and feeling very guilty for what I had
done. On the other hand, the man sitting next to me was refreshed and said that
he hadn't had such a good sleep in a long time.*

■ ■ ■

Wallach had headed the real estate group at First Capital Advisors
(FCA), a pension fund advisory firm, when he met Donald Trump in
1989. He had been asked by FCA to comment on "the state of Trump's
empire" for 30 minutes on *The MacNeil/Lehrer Newshour* on PBS. Wallach says he had protested that he didn't know much about Trump and
he didn't want to do it, but his boss at FCA thought it would be good
public relations.

"On the show I basically said if you go after too many properties at
one time and pay too much money and have too little equity, and the
market goes down, you are in trouble."

His reward? Trump sued him for $250 million.

Then he dropped the case and asked for a meeting. Wallach was mys-
tified. Trump called him directly. "Hey, I hear you're wonderful. I hear
you're a real smart real estate guy. But instead of knocking me, we ought
to work together."

Thus began a working relationship that was to last 12 fruitful years.

■ ■ ■

Wallach would later say:

"When he first hired me, I didn't feel comfortable calling him Donald, and I thought it was too formal to refer to him as Mr. Trump. So
I called him 'Boss.' That continued for the 12 years we were together.

Once he got to know me, he often referred to me as 'Abela,' which is Yiddish for Abe. It was a very endearing name that only my grand-mother had ever called me.

"Going to work each day at the Trump Organization was, at least at first, a lot of fun. You never knew whom you would meet or how the day would unfold. I often walked into his office to find him schmooz-ing with Henry Kissinger, Sylvester Stallone, or some gorgeous model or Hollywood star. Norma Foederer, Donald's top assistant adviser for many years, told me that former President Nixon often came to visit Donald after he moved to New York."

■ ■ ■

Wallach was genuinely devoted to Trump, but the GM Building would turn out to be a breaking point for him. He was very disap-pointed that the building wasn't throwing off more money. He had really wanted to build a two-story retail mall. When Trump suggested turning the property into an office condominium building, Wallach despaired. He felt they'd forgotten their original ideas; they would never make enough money in time.

He was exhausted.

"I started to have a drug habit. I needed outlets. I'm working 24 hours a day. I'm on the phone at 4:00 in the morning. . . ."

He says he began stealing credit cards.

When he was caught, Trump was gentle. He told him to stop stealing immediately, and to get treatment.

But Wallach couldn't fix himself easily.

"You can't stop an addiction. It continued until finally I said, 'I've got to leave and restore my sanity.' Donald agreed, and I asked him not to tell anybody. I said, 'Donald, here's the deal. You're going to give me a year's salary. I'm leaving and you're not to say anything to anybody about what happened.'"

Trump reflected: "I'm surprised he volunteered all that. But yes, I was very good to him—and I needn't have been. I liked Abe."

Chapter 8

The Money Hunters
and the Salesman
from Indianapolis

*Their whole world fell apart when we litigated against
them. We sued their kids. We sued their grandkids. We
were very, very aggressive. And through it all, I have to say,
Tomisue—maybe she just didn't understand what we were
doing—but she was so friggin' nice . . . it was amazing.*

—Reed S. Oslan

T he partnership of Steve Hilbert and Donald Trump came to an
abrupt end in June 2000. Hilbert was forced out of Conseco
after the company's stock tanked. It fell from a high of $58

in 1997 to below $5 in 2000. This was largely because of Wall Street's violent reaction to Hilbert's $7.6 billion 1998 acquisition of Green Tree Financial, a mobile home financing company that most analysts viewed as hanging by a thread because of unorthodox accounting methods. It booked its profits at the same time it sold its securities, thus not allowing for incorrect assumptions; for example, there was overly optimistic speculation on how soon some borrowers would pay off their loans.

But it would emerge, according to the Securities and Exchange Commission (SEC), that Conseco also had most unusual accounting practices by which its results were "grossly inflated" and that improper "top side adjustments" were made to the books.

Conseco borrowed more than $1 billion to fund the purchase of failing Green Tree, for which it paid stock; and as Conseco's stock price plummeted, it was reported that Hilbert—and 10 other Conseco executives and board members—had borrowed about $700 million from the company to purchase Conseco stock. More than 100 employees had also been encouraged to participate in this scheme. Hilbert owed $218 million, including interest.

Class action lawsuits were filed. Investigations by the SEC and Federal Bureau of Investigation (FBI) began. Hilbert got the notoriety he'd always wanted.

Trump knew that bad news for Hilbert could be good news for him in that Conseco most likely would need to find cash to placate shareholders and he would have a chance to buy the GM Building outright—and for a cheap price. But he felt genuinely sorry for Hilbert, whose friendship he had come to value.

Why did Hilbert buy Green Tree Financial? Trump couldn't understand it. "They [Conseco] spent billions and billions, and I said, 'Steve, are you sure you're doing the right thing?' He said, 'Donald, it's going to be great.' He was so convinced. I said, 'Steve, it's a trailer company; you know, they basically finance trailer homes.'

"I said [to him], 'Every time I rent trailers for, like, construction sites, by the time the building is built, the trailers are all rotted out.' I said, 'Are you sure?'"

Unfortunately, Hilbert was.

Hilbert had felt that Green Tree was the perfect complement to his insurance business because its clients were the same as his clients. They were a "cultural match," he'd told *Fortune* magazine in 1999.

The Boston leveraged buyout investor Thomas H. Lee, who had invested $500 million into Conseco—"the worst investment I ever made"—was furious with Hilbert.

Conseco's board of directors insisted Hilbert step down. He was given a severance payment of $75 million. Gary C. Wendt, the former chief executive of General Electric Capital Services, was brought in to try to turn things around.

This isn't quite how Hilbert, who is admittedly a "glass half-full" type of person, remembers things. "I made a horrible decision to leave because I thought that my persona was getting bigger than the company, because I was being thrown under the bus by all the wonderful publications.

"And then Gary Wendt came in. Conseco really didn't unravel until three years after I left."

■ ■ ■

Steve Hilbert was always a dreamer. The son of a telephone operator and a maintenance worker, he'd grown up in Terre Haute, Indiana, population 60,000. Someone who didn't like Hilbert once described the place as a "little shithole nothing of a town."

Hilbert dropped out of Indiana State University and answered an ad to sell encyclopedias door-to-door for $600 a month. He made considerably more: $19,000.

By the mid-1970s he was selling insurance for Aetna. He was its best salesman. He saw that there was an opportunity in the market if one could amass insurance businesses and cut overhead. But how to raise the money? No bank would finance him.

His father loaned him $10,000—and he charmed $3 million out of potential customers over an exhausting three years.

In 1979, Conseco was born, and it was publicly listed in 1985. From there it grew at an astonishing rate. Hilbert bought more than 20 insurance companies and ran them from the Indianapolis suburb of Carmel. At his instigation, Conseco acquired numerous other businesses: casinos, golf courses; Hilbert even invested $20 million of Conseco money with the magician David Copperfield in the hope of starting a chain of magic-themed restaurants that never materialized. At one stage, he was listed as the highest-earning CEO in the country, having taken home a total of $277 million between 1992 and 1997.

There were always rumors about "misleading accounting," but somehow Hilbert survived four attacks from short sellers.

A thin man, Hilbert surrounded himself with superlatives. His 23,000-square-foot mansion, Le Chateau Renaissance, set on 33 acres, was a temple of self-congratulation. Even Donald Trump was awed when he saw it. Indiana is a state where $300,000 is considered a vast annual salary. Locally, Hilbert was viewed as some sort of emperor.

And perhaps he too saw himself that way. In the foyer of his home there were hand-painted murals depicting the courtship of Mark Antony and Cleopatra. In another scene Hilbert was portrayed as an ancient god. Many visitors were taken aback by the overt sexuality of the "mermaid murals" painted on the children's bathroom walls. Lou Harry, the editor of a local magazine, reportedly described them as "reflecting artistic taste not seen since the [Saddam] Hussein palace was overcome by American forces."

There were a gym, a spa, a hairdressing salon, a discotheque, as well as a separate house for staff, and a replica of the basketball court used by the Indiana Pacers, who came over frequently to practice.

The estate had been commissioned with Hilbert's wife of 16 years, Louann. But in the early 1990s, Louann was replaced in unusual circumstances that have kept the local media busily entertained.

Hilbert, then in his late forties, attended a bachelor party, reportedly for one of his stepsons. At the party a 23-year-old exotic dancer with thick dark hair and what one person called "a phenomenal body" leapt out of a cake and danced. Her name was Tomisue Tomlinson—and Hilbert was smitten.

Two weeks later, Louann Hilbert (now Derrickson) told people that she learned of her husband's new relationship when the local BMW dealer phoned to ask how she liked her new convertible. Louann had no idea what he was talking about. Tomisue had received the new car.

Hilbert married Tomisue in 1994, 10 days after his divorce from Louann was finalized.

Hilbert never knocked his wife's former profession. He told *Fortune* that he "respected" the fact that Tomisue had made her living as a single mother and had not relied on welfare.

The couple acquired an 18,500-square-foot house in Saint Martin, Le Château des Palmiers, designed by Tomisue, and a place in Colorado. They owned a stable of top racehorses, and all the fillies were named after Tomisue: Tomisue's Delight, Tomisue's Indy, Tomisue's Girl, Tomisue's Gold, and Tomisue's Dancer. The duo was known for entertaining lavishly. Kool and the Gang played at one of their Christmas parties. The local sports teams were frequent guests.

The Hilberts attended their local church regularly, and gave generously to local charities, including the zoo, the theater, the orchestra, a school, and hospitals.

■ ■ ■

As Conseco cratered, the couple's opulent lifestyle came under threat.

There was the ongoing federal investigation into the unusual accounting practices of Hilbert, his CFO, Rollin M. Dick, and Conseco's rotund chief accounting officer, James S. Adams.

The SEC reported that the company had lied about its numbers in ways that inflated its stock. Dick and Adams both had to pay fines of around $100,000 and were barred from holding accounting positions for five years.

Meanwhile, the new Conseco management was trying to claw back anything to stave off bankruptcy. Gary Wendt saved $2 billion—but that left more than $6 billion of debt.

In October 2002 Wendt stepped down (but stayed on as chairman) and was replaced by William "Bill" J. Shea, a Boston banker who was brought in to manage a restructured bankruptcy, giving angry creditors equity participation in exchange for their debt.

Shea needed a special type of executive to trawl through the mess, correct it, and do battle with Conseco's former overlords.

He needed a "firefighter," a restructuring expert, someone who was tough—and basically uncharmable. He knew the ideal person for the job—he'd worked with him on various deals when he'd run the Bank of Boston.

Charles "Chuck" Cremens was something of a professional nomad, preferring to cherry-pick projects that interested him, rather than hold a

lucrative long-term position. He had previously spearheaded the investment group at a Boston REIT, Beacon Properties, and led the real estate
group at Aetna.

When he wasn't on the road—which wasn't often—he lived in the
low-key coastal town of Chatham, Massachusetts, and when he heard
the doings of what he called "East Hampton people," he would roll
his eyes. He was a detail-oriented digger who wouldn't stop until he
was done.

Shea summoned Cremens to Indianapolis in December 2001 and
asked for a quick piece of advice. Could Cremens please look at the
GM Building for four hours as a favor and make some recommenda-
tions about the sale? Cremens told him the building would fetch a
huge price, much more than Conseco was thinking of asking—over $1
billion in fact. "Will you handle it?" Shea asked the Bostonian. He kept
Cremens in the office for the whole afternoon, looking at Conseco's
figures.

Somehow—he never quite knew how it happened—the day
stretched into years and years. Chuck Cremens found himself at the
heart of Conseco, embroiled in three different complex tasks. He had
to handle the restructuring of Conseco's financial company, Conseco
Finance, and the sale of the GM Building. Subsequently, at the request
of Conseco creditors, including the renowned hedge fund manager
David Tepper, he went after the directors and officers who had borrowed $700 million of Conseco stock, and tried to retrieve what
monies he could.

All these challenges required formidable legal advice. Cremens hired
the Chicago firm of Kirkland & Ellis for the restructuring. There, he
encountered one Reed S. Oslan, a litigating partner who specialized in
disputes. He would hire Oslan to help him with the GM Building sale
and the hunt for all that borrowed money. The two men became "best
friends."

"Chuck is a brilliant, brilliant, brilliant man. He's probably the
smartest guy I've ever encountered in my life," says Oslan. "He knows
what he knows, and he knows what he doesn't know, and he's got zero
ego and he will ask questions until he's blue in the face, and then he
will figure shit out. He's so aggressive. Once he commits to a course,
he just lives it."

It would take Oslan and Cremens nearly eight years to sort through Conseco's tangled web. The ordeal would turn them into a modern, drier version of Sherlock Holmes (Cremens) and Dr. Watson (Oslan), and Oslan would find it hard to face normality when it finally ended. "It was like a circus," he later reflected. "I'd never had a case like this before."

■ ■ ■

In 2003 Steve Hilbert sued Conseco, arguing that, since he was no longer employed by the company, his contract was invalid and he no longer owed Conseco $218 million in stock loans. Cremens and Oslan sued back immediately, seeking, among other things, foreclosure on his Carmel mansion.

But Cremens and Olsan avoided focusing initially on Hilbert. Oslan would later say that the duo targeted Conseco's executives and board members tactically. They first pursued the "low-hanging fruit."

With the help of Kroll, the international security firm, they determined where the 11 directors had hidden their loot. Three paid it back right away.

But for the others, retrieving the money was a more difficult task.

Rollin Dick—who had borrowed more than $108 million from Conseco—had transferred some of his assets to the Cook Islands off the coast of Australia, where it was notoriously difficult to trace hidden money. "They have the most extreme asset protection laws in the world," Oslan says. "We found out about it, we went into court, we got it unraveled, but [Dick] was doing extreme things to try to hide his assets from us." Ultimately Dick settled. Oslan was amazed that his late first wife, "a really nice woman" who had been oblivious to his wealth, had apparently never even received so much as a watch from her husband.

The Dicks weren't the only couple with secrets. Conseco's COO, Donald F. Gonguaware, owed $39.5 million—much to the astonishment of his wife, Patricia. The discovery caused the couple to retain separate counsel to negotiate with Oslan and Cremens—and to separate as well.

And then there was the bizarre case of Conseco's vice president, Ngaire Cuneo, and her then husband Richard, who were nearly impossible to track down. Every time Cremens and Oslan turned up at the Cuneos' marital home in New Canaan, Connecticut, no one was home.

But one evening they got lucky: they found the couple moving out in the middle of the night. The two had purchased a $10.2 million home in Miami, right next to the houses of tennis star Anna Kournikova and rocker Lenny Kravitz. Oslan knew that Florida is a so-called homestead state—meaning that homes purchased there can be protected by law from creditors.

Immediately Oslan obtained a temporary restraining order and deposed the Cuneos.

It was intriguing, he told the U.S. District Court in the Southern District of Indiana (Indianapolis), that the Cuneos were moving to Miami ostensibly to be closer to Ngaire's mother—not least, as Oslan pointed out, because her mother lived in Port Charles, which is two hours' drive from Miami.

The Cuneos were forced to relinquish the Miami property.

■ ■ ■

By 2005 most of the executives, including the Cuneos, had settled. Oslan and Cremens had retrieved substantial sums for Conseco's creditors. The duo, however, knew they would never recover everything that was owed to the company. "We couldn't take a hundred percent of what they had because [then] nobody would settle. . . . It's a horse trade," explains Oslan.

There was still a large amount missing: the 200 million dollars plus owed by Stephen Hilbert, who battled them in court every step of the way. "I give them credit," Oslan says. "They fought like hell." Perhaps he used the plural for a reason. Tomisue Hilbert was an effective part of Stephen Hilbert's artillery.

The young Mrs. Hilbert turned up in court dressed immaculately, charming everyone and often accompanied by girlfriends who would accost Oslan and ask him why he was being so mean to their friend. Oslan would reply with a question of his own: why hadn't the Hilberts repaid the money they owed?

Cremens had never met anyone like Tomisue. "I think [Tomisue] thought it was a cocktail party," he would later say. Neither he nor Oslan could get over how indefatigably charming she was to them. "Did she understand what we were doing?" they wondered.

■ ■ ■

One of Hilbert's tactics was to turn all of his discoverable assets—reported to be worth more than $100 million—over to Tomisue and to declare personal bankruptcy. He only had spending money, he told the Hamilton Circuit Court, because of the generosity of his wife. Oslan cried foul, claiming "fraudulent conveyance." Tomisue Hilbert rebutted, "It's an appalling thing for them to come after my assets when I was on none of those loans."

In 2006 Tomisue was declared "joint owner" of a $400 million private equity fund, MH Equity, which was backed by a friend of Stephen Hilbert, Wisconsin billionaire John Menard Jr. Again, Oslan cried foul. He told the court: "They're going to try to make it look like [Tomisue] is a brilliant business person, but it's clear that [Stephen Hilbert] is contributing the lion's share of the work [to MH Equity] and essentially doing it unpaid." Not true, said Tomisue's lawyer, Linda Pence. "She's a very smart and very active woman at MH Equity."

Meanwhile, the Hilberts remained at Le Chateau Renaissance in Carmel and kept up their free-spending ways. Cremens and Oslan were particularly struck when they visited the house and saw the lap pool in the master bedroom. "The lap pool [was empty] and was full of clothes," recalls Oslan. "It must have been 80 feet long."

■ ■ ■

Finally, on December 7, 2006, both sides settled. The Hamilton County courthouse was packed. The Hilberts agreed that the house and its contents belonged to Conseco, which would eventually auction it for $3 million in 2010. But they held on to their 18,000-square-foot house, Le Château des Palmiers, in Saint Martin—at least for a few years. After the agreement was reached, Tomisue high-fived her friends.

Both sides declared victory. The settlement meant that a scheduled public hearing that would have aired the details of the Hilberts' finances would not take place.

The couple moved into a house worth $3 million, which, as Oslan noted, is "pretty nice by Indiana standards."

The Hilberts mailed out Christmas cards with a photograph of their cat, Mr. Whiskers, dressed in a tie and holding a bottle of Wild Turkey. The inscription read: "The Hilbert family will go on. We'll live and love and stand together beyond today, across the years. This family is forever."

Reed Oslan would later bump into the Hilberts on holiday in Saint Martin. He found them "incredibly charming," especially the indomitable Tomisue. "She comes up, she gives a hug, [my wife and I] have a drink with them. It was fascinating."

"Tomisue never sank to their level," Steve Hilbert later said. "Everyone who meets Tomisue loves her."

■ ■ ■

In 2008, the Hilberts were back in the news, this time on the front page of the *Wall Street Journal*. Tomisue's French-born mother, Suzy Germaine Tomlinson, had been found dead in her bathtub, fully clothed, after a night out in Indianapolis. Was foul play involved?

Suzy Tomlinson was 74 years old, and, it would emerge, had a life insurance policy with American International Group (AIG) for $15 million, payable to a company owned by a much younger gay friend of hers, JB Carlson. Yet at the time of her death, Tomlinson had an annual income of only $17,000.

AIG sued for fraud. The Hilberts also sued AIG, claiming they'd been duped: *they* should have been the beneficiaries of the $15 million insurance policy, not JB Carlson or his company. The case was settled under seal.

An investigation ultimately found that Tomlinson died of "accidental drowning" complicated by "ethanol intoxication."

■ ■ ■

Just as things seemed to quiet down for the Hilberts, John Menard, the billionaire with whom Tomisue "owned" the private equity fund MH Equity, filed an injunction to remove Steve Hilbert as CEO. Menard claimed that Hilbert's investments had lost 70 percent of their value. Three months later Tomisue countersued, arguing that Menard had filed against her husband only because she'd rebuffed sexual advances from both Menard and his wife Fay. Also embroiled in the debacle was Melania Trump, Donald Trump's wife, who had a marketing contract with New Sunshine LLC, a tanning and skin care company owned by MH Equity. Menard had canceled the contract. Melania Trump sued him for $50 million in damages.

Chuck Cremens and Reed Oslan read the news with bemusement. They had never understood why John Menard, whom Cremens knew as a conservative sort, would have started a private equity fund with the Hilberts. "Why the hell would a billionaire from Wisconsin give Steve Hilbert, who was being sued for fraud by us [and] was under federal investigation, $400 million to invest?" asked Oslan. "Makes zero sense. Nobody would do that."

■ ■ ■

One friend stayed loyal to Steve Hilbert over the years: Donald Trump. The Hilberts attended Trump's 2005 Palm Beach nuptials with Melania Knauss, and the local papers reported that Tomisue wore "a one-of-a-kind French silk and chiffon dress from Baracci, a Beverly Hills boutique. The pink gown featured hand-sewn Swarovski crystals on the corseted bodice. There also were crystals (Swarovski, naturally) on Tomisue's pink Escada shoes and pink purse, as well. The handbag was from her own fashion line."

Reports show that in October 2013 Trump bought the Hilberts' Saint Martin property, Le Château des Palmiers. The purchase was at the request of Hilbert, cash-stricken during his dispute with Menard. The asking price had been $19.7 million.

Perhaps Trump was showing his gratitude. Hilbert believed that Trump always should have owned the GM Building—that Conseco had wrongfully deprived him of it, and that Trump should have sued to get it back. Reed Oslan remembered the testimony Hilbert gave in the dispute with Trump as being "most unhelpful" to Conseco.

Oslan couldn't help but wonder how it had come to this. Why had Trump let the GM Building slip through his fingers? All he had to do was put down a small amount of collateral, "around $50 million," plus a letter of credit from his bankers guaranteeing he'd repay a loan of

$250 million at a time when Conseco was desperate to get rid of the building. Gary Wendt allegedly said he would have sold it for anything. Yet Trump didn't pony up.

"He should've owned it. I mean, he should've bought it. He just blew the bidding process, and then he litigated with us for four years," Oslan recalled. "It was a waste of time."

Chapter 9

Donald's "Force Majeure"

Pardon me if I get a little emotional. It's very upsetting. I've never worked this hard in my life.

—Donald Trump

I n March 2001, Gary Wendt told Donald Trump he could exercise a buy/sell agreement that had been put in place by Trump and Steve Hilbert as co-owners of the GM Building. Wendt was so anxious to get rid of the building and give something, *anything*, back to Conseco's angry creditors that he offered Trump a remarkable deal: he could buy the GM Building for $995 million, which meant Trump had to find $295 million, the surplus to the Lehman Brothers debt of $700 million.

He could even borrow this money *from* Conseco! Conseco agreed to accept an up-front payment of $50 million at closing with the rest in two notes, one for $250 million (the primary loan) at the annual interest rate of 6.5 percent and the secondary loan for $45 million at 4 percent. The primary loan of $250 million had to be guaranteed by a letter of credit from Trump's bankers at Deutsche Bank. Conseco just wanted to be certain that the deal would close.

Andrew Hubregsen, Conseco's senior vice president, drafted and signed an agreement in March in which Conseco asked to close by June 30.

Trump had clearly stated he wanted the building. But the closing date came and went and still there was no agreement, much to the consternation of Hubregsen and Wendt. Though Trump's office regularly talked to Hubregsen, lawyers for Conseco and Deutsche Bank seemed unable to reach each other, according to court documents. There was no reason given for the delay. But at Conseco, Hubregsen would later testify, they were nervous that Trump would keep negotiating and wouldn't close. People close to the transaction recalled that Trump's in-house counsel, George Ross, was extraordinarily focused on every detail.

On July 3 Hubregsen drafted another agreement, which now stipulated that the two sides needed to close by September 15. If Conseco hadn't received a letter of credit by September 15, the company could sell the building elsewhere.

Court records state that there were allegations of "foot-dragging" on Trump's part. When asked about this, Trump says, "There were problems in the market. So it took time."

■ ■ ■

Word seeped out that The Donald was hesitating. Did he not want to pay? Could he not pay? Did he need a partner? In 2000 he had approached his old friend Ben Lambert; they met and Trump told Lambert he'd pay him a fee if he found him a partner. Trump also had an intermediary call the Chicago investor Samuel F. Zell, then invited Zell to lunch at Jean-Georges in New York. Trump asked Zell if he would partner with him. Zell almost laughed. "I looked at him and I said, 'Donald, you've sued every partner you've ever had. Why would I want to be your partner in anything?'" Trump interpreted this—correctly—as: "Zell was against me because of what happened with his friend Jay Pritzker."

Zell was indeed thinking of his mentor Jay Pritzker, the late Chicago hotelier and financier. "I was around listening to Jay when Donald was in big trouble on the Grand Hyatt Hotel. Jay saved his ass, and then after he saved his ass, Donald sued him." The *New York Times* reported in 1993 that Donald had been "angry" that the Pritzkers—who had indeed given him the "curtain-raiser of his career" by partnering on New York's Grand Hyatt Hotel in 1979—asked him for his share of renovation expenses when he was at the "lowest" point of "my financial life." He filed a civil racketeering suit against them. It was eventually settled.

■ ■ ■

Trump's lawyers were haggling too long. By summer 2001 Hubregsen was seeking out other potential buyers. He contacted several New York developers, including Larry Silverstein, to gauge their interest. Silverstein forwarded Hubregsen's correspondence to Trump. Irate, Trump told Hubregsen he wanted a period of "exclusivity."

On August 6, Hubregsen received a letter, a "proposed form of guaranty" from Deutsche Bank, but Conseco felt it was insufficient. It was *not* a letter of credit, as Conseco had requested. At the bottom it even stated: "This is not a letter of a credit." Conseco officially rejected it on August 9, and then on August 24 submitted language to Trump that Conseco suggested he use for an acceptable "guaranty." Trump rejected it.

"Tempers flared," according to court documents.

Then, on September 11, 2001, two airplanes hit the Twin Towers at the World Trade Center in New York City and Deutsche Bank's headquarters nearby were heavily damaged.

The bank was unable to lend money to anyone for months, Eric Schwartz later testified. Trump had to find a new banker. That proved impossible in the short term. "No one was doing business," Trump later said.

On October 4 Conseco notified Trump that the July 3 agreement was now "null and void." Wendt and his associates had run out of patience.

In December 2001 Chuck Cremens was hired at Conseco. On January 14, 2002, not coincidentally, Conseco executives informed Trump they were exercising their buy/sell right to sell the building, for which they'd gotten a new appraisal: she was now worth $1.215 billion.

Trump had 60 days to close at the new price or he had to sell his interest in the building to Conseco (the holding company was Carmel Fifth) for $15.5 million. On March 13, Trump responded: he wasn't selling his interest, nor would he buy the building at the new price. Instead, as Sam Zell had predicted, he sued.

He claimed Conseco should have awarded him an extension after 9/11, given that a "force majeure" (an unanticipated event as in the terrorist attacks) had rendered closing impossible. Trump later said, "All the banks were out of business. I had all my financing done. It was just a question of closing. I had Deutsche Bank. I had every bank wanting to do the deal. And then, all of a sudden, you couldn't get any deal."

The case went before an arbitration panel of three adjudicators. The hearing dragged on for about a month. But before any judgment was issued, Trump disqualified one of the arbitrators, who disclosed that his firm had once represented Conseco Finance, a subsidiary of Conseco. The whole process had to start over.

■ ■ ■

In January 2003, Cremens contacted Wayne Maggin, his old pal at Eastdil, and asked if the firm could sell the building for Conseco, assuming the arbitration hearing went their way. Maggin told his boss, Ben Lambert, who wanted the business.

Out of courtesy to an old close friend, Lambert went to see Trump, along with Roy March, to tell him of Conseco's request. Trump was livid. "I felt it was just disloyal of Ben, who'd been a friend of years, to go shop the building to the other side—and I haven't spoken to him since." Lambert's view was that he was a free-agent; he had never found an equity partner for Trump, and the one meeting they'd had on the subject had been three years ago.

Within 24 hours of Lambert's courtesy visit, March recalled that someone in Trump's offices sent a box of documents to Eastdil's offices. The box was messengered back to Trump unopened, according to March. "We didn't want to create a conflict by opening it," he explains.

In March 2003, Conseco submitted an application with the United States Bankruptcy Court for the Northern District of Illinois to approve the hiring of Eastdil. Trump tried to block the appointment. He told the court that Eastdil was not capable and was too expensive. Lambert heard this while on holiday with his family in the Bahamas. "I couldn't believe it," he recalls. "Donald had been prepared to pay my fees to find him a partner—but suddenly he told a court my fees were too expensive?" Thirty years of friendship evaporated just like that.

The court ruled Eastdil could take the commission.

■ ■ ■

In May, the second round of arbitration hearings began. Trump sounded furious on the stand. "I'm the one that created the value. . . . They didn't do anything. . . . I brought the project in under budget. . . . I don't even get my $11 million [the money he put in] . . . now they're suing me for damages. . . . I'm supposed to pay them damages, and I'm the only good deal that Conseco has made in the last five years." On May 28 a ruling was issued: The building belonged to Conseco. Trump was out, but he would get paid.

Trump declared the saga a victory. "I made a lot of money, because we sold it for $1.4 billion," he later said.

And when it was over, Trump moved on. "I don't like talking about the GM Building, because I'd rather not have lost it—but I did make money on it," he said in an interview. He's not one to brood, according to Abe Wallach. "He used to say to me . . . 'It's just a deal; there'll be other deals.'"

Sometimes, it seemed to Wallach, Trump minded losing buildings less than Wallach did.

Chapter 10

Paradise, Briefly

Was I the author of that cube? No, that belongs to Steve Jobs.

—Harry Macklowe

H arry Macklowe knew that the key to really transforming the GM Building lay with Apple.

Macklowe pestered George Blankenship, Apple's vice president of real estate, until he was invited to a meeting with Steve Jobs in November 2003.

Dan Shannon accompanied Macklowe to Cupertino, California. Also at the meeting were the architects Peter Q. Bohlin and Karl Backus from Bohlin Cywinski Jackson, the designers of the Apple Store in New York City's Soho district. Macklowe recalled hitting it off immediately with Jobs. "He's wearing this black turtleneck, he's wearing black jeans . . . it was terrific. The Apple team started talking about a flagship store that would be groundbreaking in almost every aspect. It would be open 24/7."

What happened next has long been the subject of speculation and some dispute: who came up the idea of placing a 30-foot square glass cube—the world's "smallest skyscraper"—in the middle of the GM Building plaza? In that lightbulb moment, an unused basement that had caused headaches for its owners for more than 40 years morphed into what is arguably the most famous retail space in the world.

The answer, according to four people in the room—Harry Macklowe, Karl Backus, Peter Bohlin, and Dan Shannon—is that the cube was the brainchild of the late Steve Jobs. "The point of the meeting," Shannon recalled, "was that Steve wanted to show Harry what his vision was for that site. We got there and they had this beautiful wood model of the building and plaza, and there's this 40-by-40-foot glass cube in the middle of the plaza. And Harry knew immediately that that was the right answer. Our original ideas had the glass pavilion closer to the street, because the zoning laws required a street wall for that site. And the Apple team put it right in the middle, more like the Louvre. . . . Harry thought it was brilliant."

Said Macklowe: "[Jobs] presented to me and I presented to him. . . . He had this cube, which was quite different from what you see there today, and I had a cube that was quite different from what we see today as well. It took us half an hour to make a deal."

■ ■ ■

Macklowe knew that the only major flaw in Jobs's concept was the size. Forty feet was too big—not just for zoning restrictions but for the scale of the building. No one would like it—not the city, not the tenants. He also knew that talking about it with Jobs wouldn't get him anywhere. He'd have to show Apple what he meant. He invited Apple's retail development executives, Ron Johnson and Robert "Rob" Briger, to the building two weeks after the Cupertino meeting, to view a scaffolding mock-up of the cube—in the dead of night. (Regulations forbade Macklowe to build during the day.)

Around two in the morning the group met in front of the GM Building. The 40-foot cube was unveiled. They all agreed it was too big. It obscured the building. Macklowe was grinning. He then gave the signal, and the model was dismantled—only to reveal a 30-foot cube he had secretly constructed underneath.

His magic trick worked! Apple was sold on the smaller cube.

Now Macklowe had to get approval from the city's Planning Commission to put the cube in the middle of a simplified plaza. One of the ideas he was most proud of, he told the commission, he had "lifted" from the Place Vendome in Paris, where he had noticed tiny bollards in place to discourage skateboarders. He thought the bollards "just perfect" for *his* square.

Jobs phoned him. And phoned. And phoned. The Apple chief wanted continual updates. He even had Macklowe and Shannon visit Cupertino again, this time so they could all look at a stone for the plaza that Macklowe had found in Paris. Jobs created a mock-up in the Apple parking lot. Macklowe felt that he and Jobs were becoming friends. He offered him an office in the building, but Jobs declined. "He said, 'When I come to New York, I want to be in Soho. I want to be in Chelsea. I want to be surrounded by young people. . . . I can listen to what they're thinking. I want to have new ideas.'"

■ ■ ■

For Macklowe to redesign the plaza and put retailers in the bottom of the building, some existing tenants had to be malleable—and mollified. He needed CBS to change camera angles for its morning show; he needed the Lauders to relocate their company store; TPG Inc., the owner of the Bally shoe store, also had to move. "None of these people *had* to do anything," said Rob Sorin. "It's because of [Harry's] genius and charm" that they all cooperated.

"I did them favors; they did me favors," recalls Macklowe. "I think we all felt we were doing something great. Leonard and Evelyn [Lauder] said [to me], 'We can't believe what it is that you've done, and it's a pleasure to be in the building again.'"

Macklowe also got rid of Trump's Verde marble and replaced it with a white stone that looked more modern. Construction started around the base of the building where Macklowe lured, among other luxury tenants, Porsche Design. He was also busy reaching out to businesspeople he knew could afford higher office rents and whose reputations would only burnish the building's brand.

■ ■ ■

On May 19, 2006, the Apple cube was unveiled at 32 feet. It immediately drew long lines of customers and tourists. There was the cube rising with a glass elevator and circular stairs taking the crowds to the basement beneath. It was such a mob scene that Rob Sorin later kicked himself for not charging a higher "stop" or floor on the "percentage rent" of the store's profits that Apple agreed to pay Macklowe. "Apple really had no idea what this store was going to do in business per year, and we negotiated the 'stop' at a level that turned out to be horrendously low. The first year they made a million dollars a day," he says.

Still, it was worth it. The deal was the shrewdest investment of Harry Macklowe's career. The groundbreaking number of customers—the store attracted 50,000 visitors a week during its first year—would dramatically enhance the building's value and update its reputation. Though still known officially as the GM Building, many people now nickname it "the Apple Building."

At the opening, Harry was joined by his wife Linda, who was beaming. "I remember the reception that they had on a beautiful spring day for the opening of the Apple Store," says one of Linda's best friends. "And that was like Harry's defining moment. I've never seen the guy so happy. All of his friends, all of his colleagues were there. And this thing was just fantastic. And that was the only time that I ever saw Harry and Linda really mutually proud about something. [Other than that,] it was always Linda with the art collection and Harry with his business."

After 20 years of combatting salacious headlines about buildings being pulled down in darkness, Harry Macklowe had arrived. He was part of the New York establishment.

■ ■ ■

With the retail trajectory for the building looking better than anyone could have predicted, Macklowe used his charm to lure in names he deemed "appropriate" tenants to elevate the building's prestige. "We now had a very, very high cash flow with rents in the triple figures," he says.

Thomas "Tommy" H. Lee, the Boston financier who had forced Steve Hilbert out of Conseco, was an old friend of Macklowe's. He put aside the bad juju of *l'affaire* Hilbert and moved into the sixth floor.

The financier Sanford (Sandy) I. Weill was retiring from Citigroup in 2003, where he'd been the chief executive officer since its creation in

Real estate decisions are generally self-generated, having much to do with clarifying your internal vision and reaffirming your objectives. Similarly, adding support to your own convictions is, for the most part, a test of self, and more often than not, an internal challenge. A chess game of extraordinary proportion, encouragement is most welcome during this process, but rarely sought. An investor or developer thrives on having a private vision and an ability to get there. Along the way, internal courage and conviction are the unwavering standards.

Harry Macklowe

Harry Macklowe's preface to his own collection of photographs
Credit: *Macklowe Properties: Projects 1967–2007*

Harry Macklowe, left, and son Billy, New York, 2001
Credit: *April 2, 2001—The Four Seasons Restaurant Grill Room— $750,000,000 Acquisitions and Refinancings Celebration / Macklowe Properties*

(Left to Right) Billy Macklowe, Rob Horowitz, Harry Macklowe and Eric Schwartz, New York 2001
Credit: *April 2, 2001—The Four Seasons Restaurant Grill Room—$750,000,000 Acquisitions and Refinancings Celebration / Macklowe Properties*

Linda Macklowe and Harry Macklowe, 2009 Guggenheim International Gala, September 16, 2009
Credit: *patrickmacmullen.com*

(From left to right) Robert Verrone, Steve Stuart, Harry Macklowe, and Rob Horowitz
in the Wachovia Pro-am, 2001
Credit: *Harry Macklowe personal photograph*

767 Fifth Avenue in 1915
Credit: *Macklowe Properties, Projects 1967–2007*

The Savoy Plaza hotel designed by McKim Mead and White, 1928
Credit: *Macklowe Properties, Projects 1967–2007*

William Zeckendorf
Credit: *Alexandra Compain-Tissier*

Max Rayne
Credit: *by Rex Coleman, for Baron Studios;*
© National Portrait Gallery, London

Cecilia Benattar with a model of the GM building pre-construction, New York, early 1960s
Credit: *Simon Benattar*

A gold key presented to Cecilia Benattar by locksmiths on the opening of the GM building, New York, late 1960s
Credit: *Simon Benattar*

Cecilia Benattar in her office, New York, early 1970s
Credit: *Simon Benattar*

The GM building on opening in New York, 1968
Credit: *Macklowe Properties: Projects 1967–2007*

Standing: Kathryn M. Deane, Disque D. Deane Jr, Walter L. Deane, Marjorie G. Deane
Seated: Disque Dee Deane, Marjorie S. Deane
Dog: Joe
Credit: *Deane Family Archives*

Ira Millstein, 25th ANNUAL
FREDERICK LAW OLMSTED
AWARDS LUNCHEON Presented
by the Women's Committee of the
Central Park Conservancy Central Park's
Conservatory Garden, NYC, May 2, 2007
Credit: *patrickmacmullen.com*

David Simon, New York
Credit: *Don Hamerman*

Prince Nicolo and Princess Rita Boncompagni Ludovisi (formely Rita Jenrette),
Rome, Italy, Villa Aurora, January 15, 2013
Credit: *Linda Hervieux*

Tomisue and Stephen Hilbert, New York, 2013
Credit: *Tomisue Hilbert personal photograph*

(Left to Right) Rob Horowitz, Rhona Graff, Donald and Melania Trump,
in Trump's penthouse, early 2000s
Credit: *Rob Horowitz personal photograph*

The GM building with TRUMP letters on it, circa 2000
Credit: *brorson.com*

Letter from Harry Macklowe to Rob Horowitz
Credit: *Harry Macklowe*

Letter from Harry Macklowe to Donald Trump
Credit: *Harry Macklowe*

125 W 55th St. Lobby
Credit: *Macklowe Properties: Projects 1967–2007*

Macklowe exploded Smart cars, 340 Madison Ave. Lobby
Credit: *Macklowe Properties: Projects 1967–2007*

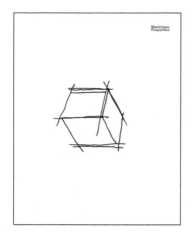

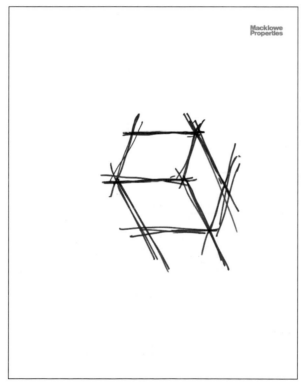

Sketches of the Apple Cube drawn for the author
by Harry Macklowe, New York, 2014
Credit: *Harry Macklowe*

The GM Building
Credit: *Macklowe Properties: Projects 1967–2007*

1998. Macklowe phoned him. Back in the 1960s, Macklowe had served as a broker for Weill's burgeoning securities firm, Carter, Berlind, Weill & Levitt.

Macklowe had an inkling he'd be nostalgic for the good old times. "I called Sandy and said, 'Last time I was your broker; now I want to be your landlord. I want to give you a retirement office.' He said, 'That's terrific.'"

Weill now has a "mammoth" office on the 46th floor, according to Ira Millstein, who still pops up to see his old friend. "You should see this office!" he says. "It's vast, with pictures of Sandy with his three yachts and various other people. So I go up to talk to him every now and then about trying to make a donation to the park or whatever."

Another friend of Macklowe's was going through a transition, which Macklowe quickly turned to his advantage. The lanky Italian-American mergers and acquisitions banker Joseph "Joe" Perella was looking for space. He had left Morgan Stanley in 2005 after clashing with the deeply unpopular CEO, Philip J. Purcell.

Macklowe approached Perella before the banker had even planned his next venture. Perella was touched by his friend's faith in him. He recalled Macklowe saying, "I want you in my building. You're going to have a great firm and I want you in the building."

"Harry, for God's sake," Perella replied, "I don't even have the money yet. I'd love to be in your building, but I've got nothing to talk about."

"You know what he said to me?" Perella asks. "'I know you're going to be able to raise the money for your firm. When you're ready, I'll have the space waiting for you.'"

Perella created a fund, Perella Weinberg, with former Goldman Sachs partner Peter Weinberg. One of their seed investors was Richard "Dick" Fisher, of the New York real estate Fisher family.

Perella told Macklowe that Fisher had a space for him in the McGraw-Hill building, at a mere $72 per square foot; leases in the GM Building were around $110 per square foot. Fisher wouldn't be amused if Perella wasted money on unnecessary rent. Macklowe decided he wanted Perella in the building more than the money. And so Perella Weinberg moved into the fourth and fifth floors at $72 per square foot.

Perella was touched. "I'll be forever in Harry's debt for the space that we have."

The building soon cultivated a reputation as Hedge Fund Central. The tenant roster included Lee Ainslee's Maverick Capital Management and Richard Perry's Perry Capital. (This concerned the lawyers at Weil Gotshal, who feared the building was fast becoming too rich for them.)

Tenants now competed to be on the highest floor. The clear winner wasn't some young hotshot firm but rather one of New York's oldest and most infamous financiers: Carl Icahn, who, like Weill, had an office the size of an entire city block. The 77-year-old founder and CEO of Icahn Enterprises became famous for keeping his office lights on at night as a warning to the rest of New York: "I'm still working."

■ ■ ■

Like everyone else in the building, Icahn was friendly with Macklowe. In November 2006, Macklowe and Icahn ran into each other in the lobby. They reminisced about a deal they'd both been involved in—the Time Warner Center, according to court records. Macklowe said he had an idea for Icahn, and he'd call him about it.

On the phone Macklowe asked if Icahn might be interested in partnering with him on a potential deal to acquire the real estate investment trust Reckson Associates. The firm owned buildings in Manhattan, on Long Island, and in New York's outer boroughs. SL Green Realty was bidding to buy it, but Macklowe thought its offer, at roughly $43 per share, undervalued the properties. If he and Icahn teamed up and outbid SL Green, they'd get a great deal. The initial offer would need to be all in cash, but Macklowe assured Icahn that raising the money wasn't a problem. "Don't worry about the banks," Macklowe said. "I've got the banks. Don't even think about it."

Time, though, was critical. They had to make their $3 billion offer by the end of November. On November 15, Macklowe and Icahn signed an agreement to each put $600 million into a joint account. Icahn added a penalty clause, to which Macklowe agreed, stating that if either party failed to do this, they'd have to pay the other $60 million.

Billy Macklowe later admitted he didn't like this unusual arrangement, but his father told him to acquiesce.

Advising the Macklowes was a banker Billy brought in named Andrew Bednar. He was one of Perella's partners at Perella Weinberg.

By late November, Icahn began phoning the Macklowes. Where was their money? They were scrambling. Over Thanksgiving Harry made an SOS call to Rob Horowitz on his cell phone. Horowitz immediately called both Steve Stuart at Fortress and Eric Schwartz.

Fortress promised to lend Macklowe the $600 million—but according to Horowitz, they were not comfortable with him putting the money into a joint account with Icahn. Fortress wanted control, so instead the money was posted to a separate account with Bear Stearns. They told Macklowe he could access it if the joint bid was successful.

This was not what Icahn had requested. He phoned the Macklowe offices looking for both Harry and Billy. "What the hell is going on here? You have got to put up your money!"

Macklowe was cooling on the deal. Someone at Deutsche Bank had told him that the Reckson portfolio was worth far less to him than he thought.

"He gave Fortress back the $600 million, and Fortress said, 'That's fine, but you owe us $606 million.' Six million was the fee," Rob Horowitz explained. "So Harry wrote them a check for $6 million. He had the money outstanding for one week."

■ ■ ■

Icahn went ahead and made an offer that was not nearly as attractive as the one he'd discussed with Macklowe. It was a combination of cash and stock, rather than all cash. He lost the deal to SL Green.

He later sued both Macklowes for $60 million, since that was the agreed penalty. The case was fought over the finer points of contract law, and the Macklowes prevailed.

But the Reckson deal would mark a pivotal moment in the life and career of Harry Macklowe, for two reasons. The first was the insertion—albeit in a mild way—of a banker, namely Andrew Bednar, who was not part of Macklowe's inner circle. The second reason was that in order to line up the financing from Fortress, he had to show the hedge fund his financial statement of $2.7 billion.

Both these facts would play a vital role in the biggest mistake Macklowe ever made.

Chapter 11

Mr. Toad's Wild Ride

Think about it. An individual with $50 million in cash basically bought $10 billion worth of real estate. . . . That's leverage.

—Michael Fascitelli

B y the end of 2006, Harry Macklowe was the sole owner (with the bank) of the GM Building. In 2005 he'd bought out Steven Mnuchin and Vornado and, in 2006, their replacement—a German pension fund called Jamestown. Deutsche Bank now had a five-year loan on the building for $1.9 billion at a fixed interest rate of just over 5 percent.

Macklowe was busy buying and refinancing other buildings, too. Rob Horowitz wrote down their new deals—all financed by Deutsche Bank—on his A4 lined paper which served as the only record off of which he worked. Who cared about the methodology of the record keeping? They were all getting very rich.

Horowitz documented the refinancing of a sparkling, redesigned office building at 340 Madison Avenue, which Macklowe marketed with his usual panache. He drove to Canada with some colleagues, brought six Smart cars over the border, and disassembled one of them, displaying its parts in the building's entrance to show how "iconic design" works.

He bought a potential hotel site on Madison Avenue and 53rd Street. And in early 2006, Macklowe purchased the Drake Hotel on Park Avenue at East 56th Street for $400 million. (The Drake was famous for housing rock bands like The Who and Led Zeppelin in the 1960s and 1970s.) Deutsche Bank provided the financing. Harry planned to demolish the hotel and build a condominium tower.

He encountered opposition in a tenant named Raphael Schwarz, a tailor who wouldn't move from his atelier on the fifth floor. The *New York Post* recounted how Macklowe paid Schwarz a "get-to-know-you visit"; he assured Schwarz they had several rabbis in common, which Schwarz said was impossible, since he wasn't Jewish. Ultimately, however, Schwarz moved.

But all of this was the "same old." Those who really knew Harry Macklowe suspected it wouldn't be long before he placed a bet that no one else would consider. His appetite for risk was that big. "As good as [most] real estate guys are as transactionalists, that's how poor they are as conceptualists," says Sam Zell. "That's why they keep getting caught in oversupplies. Because what they do requires such a micro focus, their ability to then go macro is limited."

Even the GM Building—Harry's greatest triumph, the thing that had transformed him—was not enough. He outgrew it. He needed more fame, more wealth, more *everything* to cement his place in the pantheon of real estate families. Doug Harmon described him as the perfect "mark" for the right "professional gambler."

■ ■ ■

Jonathan "Jon" D. Gray possessed a charismatic energy. In 2006 he was 36 years old. He was understated in his appearance, preferring watches from Walmart and off-the-rack suits. He had earned degrees in both English literature and finance at the University of Pennsylvania. He enjoyed telling people that he'd met his wife in a Romantic poetry class—and that he was the only student in his college crowd who didn't wear Birkenstocks.

Gray was ambitious, fiercely so. He was, in 2006, the head of the real estate group at Blackstone, a huge private equity firm. Under his watch Blackstone had been placing far more emphasis on real estate, moving beyond buying and selling individual properties into a much bigger scale, buying and selling real estate companies, a business with much bigger margins.

His friend Roy March planted an idea in his head that wouldn't go away. He should try to buy Equity Office Properties (EOP), the biggest public landlord of commercial office space in the country, worth about $41 billion. EOP had 662 prime buildings around the United States.

EOP was owned by Sam Zell, the so-called "grave-dancer" because of his penchant for buying distressed properties cheap. Zell had already hinted publicly that he thought the market was ripe for trading. "Prices of office buildings in Manhattan are selling at significantly less than their replacement cost," he told the *New York Sun* in May that year.

Even so, Zell would later say that he had sold EOP only because Gray had made an offer he couldn't believe, an offer he couldn't—on one level—even understand. "I couldn't justify what I was selling to Blackstone," he said.

■ ■ ■

The process began, according to Gray, when Roy March came to see him in the summer of 2006 along with Jordan Kaplan, the president and CEO of Douglas Emmett, a California real estate investment trust. Kaplan mentioned casually that he'd pay a capitalization (cap) rate of four for the Los Angeles portfolio of EOP. This translated to 25 times cash flow, or, put another way, a 4 percent cash return. It was two or three times the going rate. "We saw we could buy this company on the screen a lot cheaper than you could sell it on the street," Gray said.

Gray asked March to price out what he thought it would all be worth. By November he was ready to bid $47.50 a share for EOP—at

$35.6 billion, it was the most Blackstone had ever risked in a deal. Gray couldn't afford for anything to go wrong. What would be disastrous would be for him to get stuck with overvalued assets in a market that then turned down.

Zell was equally cautious. "The key," he would say later, "was negotiating the breakup fee" (the penalty amount EOP would have to pay Blackstone if it decided to go to another buyer). Initially it was $200 million—deliberately "minimal" from Zell's point of view.

What Zell wanted was an auction. And the rival purchaser he had in mind was his old friend Steve Roth at Vornado. Back in the summer Roth had suggested to Zell that the two firms merge. This way Zell could keep control. But Zell didn't want control. He wanted *Godfather* money—as in an offer he couldn't refuse—for him and his shareholders.

Gray knew the bidding war would be like a "sporting event" with much public interest and media comment following his opening offer. This was, after all, the largest leveraged buyout (LBO) ever. What he was hoping was that by making the opening bid in November—knowing that Zell had a shareholder meeting on February 7 and would be under pressure from his board to maximize value—Gray had given himself the advantage of time that competitors would not have.

He was already working with his team in a conference room, assembling information he would need to get the financing perfected, and crucially the same information ready to make available to buyers once he was allowed to waive his confidentiality agreement by Zell.

The clock ticked. To Sam Zell's consternation, he didn't hear anything from Vornado. What was going on? He was worried that Blackstone might be stifling competition. It wasn't, though. Zell called Roth: "Where the hell are you?" Roth explained that Vornado was struggling finding partners.

Finally, on January 15, 2007, Zell heard a rumor. Vornado was going to bid. It had gotten Walton Street Capital and Starwood Capital Group Global on board. Zell e-mailed Roth: "Dear Stevie, Roses are red/Violets are blue/I heard a rumor/Is it true? Love and kisses, Sam."

He received a reply: "Sam, how are you?/The rumor is true/I do love you/And the price is $52."

The auction was under way.

On January 22, Blackstone upped the ante to $53.50 per share—provided that Zell agreed to increase the breakup fee to $700 million, 3 percent of EOP's market capitalization. Zell said yes if Blackstone got to $54 per share.

Gray agreed. But it was a dizzying price.

Gray knew there was only one way he could afford what was now looking like a bid close to $40 billion. He was going to need to sell some of the assets simultaneously as he bought them, this way considerably lessening the price for Blackstone and the massive cost of transfer taxes. The biggest chunk was the New York portfolio, which was worth, he thought, around $7 billion. $180 million in transfer taxes would be avoided.

So Gray asked Zell for his permission to market the New York buildings. Zell agreed.

■ ■ ■

Harry Macklowe first went to see Jon Gray on a Friday in late January. Roy March had planted the idea of buying EOP's New York portfolio in Harry's head during a visit ostensibly to talk about renovations at 1330 Sixth Avenue, which Harry had recently bought. That was "the hook," as Gray would later tell people. March dropped 1301 Sixth Avenue, one of the EOP buildings, into the conversation.

Macklowe was mesmerized.

Gray knew Macklowe was the most likely—and ready—buyer on the short list of three he had made with Roy March, Blackstone's broker. The other two were Mort Zuckerman and his REIT, Boston Properties, and SL Green—but Harry, Gray reckoned, was the one who would want the EOP portfolio, despite being the minnow of the group.

"It" was, after all, quite a prize: Seven million square feet of prime real estate in New York City for seven billion dollars. The buildings in the portfolio included the Park Avenue Tower at 65 East 55th Street and Worldwide Plaza on Eighth Avenue and 49th Street. Trophies like those come only once a lifetime, Gray would later tell people.

From Gray's perspective Harry was the most flexible bidder on account of not being answerable to shareholders; he could move with lightning speed—which was essential. In many ways the scenario was a replay of his bid for the GM Building three years earlier. The parallels were eerie. It was the same broker (Eastdil). It was, again, the biggest deal anyone had ever conceived of, but it would be done four times as fast.

Harry told Gray and Gray's right-hand man, Anthony Myers, that should Blackstone end up as the buyer (and seller) of EOP, he wanted Gray and Myers to know he thought he could get financing for roughly $7 billion for the New York portfolio. Seven billion dollars was the right price.

There was only one problem. Harry had Googled EOP to look at the list of buildings before talking to Gray. Having agreed to the price, he then went though his list, which included an eighth building, the so-called Verizon building at 1095 Avenue of the Americas, that wouldn't actually be for sale for another two years. There was total silence for a few moments until someone said to Macklowe, "Harry—you've got an extra building on your list."

Myers, for one, feared that any deal died right there, since the price wouldn't be shifting, and Harry would have to pay it for one less building than he'd reckoned.

But Macklowe appeared to get over the extra expense extraordinarily quickly.

They agreed on a pro rata price of around $7 billion. Macklowe asked Roy March to get Billy up to speed on what was going on. The younger Macklowe peppered March with questions as he drove into the city on a Sunday. Rob Horowitz called Eric Schwartz and started talking about financing.

■ ■ ■

The next two and a half weeks—the countdown period—would come to be known within Blackstone as "Mr. Toad's Wild Ride."

Roy March came up with the label—a chapter title from Kenneth Grahame's children's book *The Wind in the Willows*—as he warned both Gray and Myers that negotiations with Macklowe would not be smooth, but that Macklowe would get there in the end. Macklowe wanted the buildings "worse than anything."

March promised Gray he would act as a facilitator. "Harry can pull this off," he said, "but you have to understand, we're gonna go on a wild ride."

What Gray and Myers understood this to mean was that "Harry will show up, from one day to the next, and you're never quite sure with Harry who he is or what he's gonna do, and you just gotta be prepared."

As if Macklowe wasn't complex enough, Gray soon found he also had Harry's son to contend with. For the first time, Billy was to take the lead in executing a Macklowe deal. From Gray's point of view he was risking his career and an unprecedentedly large amount of money—and Blackstone's stellar reputation—on perhaps the trickiest, least predictable father-and-son act on the planet. "I would never have taken the risk that Jon Gray did," says EOP's then CEO, Richard D. Kincaid, who watched the whole drama play out from Chicago.

■ ■ ■

On Sunday, February 4, with just two days to go before the EOP shareholder vote, Gray was watching his home team, the Chicago Bears, play the Indianapolis Colts in the Super Bowl when his phone rang and he heard that Vornado had parried again. They were now at $56 per share but the deal was "softer" than he'd anticipated. It was not all in cash, which was what Zell wanted—and the offer was not legally binding.

Gray saw his chance: he could win this. Blackstone would deliver a $55.50 per share binding all-cash offer. He knew Zell would take it and submit it two days later for a shareholder vote. He had to get ready to close by the week's end. He needed Macklowe ready with his $7 billion in the next five days. The timing was critical.

Gray called Macklowe, who in turn called Rob Sorin, who was watching the football game in New Jersey. At midnight Sorin and Rob Horowitz gathered in the law offices of Simpson Thatcher, Blackstone's lawyer, along with Anthony Myers and Billy and Harry Macklowe.

■ ■ ■

Sorin recalls his immediate reaction that night as Harry told him, "We are buying EOP." "I was terrified," says the lawyer.

Sorin felt it was too much money too quickly, that the lender's terms would be extraordinarily onerous even for "gung-ho Harry"—and they didn't know the properties they were buying well enough. They still hadn't finished their due diligence. The leases on these buildings were long-term and there was no obvious profit to be made for at least five years.

But Harry had made it clear there was no stopping him. Billy Macklowe, too, was being unusually assertive, says someone in the meetings. "He was very rah-rah." This worried other members of the Macklowe team. "The biggest, trickiest deal of Harry's career? It was completely the wrong time for Billy to try to carve out an identity for himself," one of them would later say.

By Tuesday, Eric Schwartz had given Rob Horowitz Deutsche Bank's final terms: Deutsche Bank would loan him $5.8 billion—with a term of one year. The EOP buildings would serve as collateral. The bank fees from such an enormous loan would exceed $100 million. That left $1.2 billion for Macklowe to scrape together. Who would lend him $1.2 billion? There was a very short list. The obvious candidate in Horowitz's mind was the hedge fund Fortress, which had recently lent Harry money for the aborted Reckson deal. That close, good relationship with the managing director, Steve Stuart, Eric Schwartz's golfing buddy, paid dividends.

Stuart presented a proposed term sheet that was just over a page long. It agreed to lend Macklowe $1.2 billion for a one-year term at an interest rate of 15 percent.

But—and it was a big *but*—not only would Macklowe have to pay it back in full in precisely 12 months, but it was collateralized by everything owned by Macklowe Properties (including the GM Building, which Fortress had valued at $2.8 billion), and on top of this, printed in bold, was a clause stating that Macklowe had to guarantee it personally. Should he default, Harry Macklowe would owe Fortress every work of art, every piece of his boat, every house, even the shirt off his back. Stuart took this term sheet to his boss, Peter "Pete" L. Briger Jr., a former Goldman Sachs partner with a reputation for being taciturn and tough.

Stuart showed him the paper and said: "We can do the world's largest hard-money loan with a bunch of collateral that we think is real and a personal guarantee, you know, for a billion-two."

Briger agreed to do it.

■ ■ ■

Rob Sorin watched Harry and Billy sign the Fortress deal, but told them he didn't like the terms. "Briger is a hard-money lender. You're playing with fire. . . . They're very tough. When I say hard money, I mean they're lenders of high risk, not necessarily last resort, but pretty close to it."

Even Rob Horowitz had his reservations. He worried about the EOP buildings, the lack of rent revenue. He'd been doodling on his A4 paper. How would they repay the loan that fast?

The team at Blackstone was worried as well. Gray called both Eric Schwartz and Steve Stuart to check that they were really financing Macklowe. "Harry's a wealthy guy but he's not Boston Properties, and this was seven billion dollars . . . and it was 99 percent financing, so anything could go wrong."

Mike Fascitelli heard what was happening and thought they'd all gone mad. The risk was extraordinary, he felt, a sign the market was completely overheated and that a downturn was inevitable. He told Harry that to finance it for one year "you gotta be out of your mind" and that Eric Schwartz must have "lost his brain" to make such a big loan. Even so—just in case—he was going to take a small mezzanine part of their debt. If Harry were to lose the GM Building, once again Vornado wanted to be able to buy it.

Macklowe went on singing and cracking jokes as usual. He now says he believed he was covered. "Truth to tell, Deutsche Bank told me they would consolidate everything." He believed Deutsche Bank had his back after all these years, all those deals. They'd refinance the Fortress loan. "Fifteen billion dollars is a lot of financing."

Once Harry had "blessed the deal," he left the bulk of the paperwork and haggling up to the lawyers—and Billy. There was a lot to be done in just days.

Billy Macklowe was clearly stressed, remember executives who negotiated with him. They also remember "a great deal of shouting and swearing."

They didn't have much time to complain, though. Every day, as the clock ticked down to February 9, Jon Gray was asking Anthony Myers how close they were to a deal. Every day Myers worried they couldn't get there. The Macklowes were still doing due diligence.

They'd come apart on the price. Roy March was on the phone to everyone, reporting back to the Blackstone executives on the Macklowe "body language," reassuring them that even though it might not look like it, Harry Macklowe would close.

■ ■ ■

For a reason Myers never fully understood, Gray interrupted him two days ahead of the closing scheduled for Friday, February 9, and told him to march with him to the law offices of Simpson Thatcher. They were signing *now*. "Get your jacket; we are closing," Gray said. Myers protested that the paperwork was not ready—not even close. There were so many outstanding items still to be resolved.

But he went with Gray down the street to the offices of Simpson Thatcher. There the room was crowded with lawyers as well as all the expected players: both Macklowes, and Rob Sorin. Eric Schwartz was giddy. He said to Myers, "You realize that you guys have probably created about $150 billion of underwriting that's going on simultaneously on the street right now."

Myers said, "Yeah, I get it. I've been a little busy, but you're right. That's an amazing thought."

Harry Macklowe was grinning broadly and taking photographs.

The legal papers were produced for him and Billy to sign, and he got out his pen with a flourish. But then he stopped. He turned to his lawyers and said, "My name's in here. Why's Billy's name not on the signature page? I want Billy to sign this as well. This is important."

Billy Macklowe looked uncomfortable. Why? Was it because he didn't want to sign? He didn't want to do this deal? Or because he'd been left off? And why was the elder Macklowe so insistent he sign?

"Billy was tense, tired. Harry was calm. Something was off between them," one person said.

A new page was printed and both Macklowes signed.

■ ■ ■

The monies got held in escrow accounts.

Back at Blackstone's office it was "battle, battle, battle" to close out all the legal issues by the official closing deadline of 11:00 A.M. Friday.

That was when $39 billion had to be wired. And at 11:05 A.M. on Friday, Anthony Myers didn't have signatures from Billy.

Forty-or-so bankers were due to simultaneously dial in and await the signal to wire their money. Federal regulations won't permit more than $1 billion to be wired in one transaction, so Blackstone had arranged for the $39 billion to be broken up. But Deutsche Bank, on behalf of Harry Macklowe, needed to be ready with his wire at the same time.

The coordinator was busy lining up the wirers like an air traffic controller. "JP Morgan, are you ready? UBS, are you ready?" On and on, until "Deutsche Bank? Deutsche Bank? Deutsche Bank? . . ."

Silence.

It was now 11:15.

Jonathan Gray burst into Anthony Myers's office. "Where the fuck is Harry?"

Myers called Billy Macklowe. "We've got 40 banks and $40 billion waiting," he told him. "Why aren't you on the phone confirming?"

Billy said Rob Sorin was still reviewing the contract.

Myers told Billy to tell Sorin the clock had run out.

The roll call on the phone began again.

"Deutsche Bank, are you there?"

This time they were there.

And the biggest leveraged buyout in history was done.

Chapter 12

Tick Tock—A Year
on the Clock

I remember the clock ticking; I remember him scrambling.
—Doug Harmon

They had a dinner at Cipriani at Grand Central Station to celebrate the closing, but it wasn't like the fete in the fall of 2003:
This just didn't have the excitement and the optimism of when
they closed on the GM Building. . . .

The GM Building!

What had they done?

Harry had risked his biggest trophy, his most prized possession, the
building that, for him, was so much more than bricks and mortar; it was
the cocoon that had changed him from a caterpillar into a butterfly. He'd
also risked his personal fortune—and Peter Briger surely knew, as he

extracted the promissory note with a personal guarantee, that if it came down to it and Harry couldn't repay the $1.2 billion plus interest within a year, Harry would have to choose between the two. Which would he forfeit? The building, which, at Fortress's valuation of $2.8 billion didn't cover his obligations since it had debt of $1.9 billion on it? Or his personal assets—his houses, his boats, Linda's art?

Rob Sorin reflected: "Maybe people just didn't want to admit that and say, 'Oh God, what did we just do? Did we really close a $7 billion deal in nine days or whatever it was?

"If you think of it that way, you'd ask, 'Are you crazy?'"

■ ■ ■

The next day, Horowitz sat with Harry and Billy in the Macklowe offices. "Okay, so we bought [the EOP assets]. Now what do we do?" he asked.

Would Harry sell his new purchases? There was plenty of interest. He could get more than he paid for them.

The answer was no.

Harry wanted to study the buildings closely and see what opportunities there were. "Define" them is the real estate jargon for this.

Horowitz pointed out they could still hit the brakes, pull out; they'd lose their deposit but that was many millions, not billions. But the Macklowes—both of them—said no.

On February 13, Billy Macklowe spoke proudly about the new purchase at a lunch for the Young Men's and Women's Real Estate Association, saying that he and his father had moved so fast because they believed that nothing kills a deal more than "lack of speed." He talked about the new portfolio of buildings as being "five generational"—it was only then, the New York Observer reported, that his father, who was in the audience, stopped staring at the floor and glanced up at him quizzically.

■ ■ ■

The Macklowe plan, according to Sorin, Schwartz, and Horowitz, was to find an equity partner with whom to share the assets, the GM Building included, and offload the debt. Deutsche Bank had been tasked with this. It had been part of the discussions when the bankers had agreed to make Harry the loan of $5.8 billion.

A source on the Deutsche Bank team stresses they'd been clear to Harry that Macklowe Properties had to make some essential changes if Deutsche Bank was to find an investor. One of the talking points had been the necessity of hiring a credible CEO—someone of the caliber of Mike Fascitelli—now that the assets under management were so vast. But Harry didn't move. Everyone kept waiting—and waiting. Could he not bear the idea of having an outside partner? Was Billy preventing him? The general perception was that Billy, encouraged by his mother, wanted to assume much more responsibility. A *Fortune* magazine article would report that father and son ended up in counseling because of this conflict.

Linda was also openly livid about the personal guarantee. "She was furious with Harry for doing it and she didn't care who knew," one of her friends said on the condition of speaking anonymously. Her criticism of her husband was even reported in the *New York Times*. She told Rob Horowitz that she blamed him for advising Harry badly—which, he felt, was unfair. "No one could have stopped Harry on that deal."

Harry seemed uncharacteristically paralyzed and silent, unwilling to share the pressures of what was clearly a growing power struggle in his family. His advisers were dismayed. "It was very unfortunate that right at the moment when Harry made the biggest deal by far, in terms of money, of his career that suddenly his family situation got a lot more complicated," one of the advisers would later say, on the condition of speaking anonymously.

Mike Fascitelli believed he understood what was happening. "Harry had put their money in Linda's name," he said. "He's done it before. . . . [to protect himself]. It became obvious to all of us that she was calling the shots."

■ ■ ■

Joe Perella saw the sale of EOP on the tape and was dismayed when he heard how Macklowe had paid for the buildings. He rushed up to his landlord's offices with his younger partner, Andrew Bednar.

Perella recalled: "[Harry] was a friend I cared about deeply." He thought he saw a way to solve this. Through his cofounder and former Morgan Stanley colleague, Tarek "Terry" Abdel-Meguid, Perella had five seed investors in the Middle East who included sovereign wealth funds such as that of Sheik Mohammed of the United Arab Emirates.

Perella told Macklowe: "You've got to get permanent financing. . . .
You've got to build up a team. . . . Go to the Middle East, put together a
portfolio and a proposal and say: 'You can enter the big-time real estate
market in the United States, partner with me, and I will put all of my
buildings into the partnership. The only thing we have argued about
is what are they all worth today? It will be 50/50, and I'll manage it
for you.'"

"I told him, 'Go right away. Go to the Middle East right *now*.'

"Macklowe said, 'Yes, yes.' But Macklowe didn't move."

Perella was frustrated. He warned his friend not to underestimate
the business savvy of the foreign investors. "I said, 'don't think there's
a bunch of graybeards over there living in a tent and you're going to
go over there with a wheelbarrow and they're going to fill it up with
money saying, 'tell us when to stop, Harry.'

"That's not how it works. These people have very astute people advising them, and you've got to go to them with a deal that makes sense
and is attractive."

Perella told him repeatedly that he had to offer *all* of his portfolio
to investors.

But there was another impediment. The younger Macklowe, recall
many people who were in meetings with father and son, was vehement
that only the EOP buildings could be offered up to equity investors. All
the others—the GM Building, the buildings he and his sister Liz had a
stake in, the so-called "legacy portfolio" worth north of $2.7 billion—
could not be included.

The problem with this was glaringly obvious. No serious equity
investor would want to purchase equity in only part of the Macklowe
portfolio. The fear would always be that the Macklowes would give
preferential treatment to the buildings they owned exclusively. It would
create a conflict.

Eric Schwartz had no idea that the Macklowes were conversing with
Joe Perella or Andrew Bednar—and Perella never knew that Macklowe
already had an agreement in place with Deutsche Bank to find an equity
partner. He simply wanted to help his friend.

The two banks had competing strategies. Deutsche Bank told
Macklowe it would require him to put in around $500 million and
the bank would find him a partner in the Middle East for $2.5 billion.

Perella Weinberg had lower equity requirements. Terry Abdel-Meguid had unbeatable relationships in the region. Even Schwartz would be forced to acknowledge that.

So late that summer Harry Macklowe made a small first step. He fired Deutsche Bank's investment banking arm as the group responsible for raising equity and asked Perella Weinberg to put together a book and raise money in the Middle East. Rob Horowitz had to act as the messenger to Deutsche Bank. "I said, 'Guys, Harry doesn't want to use you. He wants to use someone else. Do you guys give a shit?'

"They said, 'Okay, Rob. No problem.'"

But Harry had waited too long. Perella knew that they had lost crucial time. The markets were beginning to turn.

■ ■ ■

In September, Andrew Bednar went with Harry and Billy to the Middle East to market the seven EOP buildings. Bednar would tell people he thought the meetings went very well but that no agreement could be reached "on price."

Joe Perella was less tactful. "The vultures had got there first," he would say. What he meant was word had spread that "Macklowe was under pressure." The rival real estate developers who thought they could feed on his carcass told the Middle East investors to hold off. If the markets kept falling they'd be able to buy the buildings—especially the GM Building—far more cheaply when Macklowe was forced to sell off his assets when the loans to Briger and Deutsche Bank came due.

Billy Macklowe, Perella remembers, became increasingly emotional as time ticked by. "He was in tears," recalls Perella.

But Harry Macklowe seemed to live his usual life. He and Linda closed on a $60 million apartment at the Plaza, across from—and looking out on—the GM Building. He would later say he always believed that Deutsche Bank would be there for him to re-finance. "I had their word."

He went sailing on *Unfurled*. He invited a group of bankers and brokers, as well as Roger Cozzi, the new managing director at Fortress, out to East Hampton to play golf. On the helicopter ride out there one of the bankers quipped, "Harry knocked down a building in the middle of the night. Do you think he'll kill his bankers on a plane?"

He didn't appear to have the sense of impending crisis everyone else felt. Schwartz's team was working around the clock, as Deutsche Bank felt the pressure and it seemed like it would lose money on its giant loans. It was no longer time for golf.

On August 14, Joe Perella had a meeting with the mortgage lender Countrywide Financial, where the CEO, Angelo Mozilo, told him about an impending housing crisis. "Angelo Mozilo scared the living hell out of me with his description of what was going on in the country at that time and his inability to get people or the Feds to focus on what he called a looming housing crisis."

Perella recalled, "I came back from my meeting on a Monday. We had a corporate meeting and I said I've been in this business for 35 years, and I've never had the you-know-what scared out of me more than that day. I said all I could do is relate it to my mother and father growing up in New Jersey. They are religiously making their mortgage payments on their house every month. The American system of savings for hard-working middle-class people was you bought a home, you made your mortgage payments, and the mortgage was paid off in 20 years. When you retired, you had this nest egg that you got from selling your house and you moved to Arizona or Florida.

"I said [at my partners' meeting] these millions of people right now in America are going to wake up and find out that that nest egg doesn't exist because the prices of real estate will collapse and their savings will be wiped out. The one thing I don't know is how it will affect their behavior, but it sure as heck is going to put the country into a nosedive.

"It was clear a real estate bubble that affected everyone in America was about to burst. It wasn't sustainable."

■ ■ ■

In October the junior loan on the Drake Hotel came due. Deutsche Bank had sold the mezzanine layer to Vornado, SL Green Realty, and Cerberus Capital Management. Harry owed $180 million. He had personally guaranteed it. The troika wanted their money.

Harry didn't want to pay. Rob Sorin didn't want him to pay, either. At this point the lawyer felt that "any money was better off in Harry's pocket. We could sort out how to work it all out down the road, when the EOP loans came due."

But Eric Schwartz told Harry he could not get an extension on his behalf. If he didn't pay, he would lose the Drake Hotel.

So, reluctantly—and against Sorin's advice—Harry paid, hoping that the gesture would curry favor with Deutsche Bank. "I was investing a couple hundred million dollars more in the deal," he would say. In his mind, they all still had a deal. But he was the only optimist left.

Rob Sorin was by now highly skeptical. He feared that Deutsche Bank had too many troubles of its own to assist Harry anymore.

In Sorin's mind, Harry had only two options left to save the GM Building: "There was either the nuclear option, which is to file for bankruptcy or something equivalent [which Sorin most emphatically did not endorse—"Harry would never have worked again; no one would have lent to him"], *or* to try to negotiate a restructure."

On Sorin's advice, Alvarez & Marsal, a firm specializing in corporate turnarounds, was brought in to help restructuring—and to prepare to negotiate with Pete Briger, come February. Sorin wanted Alvarez & Marsal to be the front team.

Harry Macklowe now wished he was on a different planet. "How do I get out of this shit?" he asked Rob Horowitz.

■ ■ ■

Horowitz believed he had a solution that did not involve Alvarez & Marsal: It was Eric Schwartz. Horowitz truly believed Deutsche Bank might roll the dice one last time, despite what had happened with the Drake Hotel. He told Harry the bank would buy all Harry's debt—including the Fortress loan—in exchange for a 10 percent ownership interest in all of the Macklowes' legacy assets.

On November 10, Horowitz wrote Billy and Harry an e-mail:

> Guys . . . I think it is in our best interests to have a private meeting, the three of us with Eric and maybe Jon [Vaccaro, Eric's boss] to discuss strategy. I know that Rob S and the [Alvarez & Marsal] advisors are telling you they don't control our fate, but I am hearing otherwise from Harvey [Uris, Deutsche Bank's outside counsel]. . . .

I truly believe Eric is more concerned about [you than the other] advisors will be. I think we should have a meeting before it's too late. . . . The only people who can make a deal here are you both, me, and Eric. If we lose that opportunity we will regret it.

On November 12, he wrote again to Harry and Billy, this time a 12-page e-mail, which he decided to print and fax directly to Harry.

As we discussed over the last few weeks . . . [it is my] recommendation we meet privately, the three of us with Eric, and maybe Jon, to discuss strategies with the global recap. Although Rob Sorin and the A and M advisors are providing you with options, I believe our fate rests with Eric; it's my strong belief Eric is more concerned with MP [Macklowe Properties] than our non-legal advisors. . . .

Horowitz also mentioned that Fried Frank, in his opinion, was not giving Macklowe the best advice. "They were telling him to pay off his loans. Why do you need a lawyer to tell you to do that? It would be like you paying a lawyer to tell you to pay off your credit card bill."

On Saturday, November 17, he wrote to the duo again. "Guys . . . I believe that something could be worked out in exchange for equity kickers. . . . This is your call. I want you to meet with them."

Two minutes later, there was a reply from Billy.

"No."

■ ■ ■

Rob Sorin would later say that Horowitz was overstepping, "that he wasn't being paid" to act as Harry's restructuring guru, and that although everyone believed he'd done a great job—he'd made everyone millions, walking a tightrope between Deutsche Bank and Harry—in the end he was, as Sorin said, simply "a broker."

Sorin also says that he and the Macklowes had met with Eric Schwartz and Jon Vaccaro but that the meeting hadn't gone anywhere. Schwartz didn't have the authority from the bank in these tough times to follow through on his offer.

"Believe me, if they'd offered to buy all of the debt in exchange for a 10 percent ownership interest, I'd have taken that very seriously," Sorin says.

So Sorin was upset when he read Horowitz's memo, which basically trashed his legal advice and tried to end-run his solutions. He called Horowitz and reamed him out. Horowitz, in turn, was furious that his memo had been leaked to Sorin.

They'd get over it, but the friendship was tested.

Unlike Horowitz, Sorin had been careful to steer a more neutral course between Macklowe father and son. Billy had even joined a small group in Las Vegas for Sorin's 50th birthday that fall.

Increasingly, Horowitz found himself shut out of meetings in the GM Building. He heard that Billy now called him "Deutsche Bank's spy." "I heard that [Billy said] 'Rob shouldn't be involved in our private meetings, because he'll run back and tell Deutsche Bank'—which really wasn't the case. I was always pro-Harry; he was the one who paid me a lot of money."

But Billy prevailed. By January 2008, Horowitz was bounced from Harry Macklowe's life.

■ ■ ■

As the new advisers replaced the old, Harry seemed to recede into the shadows of his own organization. It looked like Billy was now in charge. According to Rob Sorin, this was a deliberate tactic both he and Harry supported. Lenders' memories are fickle—especially in a tanking market. Harry was now no longer the visionary who had transformed the GM Building. Rather he was the loose cannon who had borrowed billions of dollars and might file for bankruptcy rather than pay it back. Billy, on the other hand, didn't have that track record. In fact, Billy had no track record—and right now that was almost helpful—at least to his new bankers, Citigroup, led by Paul Ingrassia. From now on Billy Macklowe became the front person in negotiations to find a new partner who would somehow save the day.

But time was running out.

On February 9, Harry Macklowe defaulted on both the loan to Fortress and the loan to Deutsche Bank. Would he file for bankruptcy and fight? Deutsche Bank was losing money by the day. The bank wanted to settle, and get something, *anything*. By the end of the month, it had gotten a deal. The bank took back the seven EOP buildings and sold them gradually.

Pete Briger gave Macklowe an extension of four months (earning more interest). But he wanted to know Fortress would get paid. In exchange for the extension he insisted that Harry put the GM Building on the market immediately.

Harry listed the GM Building with brokers CB Richard Ellis for $3.5 billion.

Harry was still so confident it was all going to turn out well that he turned down an offer of $3.1 billion from Larry Silverstein.

Billy, meanwhile, was in talks to find a last-minute equity partner. The Canadian pension fund Omers Private Equity was a natural option since it already owned a piece of the Fortress loan. In meetings held either in Toronto or in the GM Building in New York, Billy, Andrew D. Trickett (Omers' senior vice president), Paul Ingrassia, and Jonathan L. Mechanic (Fried Frank's top real estate lawyer), as well as Rob Sorin went back and forth as to what a merged company would look like.

While Omers would own the new company, Billy wanted to manage it. The economics would have changed for him, but he'd still have his place in the market, and the Macklowe name would mean something.

Omers said it wanted the ability to fire Billy if this arrangement didn't work out. They offered to pay him a salary of around $1 million a year, a figure that, people recall, visibly upset him.

Still, the talks kept going for six weeks. Omers wondered whether Briger would be interested in rolling some money into the deal. The financier flew in from Vail in his jeans to a meeting at the GM Building and asked with a bored expression and an irritated tone, "What am I doing here?"

He pointed at Andrew Trickett from Omers. "You should be figuring this out. Why do you need me here?"

He was deliberately squeezing them: reminding them who was in control.

Billy Macklowe was calm. "We've been friends a long time. Our families have known each other a long time. We hoped we might have a reasonable conversation," people recall him saying.

Briger stayed for a full day of meetings.

But six weeks into negotiations, the issue of control was still unresolved. Omers felt that this had to be sorted out to their satisfaction before pricing—and they were not yet comfortable.

Suddenly the Macklowes inserted a new clause into the term sheet that had to do with Harry Macklowe's potential personal tax liabilities.

The Omers people were surprised. "What is this?" they asked.

Citigroup explained that Macklowe needed to retain a "sliver interest" in the limited liability company that would be set up as the acquiring vehicle in order to defer a "very painful" capital gain of hundreds of millions of dollars that would ordinarily be due if he did a straightforward sale. The "sliver interest" would explicitly be passive and have no voting rights, but even so the Canadians were surprised.

They phoned tax attorney Martin Edelman at Paul Hastings for tax advice and learned that this kind of thing is a regular occurrence in American real estate deals.

There are all sorts of tax loopholes for real estate investors that would strike many regular income taxpayers as deeply unfair. The main three: First, there is so-called depreciation, which declares that a building, no matter how profitable, wears out and declines to a value of zero over 39 years, which allows an investor to write off, as a tax loss, around 2.5 percent of the building's value every year. In other words, for every year he owned the GM Building, Harry Macklowe was being credited with a tax loss of millions—even as its value went up by a billion dollars! Second, there are the 1031 exchanges whereby if you sell a building and buy a replacement property you avoid capital gains taxes altogether. Macklowe couldn't do this because he didn't have the liquidity. But third, there *was* the "sliver interest" clause—known as a contribution/debt-financed distribution scheme—which Macklowe hoped to use here.

Omers was not comfortable with this proposal. The Canadians didn't know the Macklowes well. They didn't want anyone having a "sliver interest." They weren't the pushovers the Macklowes might have hoped for. "I guess they found we were less 'Canadian' and more 'Goldman Sachs,'" Trickett would later tell people.

The talks ended. It was now March. Briger needed to be paid by May.

■ ■ ■

There were two serious contenders who knew Harry Macklowe well enough to consider giving him the "sliver interest" and other tax considerations he needed to keep his personal wealth unaffected by the building's sale. They were both public REITs, so they could, in a series of complex steps, issue him units in an "operating partnership" as well as "guarantees." One was Boston Properties, the behemoth run by the clever, articulate entrepreneur Mortimer Zuckerman.

The other was Vornado. Could Steve Roth and Mike Fascitelli finally lay their hands on the prize that had eluded them for so long?

■ ■ ■

In April and May, Fascitelli negotiated with Harry, Billy—and Linda, who now didn't even pretend to be in the shadows.

Once again, Fascitelli was not prepared to offer more than what he thought the GM Building was worth. "I loved it at $2.4 billion," he said. He also didn't want any of Macklowe's other "legacy assets." He "hated them"—unless, that is, he could get them for a cheap price. The GM Building was the prize. Even in these roiling markets, she remained a trophy property. He knew that Boston Properties was ahead of him in talks. He was playing an intensive game of catch-up.

For three weeks, he negotiated with the Macklowes, culminating in a marathon five nights in a row in May during which he operated a so-called war room at Fried Frank's downtown office. Jonathan Mechanic, a legal rainmaker in New York real estate, was now in charge, running between the Macklowes, Vornado, and a separate room where the Boston Properties team was installed.

The drama of those five nights was worthy of both a *Dallas*-style soap opera and a Shakespearean tragedy. Fascitelli saw the family run the gamut of emotions in those final days and hours. There was Harry, like King Lear, stumbling about, desperately looking for any way to restructure—any way to hold on to the building that had made him— and, he hoped, that could make him again.

But his family was in revolt. Daughter Liz Swig was there with Billy and Linda. Feelings were raw. "They were all yelling at Harry," recalls Fascitelli.

They were yelling because they didn't want him to gamble; they didn't want him to keep looking for ways to restructure to save the building. "Billy was talking [to me]," Fascitelli recalls. "He said, 'My father, he's lost his mind.'"

Fascitelli snapped. "I said [to Billy], 'Well, was it his money to start with or your money?'

"I feel like I'd slapped the shit out of him."

■ ■ ■

"He [Harry] wanted to merge into Vornado. He wanted me—us—to finance the whole company and be a creditor to Macklowe. I spent 40 hours on that at Macklowe's office and two to three weeks there trying to make a deal," Fascitelli said.

But by mid-May, Fascitelli had run out of time. He wasn't in control—nor was Harry.

Someone else was, says Fascitelli. "In the end, Linda called the shots."

■ ■ ■

Linda Macklowe, in tears, told Fascitelli she didn't want any more "risk."

"We've got to pull the trigger and sell the GM Building now," she told him. "We can't take the risk. We can't go through any other structuring."

It was at this moment that Fascitelli recognized that here, finally, Harry's decision not to leave his wife—and vice versa—had come home to roost. "Look, they could have split up. She could have taken the half and said, 'screw you.'"

They didn't.

"Harry didn't protect himself; [he] put a lot of the stuff in other people's names and they basically said, 'Okay, so it's in our name, we're going to control it.' That was his miscalculation."

Now Linda was going to use her leverage. All their money, homes, the art, the beloved boat—they weren't his to gamble with; they were hers.

He'd have to pay Briger with the GM Building.

Linda Macklowe laid out what was going to happen: Harry was going to sell the GM Building and three other buildings to Boston Properties—which was prepared to accommodate his tax requirements—so that he could pay off Briger.

He would get to keep—or *they* would get to keep—all their wealth, including her art collection; but his legacy, his dream, was over. He was a broken man. Fascitelli found it hard to watch. "Linda forced Harry to do it. She teamed up with his two kids and they had Harry by the—they forced him to sell it. Harry will never forgive her.

"He had been reduced to, unfortunately, a very old man."

■ ■ ■

On May 24 it was reported that Boston Properties, in partnership with a Dubai fund, Kuwait and Qatar Investment Authority money, and Goldman Sachs, would be buying four assets from the Macklowes for $3.95 billion. The GM Building sold for $2.9 billion—the highest price ever for a single office building—and the sale also included 540 Madison Avenue, 125 West 55th Street, and Two Grand Central Tower. Harry Macklowe received $650 million in non-taxable cash and $10 million worth of units that he could convert into stock.

In return, public filings show, Zuckerman agreed not to sell the building for nine years. Any earlier sale would trigger Macklowe's capital gains.

He paid off all of his debts.

■ ■ ■

Rob Sorin figured Harry had taken the only sane course. "He was better off doing what he did than making a deal with Vornado. Look, everybody's out for themselves. The Vornado offer made no sense. We sat with them. We talked to them, but it made no sense.

"In the end, he avoided personal bankruptcy. He paid Briger back every penny that Briger asked to have paid back. In a lot of ways, he maintained his reputation."

■ ■ ■

But even Sorin felt the pain of the moment when Harry Macklowe officially gave up the GM Building.

Harry walked into the downtown offices of Fried Frank with Linda and Billy. He looked like he might cry. Mort Zuckerman had the tact to stay away.

Sorin recalled, "It was tragic for several reasons, but one of the main reasons, I think, is because it was incredibly, incredibly successful even under the circumstances. Harry bought the building for $1.4 billion and he sold it five years later for $2.9 billion. That in and of itself is remarkable, even though it was not sold at its peak value.

"Harry didn't put a penny in his pocket. It all went to pay Briger. It was probably the saddest closing I've ever attended.

"It was tough."

Chapter 13

The Fall That Wasn't

I did not want this story to be about me. . . . I'd learned my lesson. I wanted this to be about the building.

—Harry Macklowe

Mort Zuckerman kept Harry Macklowe on as a tenant in the building of Harry's dreams. To this day Macklowe has the same corner office on the 21st floor. He keeps it white, minimalistic, save for the photos of his family on the walls.

Liliana Coriasco still acts as his office sentinel from her perch outside his lair. But Macklowe Properties is much reduced from what it used to be. There are only a handful of executives. And there is no Billy. In 2008, right after the sale of the GM Building, he denigrated his father in the *Wall Street Journal*. He said he had disagreed with his father privately, all along, about the Equity Office Properties (EOP) deal, about giving Pete Briger his personal guarantee. "You should always be opposed to recourse," he said. "There's not a lot of complicated math around that."

He said he had wanted to "exit" the EOP deal as soon as it was done. "The issue was my father seeing the victory of the deal as closing the transaction; I saw victory as exiting the transaction."

After they'd gone to the Middle East, he said he'd told his father to "step aside. . . . We had a series of very specific conversations."

He told the *Journal*, "There's a new way of business going forward."

Harry Macklowe's friends and colleagues—even many of his competitors—were horrified.

Rob Horowitz called the *Journal* reporters to complain; Ben Lambert offered Harry his "condolences." Even Rob Sorin wondered aloud, "Why does anyone do something like that?"

On June 12 it was reported that Harry Macklowe, then aged 71, would "step down" from his company. But even that didn't mend the rupture with his son. On May 17, 2010, it was reported that Billy Macklowe was leaving to form his own company, William Macklowe Company. He was taking a dozen staff with him.

Harry Macklowe was left working in the background, but he had many things to occupy him. One was his daughter Liz's acrimonious, high-profile divorce from the real estate scion Kent Swig. "Divorce is so fucking expensive," Macklowe moaned one afternoon, looking at a pile of legal papers.

And then there was 432 Park Avenue, the former Drake Hotel. He'd had to sell it, of course, like everything else, but he'd kept a stake. He'd insist it was a "significant amount," but no one believed him.

Harry Macklowe no longer worried about what other people thought.

"You've had an interesting career," Zuckerman had said to him as they finished up the GM deal.

"At first I was very hurt, and then I took it as a challenge," Macklowe said.

■ ■ ■

Initially it was speculated that Mort Zuckerman was repeating history with the purchase of the GM Building. The *Wall Street Journal* commented that it was an unusually "flashy" acquisition for Boston

Properties, and the question was raised whether Zuckerman might have overreached. Was he "an aging mogul grasping for glory in his twilight years?" asked a report in the *Real Deal*. It was observed that the building still had $1.9 billion of debt on it, and that many of the tenants with the most space had long leases.

Weil Gotshal, which now had the most space, had a lease that did not expire until 2019 and paid only $45 per square foot; Estée Lauder's lease wasn't due to expire until 2020. The new asking price was a mammoth $150 a square foot, but it was going to be a long time before Zuckerman would be able to get that.

But Zuckerman knew exactly what he was doing. The building yielded a return for him from day one. And tenants did move out. "This is what real estate is all about," he would say later, amused and bemused that he'd been underestimated.

Boston Properties had bought only 60 percent of the building. Zuckerman did not have Harry's aversion to partnerships, particularly ones that could spread the risk. The remaining 40 percent of the building was owned initially by Middle Eastern money—some of the same people Harry Macklowe had wooed in vain earlier. The Kuwait Investment Authority (KIA)—which had partnered with Disque Deane—was back. The KIA and Qatar Investment Authority shared 20 percent with Goldman Sachs; a Dubai fund had the other 20 percent.

Zuckerman has always been viewed as being apart from the flashy, trashy folks who comprise so much of his industry. He is that rare thing in that world: a bona fide intellectual with a passion for politics and media—and a steady track record. He invests in four cities only, each with what he termed geographic "constrictions": New York, Boston, San Francisco, and Washington. The constrictions, he said, mean that supply is limited so that demand will always drive prices up.

In 2006 and 2007 he was busy selling while everyone else was buying, a move, he later said, that put him in a perfect position to pay for a trophy building like the GM Building when it came on the market under duress.

The GM Building, he said, was the best building in New York City. "And New York City had the best buildings in America . . . deduce what you will from that." When asked why he didn't simply pronounce it the best building in America, he laughed. "Others may say that. . . . But at

Boston Properties, we are low key—we are lower key than some of the people you've written about [in this book]."

It also held a personal appeal: "Whenever I want to cheer myself up, I just take a walk around the Apple Store," he said. "They make $665 million a year for 10,000 square feet—in a windowless basement." He smiled. "Think about that."

■ ■ ■

In 2013 it was announced that yet again the building was in new hands—sort of. Zuckerman was keeping his 60 percent, but a new partnership of Chinese and Brazilian money was buying the other 40 percent piece—at a valuation of $1 billion. Goldman Sachs and the Middle Easterners had made money on their share and were cashing out. The tower was now worth $3.4 billion. As of 2014, it was worth close to 40 times what Max Rayne had paid for it in 1964. It was worth more than any single privately owned office building in the country, possibly in the world.

Fittingly, given her history, her new co-owners both came with backstories of grand accomplishment, struggle, and glamour.

Brazil's Safra family invested through their firm, M. Safra & Company. The Safra banking dynasty is one of the richest—and most mysterious—in the world. Most famously, one of the family, Edmond, died in highly unusual circumstances in Monaco in 1999, found in his penthouse, along with his nurse Vivian Torrente, having apparently locked themselves in a bathroom while a fire raged. In December 2002, another of Edmond's nurses, Ted Maher, was convicted of lighting the blaze—but a cloud of suspicion hung over his widow Lily, a woman Edmond's brothers, Moise and Joseph, had always resented.

The Safras joined forces on the GM Building with Chinese developer Zhang Xin, the cofounder and CEO of SOHO China Ltd, the biggest developer in Beijing's business district. Zhang is a self-made billionaire who invested private money in the building. She was born in Bejing and at 14 moved to Hong Kong with her mother, where she worked in a garment factory. She saved enough money to move to England, where she earned an undergraduate degree from Sussex University and a master's in economics at Cambridge. She worked for investment bank Barings, and then Goldman Sachs in New York. She returned to China, where she met a budding developer named Pan Shiyi. They married and, with very different skills and outlooks, they forged a multibillion-dollar development empire.

Fortunes in China are never made without rumors of corruption, and theirs was no exception. Zhang bought the piece of the GM Building amid talk of alleged money laundering.

No one quite knew all the facts, nor did they really care. Whatever the source of her fortune, Zhang, with a net worth of $3.6 billion, was a safe bet. In November 2013 she and Pan bought a $26 million town house on East 74th Street, beating out Brad Pitt.

Mort Zuckerman said he had "cherry-picked" both of his new partners. "They are solid investors who would be there for a long time to come," he said.

That the tower was seen as a trophy by global investors was fitting, given the international iconic importance of Apple, of General Motors, and of the white tower itself. From his offices over on Park Avenue and 52nd Street, Jonathan Gray looked at the building. "Is there another tower like it, not just in America, but in the world? Has anything risen so much in value?"

He shook his head. "I don't think so."

■ ■ ■

As the GM Building's fortunes soared, so, unexpectedly, did Harry Macklowe's. He and Linda made a point of carrying on in their private life as if nothing had happened. They never publicly talked about what Billy had said in the newspapers. Harry continued to invite his son to play golf. In fact, Harry never publicly talked about any of his family members in anything but a supportive manner.

Billy Macklowe bought and sold a couple of buildings that were reported to be "a far cry from" the "daring" investments of his father. He tried to patch things up in public, saying he and Harry had more quality time together these days. His wife Julie posed naked in an advertisement in *Vogue* promoting her cosmetics line, vbeauté. She and Billy often appeared in society columns.

Harry and Linda started to entertain in their new apartment, in which she finally showed off their art. Every spring they gave a party for 300 people. Guests included the Lauders, the Perellas, the Swid family—many of the boldface names in New York's social and art crowd. People noticed that the champagne flowed at the parties and that there was barely anything missing from the art collection, much to the chagrin of the experts at the two major auction houses, who had read the bad press about EOP and hoped, in vain, they'd have inventory to sell.

Harry kept his homes and his boat—and even ordered a new one to be designed by the Argentinian designer Germán Frers. And Linda kept on collecting art. Dealers noticed one major difference in the way she purchased, though. She did it "unilaterally"—without checking with Harry.

Slowly, the name Harry Macklowe started reappearing in the real estate pages. The Drake, or 432 Park Avenue as it was now known, was becoming a story. And so too was Macklowe.

In October 2013, Charles Bagli, the New York real estate chronicler of the *New York Times*, came to take a look at the Drake. "Harry Macklowe Gambles Again," read the headline. There was a photograph of Macklowe atop his building. "Is this a comeback?" he nonchalantly asked in the interview. "I never really went away."

The story told of how Macklowe had put together this tower, hired the architect Rafael Vinoly, and got to work designing what would be the tallest skyscraper in Manhattan. At the base would be retail. The rest would be the most expensive apartments in the city; the penthouse would be priced at $95 million. It would be, according to Harry, the "highest-grossing residential building in the USA." It was part of what was becoming known as Billionaires Row since Gary Barnett, the CEO of the development group Extell, was ahead of Macklowe by a little over a year, having already announced plans for a luxury residential building close by, on Park Avenue South.

Macklowe was delighted that all his hard work was finally coming to fruition—he said he had sold more than a billion dollars' worth of apartments—and that his public relations strategy of keeping quiet had worked. "I wanted to do [my project] quietly, without letting anybody know. It's only when you come out of the ground that people know you're real.

"That's why for two years I wouldn't give an interview. I wouldn't speak to anybody. I didn't give a shit what pressure I was put under. I wouldn't do it. And everything that I've said about that for that marketing, for capturing your imagination, for capturing Charles Bagli's imagination, for capturing my partner's imagination has come to be . . . 432 Park Avenue is bigger than you, bigger than me."

To coincide with Bagli's article, Macklowe had produced both a glossy magazine and a film promoting 432 Park Avenue. He showed off both with a boyish giddiness. The video focused on the themes of luxury, architecture, dreams, heights, perfection—and typically included some Macklowe humor; he appeared wearing a monkey costume—King Kong's.

The sales magazine was also a glossy paean to the billionaire lifestyle; it featured articles by well-known writers. Ingrid Sischy, the editor of the Italian, Spanish and German versions of *Vanity Fair*, had been a consultant. Tobias Meyer, then the head of contemporary art for Sotheby's, posed in front of a painting by Mark Rothko, *No. 1 (Royal Red and Blue)*, that he sold for over $75 million. There was a feature on Perini Navi yachts, Harry's favorite; a feature on tightrope walker Philippe Petit; and one on Simon and Garfunkel. He wasn't just pitching *any* affluent lifestyle to would-be buyers of apartments at 432; he was pitching himself, his tastes: his love of slender ballerinas, of clean architectural lines and contemporary art, and of old black-and-white Fred Astaire movies.

The magazine was called *432*—but it might have been more aptly titled *Harry!*

■ ■ ■

As he got more and more engaged in 432 Park—and a new project, One Wall Street, which he bought from Bank of New York Mellon in May 2014 for $585 million, Macklowe talked less and less about the GM Building—although he said, in a rare moment of contemplation, that it was never far from his dreams. "Was there any way I could have kept the GM Building?" he mulled in the summer of 2013. "I ask that so often, and it's a difficult game to play. . . . There were mistakes made, but I don't know. Was it hubris? I don't know.

"Listen, I did what I was supposed to do. It cost me a lot of money, and it certainly cost me a lot of criticism and embarrassment in the business. Many people may say—and I think it's justified—I should've been more conservative. But being a little more optimistic and pushing—it's worked in the past. That's optimism. And maybe [this time] it wasn't as well thought out as it should've been. It's unfortunate. Business turns. Business always turns.

"I've made billions and billions of dollars. And the accomplishments have been wonderful. They weren't as safe or as prudent—perhaps my planning wasn't as good as it should've been.

"Having said that, though, the number of buildings that I have built—the creations that I've been able to create, and those that will [have a] long life after me—is very satisfying.

"You know what I'd call your book? *The Impossible.*

"This building, the GM Building: It's impossible."

Chapter 14

Aftermath

Real estate is basically a circle of men holding a revolver to each other's heads.

—Industry proverb

Perhaps because people saw some part of themselves reflected in Harry Macklowe and his cautionary tale—and because in the strange, incestuous web of real estate so many people were, in some way, connected to what happened to him—many were thrilled to see Harry rising again. It meant good news for everyone. Jonathan Gray chuckled, "Will he go and put it all on red 17 again? Maybe."

At this point in his life, Harry Macklowe had earned the prerogative to do so. He was the unofficial lord of the Liar's Ball, a warrior who had survived the worst—and was now back in contention.

As for the others in his circle, well, true to form, they kept on scheming—though not without reflecting on what the story of the GM Building meant to each of them.

Jonathan Gray was widely considered to be the heir apparent at the Blackstone Group. The Equity Office Properties (EOP) deal cemented his place in the hierarchy of the storied private equity firm. And even though every purchaser of EOP ended up losing money in the short term, Gray was quick to note that, in the long term, prices came roaring back. The price Harry paid for EOP no longer looked unrealistic—something Macklowe was glad to hear when it got back to him. "His mistake was not the price he paid . . . it was the way he financed it," said Gray.

Donald Trump still felt irritated about losing the GM Building, but was glad he made money out of it. He felt gratified when Macklowe asked to see the blueprints for the lease Trump has for the Gucci store on Fifth Avenue at the base of Trump Tower. He warned Harry he couldn't possibly expect to do so well on Park Avenue.

At EOP's offices, **Ben Lambert** and **Roy March** were happy for their old friend. They'd made a killing with EOP. And Macklowe didn't harbor a grudge. In fact, he phoned Lambert as ground was broken for 432 Park Avenue. "Ben, come on over," he said. Macklowe wanted to take a photograph of the two of them pouring cement into the ground, for posterity.

In 2012 **Doug Harmon** was the broker on the sale of the Sony building on Madison Avenue. He was bemused to see Harry "on the verge of tears" when it looked like he might not get it. (He didn't.) "He's very clever in that regard . . . he said, 'This is my phoenix. I need this deal; don't you understand?'" Macklowe was still the consummate actor.

Mike Fascitelli left Vornado in February 2013. He wore a T-shirt that stated "Trophy Husband," played golf, and figured out his next move. He would tell Harry Macklowe that "where I come from, if you don't pay your debts, you end up dead . . . from that perspective Pete Briger was very nice to you."

Pete Briger stayed on top at Fortress. But he would tell people that he wished he'd come out looking "softer" in the whole affair. "How come I looked like the bad guy?" he asked. All he'd done was make a loan and get his money back. He wanted it known that he too had gone through a tough time in the Great Recession. "I had never worried about work on weekends until 2008. But then I found I had to do something to take my mind off of it: I learned how to fly and to snowboard. . . . They were crazy times."

Rob Sorin continued to advise both Harry and Billy, staying on excellent terms with both.

Eric Schwartz left Deutsche Bank. In January 2008 a loan on the brand-new Cosmopolitan hotel in Las Vegas was defaulted on. Deutsche Bank lost more than $2 billion. Schwartz went to work for the Wall Street financier Lewis Ranieri and ran a real estate fund. In August 2014 he moved to Cantor Fitzgerald. He played golf most Fridays with his buddy Rob Horowitz.

Rob Horowitz carried on wheeling and dealing from offices by Grand Central Station. He met Harry once for a drink and they reminisced but tried to keep the conversation light. He misses the golden days.

Rob Verrone left Wachovia in 2008. He started Iron Hound Management Company, a real estate advisory and lending business.

Stephen Hilbert was busy and upbeat even about the lawsuits with John Menard. He remained great friends with Donald Trump.

Chuck Cremens was appointed the CEO of Spirit Finance and supervised the real estate investment trust's restructuring. He had to move to Arizona for two years. He hired **Reed Oslan** to litigate on behalf of Spirit.

Rita Jenrette was featured in a story in the *New Yorker*, which depicted her new life as the Principessa Rita Boncompagni Ludovisi; she had met her new husband when she acted as his real estate broker. She lives in a castle near Rome and hosts Woody Allen and other luminaries at dinner parties.

Abe Wallach settled in Southampton, and, in 2012, married his partner of 18 years. He retained an international consulting business but, at 73, also made time to travel, vacation, and relax.

Sheldon Solow took the lawsuit against Conseco to court. Depositions were heard in 2008. The case was dismissed in 2009. Sheldon Solow was not declared the rightful owner of the GM Building.

David Simon became one of the most respected real estate executives in the country. The Simon Group is now the largest commercial REIT in the United States.

Disque Deane faded from public view but not from the thoughts of his children. "He ripped us off like a Band-Aid," said Kathy Deane. "That's something to live with."

Simon Benattar ran his late mother's business, NIOT, in Toronto. To this day he is sorry her memoir *Structures* was never finished.

Robbie Rayne ran his late father's charitable foundation. "London," he reported, "is a far more civilized place to live than America."

Sam Zell thought that being a real estate developer is the hardest job in the world. "Think about corporate America. I'm IBM and I'm going to go acquire Oracle, okay? Well, if I'm going to go acquire Oracle, first thing, I'll have 400 guys study the shit out of it for three months, and then I'm going to ground with 27 different pro formas. But the real estate guy, Harry Macklowe, walks up to the building, looks at it, and says, 'You know, if you did this and you did that . . . .' They're very different animals.

"The CEO of IBM makes a bad acquisition and maybe his bonus gets cut—most likely not. In the real estate scenario, if you make a bad deal, it gets your ass empty. The world is full of skeletons of real estate guys who made the wrong decision.

"Don't call them cowboys."

Ira Millstein remained on the 32nd floor in the GM Building. He reflected that the building had met all his expectations for Weil Gotshal. "It was and is the place to be," he said.

Note about the Sources

I spoke with Billy Macklowe on the telephone in the summer of 2013; he was polite—but he told me he wanted to get a "clearer direction" of where the book was headed before deciding whether to participate. Ultimately he decided not to.

Harry Macklowe phoned me to say that his wife and son were pressuring him not to speak. I told him the truth: that this book is not about his wife or his son, or, for that matter, his daughter—except in one regard: the pressure they came to bear on him to sell the building that signified, more than any other, the sum of his achievements, and with which he most personally identified.

That they had exacted this price from the family patriarch was already public knowledge. Still, just how they had battled it all out—the details of those agonizing last weeks and nights—remained largely private, until the cast of this book stepped forward and put the pieces together.

Acknowledgments

I am grateful to my protagonists for their time, especially Harry Macklowe, who talked so vividly and so poignantly—and also to Donald Trump, who met with me several times. Thanks, also, to David Simon, Steve Hilbert, Mort Zuckerman, and Samuel Zell. Then there are the relatives of the building's deceased owners who entrusted their parents' legacy to me: Simon Benattar, Robbie Rayne, and Walter and Kathy Deane.

The book didn't really find a heartbeat until I found my supporting cast, so I am in debt to Rob Horowitz, Rob Sorin, Eric Schwartz, Rob Verrone, Mike Fascitelli, Steve Stuart, Pete Briger, Liliana Coriasco, David Boies, Ben Lambert, Roy March, Doug Harmon, Wayne Maggin, Jonathan Gray, Anthony Myers, Steven Mnuchin, Andy Hayes, Hans Mautner, Tom Zacharias, G. Martin Fell, Warren Hamer, Roz Jacobs, Dan Shannon, Peter Bohlin, Rhona Graff, Mark Walsh, Charlie Schoenherr, Rod Johnson, Jim Nagy, Joe Perella, Joe Forstadt, Andrew Bednar, Mary Wells Lawrence, Leonard Lauder, Lester Crown, Abraham Wallach, Principessa Rita Boncompagni Ludovisi (formerly Rita Jenrette), Charles Cremens, Reed Oslan, Geoffrey Wharton, Harvey Miller, and the fascinating and inimitable Ira Millstein.

My first-rate team of editors and researchers exhibited staunch stamina and professionalism: Bob Roe, Lisa Santandrea, Lee Smith, Maggie Boitano, Ed Frost, Katherine Wessling, Jenifer Bloodsworth, Gina Fitch, and Stan Friedman.

The team at John Wiley & Sons, Pamela Van Giessen, Emilie Herman, Evan Burton, and Tula Batanchiev, deserves a prize for sticking with me over what has been, to use Rob Sorin parlance, an "interesting" few years. And for introducing me to the talents of Lia Ottaviano.

My agent Andy McNicol is not just outstanding at her job, but a terrific friend.

Caroline von Reitzenstein and Gabriela Svec are indispensible allies, supporters, and facilitators. Austin Cohen, and Lorcan and Orlando Doull have been, and are always, my cheerleaders, my friends, and my comic relief.

This book is dedicated to Richard Cohen because he believes in me with such remarkable conviction that he leaves me no choice but to get the words out of my head and onto the page in what is, I hope, their best possible form.

Notes

Preface

Page xi   *Every year, toward*   Daniel Edward Rosen, "An Evening at the Liar's Ball: Raucous Behavior! Bottles of Colgin at the 21 Club! Talking over the Cardinal?" *New York Observer*, January 17, 2012.

Page xi   *The senior U.S.*   Daniel Geiger, "Mayor de Blasio to Party with Real Estate," *Crain's New York Business*, January 15, 2014.

Page xi   *The dignitaries sit*   Author's observations.

Page xi   *Senator Schumer grins*   Ibid.

Page xii   *Every year, for*   Ibid.

Page xii   *"It almost doesn't*   Daniel Edward Rosen, "An Evening at the Liar's Ball: Raucous Behavior! Bottles of Colgin at the 21 Club! Talking over the Cardinal?" *New York Observer*, January 17, 2012.

Page xii   *To an outsider*   Author's observations.

Introduction

Page xvii   *The most expensive*   Hiten Samtani and Guelda Voien, "GM Building: Who Works in the Country's Most Valuable Trophy Tower?" *Real Deal*, April 1, 2014. http://therealdeal.com/issues_articles/the-billionaires-nest/. Hiten Samtani, "NYC's General Motors Building Is Now the Most Valuable Office Space in America," *Business Insider*, June 3, 2013, www.businessinsider.com/stake-sold-in-nycs-general-motors-building-2013-6. John Koblin, "The Ten Most Expensive Buildings," *New York Observer*, April 9, 2007.

Page xvii   *Tammany Hall scoundrel*   Kenneth D. Ackerman, "Boss Tweed: The Corrupt Pol Who Conceived the Soul of Modern New York" (Falls Church, VA: Viral History Press, 2011). Christopher Gray, "A Plaza Evolves from Oversight to Landmark," *New York Times*, July 23, 2006.

Page xvii   *Harry S. Black, America's*   Alice Sparberg Alexiou, *The Flatiron: The New York Landmark and the Incomparable City That Arose with It* (New York: St. Martins Griffin, 2013), 254. "H. Black Ends Life in Home: No Motive Revealed," *New York Times*, July 20, 1930s.

Page xvii   *Then there was*   Chris Welles, "A Big Man on a Thin Edge: Bill Zeckendorf's Big Plans Gone Blooey," *Life*, February 12, 1965. Michael Stern, "William Zeckendorf, Real Estate Developer, 71, Dies," *New York Times*, October 2, 1976. William Zeckendorf and Edward McCreary, *Zeckendorf* (New York: Holt, Rinehart & Winston, 1970).

Page xvii   *There followed the*   "More Than Meets the Eye in GM Skyscraper," *Fortune*, February 1965. "Obituary of Lord Rayne, Businessman and Patron of the Arts Who Dispensed Millions of Pounds," *Daily Telegraph*, October 11, 2003. David English, "House-wife Tycoon," *Daily Express*, August 26, 1964. Interview with Simon Benattar.

Page xvii   *"Housewife tycoon"*   David English, "Housewife Tycoon," *Daily Express*, August 26, 1964.

Page xviii   *Disque D. Deane, a*   Interview with Walter and Kathy Deane.

Page xviii *David Simon, the* Interview with David Simon.

Page xviii *Stephen "Steve" C. Hilbert, the* Shawn Tully, "A Deal Too Far," *Fortune,* November 8, 1999. Thomas Wyman, "Making of a Mogul," *Indianapolis Star,* April 29, 2000. Interview with Reed Oslan. "Lifestyles of the Rich and Famous: A Monet over the Mantle, His-and-Hers Harleys, an Indoor Basketball Court: How Insurance Mogul Steve Hilbert Spends Indy's Biggest Paycheck," *Indianapolis Monthly,* November 1995.

Page xviii *His partner was* Interviews with Steven Hilbert and Donald Trump. "Trump Buying the Landmark G.M. Building," *New York Times,* May 31, 1998. Mason King, "Conseco, Simon Ties Propel Skyscraper Sale," *Indianapolis Business Journal,* June 8, 1998.

Page xviii *That he made* Interviews with Harry Macklowe and Rob Horowitz. Alan Feuer and Charles V. Bagli. "Harry Macklowe Gambles Again," *New York Times,* October 4, 2013.

Page xviii *"Rough riders"* Interview with Harry Macklowe.

Page xviii *"This is not* Interview with friend of Linda Macklowe.

Chapter 1 Stealing the Spotlight

Page 1 *They were there* Clyde Haberman, "NYC, When Big Names Take a Tumble," *New York Times,* June 27, 2003.

Page 1 *Their disappearance immediately* Interviews with Charles Cremens, Roy March, and Reed Oslan.

Page 1 *Bizarrely, some of* Interviews with Roy March, Charles Cremens, and Reed Oslan.

Page 2 *Their proud owners* Author's observation.

Page 2 *The glass box of* Eric Herman, "Trump's Making a Deal: The GM Building Goes Up for Sale," *New York Daily News,* June 14, 2003.

Page 2 *There was the plaza* Interviews with Dan Shannon and Harry Macklowe. David Dunlap, "A Cube in the Land of the Wheel," *New York Times,* March 2, 2005. David Dunlap, "Making Peace with a Prominent Hole in the Ground," *New York Times,* October 23, 2008.

Page 2   *But the building's*   Clyde Haberman, "NYC, When Big Names Take a Tumble," *New York Times*, June 27, 2003.

Page 2   *For five years*   John Tierney, "Towering Case of Trump Writ Large," *New York Times*, October 18, 1999. Paul Goldberger, "A Reversal of Fortune," *New York Times*, August 7, 1978. Ada Louise Huxtable, "The Newest Skyscraper in Manhattan," *New York Times*, October 1, 1968.

Page 2   *The brass letters*   David Dunlap, "Courtyard Is Rising with New Look," *New York Times*, June 30, 1999. John Tierney, "Towering Case of Trump Writ Large," *New York Times*, October 18, 1999. Robert Burgess, "Trump's Name on GM Tower Peeves Tenants," *Commercial Appeal*, October 14, 1999.

Page 2   *The sunlight had*   Interview with Harvey Miller. John Tierney, "Towering Case of Trump Writ Large," *New York Times*, October 18, 1999.

Page 2   *When he heard*   Interviews with Ira Millstein and Harvey Miller.

Page 3   *Some of the*   Interviews with anonymous tenants. John Tierney, "Towering Case of Trump Writ Large," *New York Times*, October 18, 1999.

Page 3   *The building*   Interview with Ira Millstein.

Page 3   *She had been*   "Developer Acquires Site for GM Building in Midtown New York," *Wall Street Journal*, October 29, 1964.

Page 3   *Then the biggest*   "Fortune 500 (1964)," *Fortune.com*, http:// archive.fortune.com/magazines/fortune/fortune500_archive/ full/1964/. Retrieved June 24, 2014.

Page 3   *GM had occupied*   Interview with Robert Rayne. Laurence G. O'Donnell, "GM Now Half-Owner of Firm That Will Build Its New Headquarters," *Wall Street Journal*, December 16, 1964. "A New Vista on Fifth Avenue," General Motors (brochure).

Page 3   *An entire city block*   Ada Louise Huxtable, "The Newest Skyscraper in Manhattan," *New York Times*, October 1, 1968.

Page 3   *The blue-chip*   "Tower of Power," *Fortune*, November 8, 2007.

Page 3   *Trump didn't usually*   Interview with Abraham Wallach.

Page 3   *In 1998 he*   Interviews with Stephen Hilbert and Donald Trump. "Trump Buying the Landmark G.M. Building," *New York*

Times, May 31, 1998. Mason King, "Conseco, Simon Ties Propel Skyscraper Sale," *Indianapolis Business Journal*, June 8, 1998.

Page 3 *He took out* Interview with Robert Horowitz.

Page 3 *The building's white* Interview with Donald Trump.

Page 3 *There were plaques* Interview with Robert Horowitz. David Dunlap, "Courtyard Is Rising with New Look," *New York Times*, June 30, 1999. John Tierney, "Towering Case of Trump Writ Large," *New York Times*, October 18, 1999.

Page 3 *He tried to* Interview with Ira Millstein.

Page 3 *In 2000, Hilbert* "Next for Conseco," *Indianapolis Star*, April 29, 2000. Jonathan Berke, "Conseco's Hilbert Resigns," *Daily Deal*, April 28, 2000. Shawn Tully, "A Deal Too Far," *Fortune*, November 8, 1999. Leslie Eaton, "Conseco and Green Tree, an Improbable Merger," *New York Times*, April 8, 1998. Debra Sparks, "Conseco's Morning After," *BusinessWeek*, June 4, 2000.

Page 3 *Conseco went* Floyd Norris and Alex Berenson, "Conseco Files for Bankruptcy Protection," *New York Times*, December 19, 2002.

Page 3 *Trump negotiated to* Depositions of Donald Trump and Andrew Hubregsen, *Donald J. Trump v. Carmel Fifth, LLC*, State Supreme Court of New York, County of New York. Joseph Hallinan, "Talks with Trump to Sell GM Building Stake," *Wall Street Journal*, June 9, 2000. Bill Hornaday, "Carmel, Ind., Firm to Sell Share of New York City Building to Donald Trump," *Indianapolis Star and News*, July 12, 2001. "Trump Agrees to $295M Deal," *Bloomberg News*, July 12, 2001.

Page 4 *But in the fall* Testimony of Donald Trump and Andrew Hubregsen, *Donald J. Trump v. Carmel Fifth, LLC*, State Supreme Court of New York, County of New York. "Trump, Deutsche Reworking GM Building Loan," *Commercial Mortgage Alert*, October 22, 2001. Peter Grant and Joseph T. Hallinan, "Trump Sues Conseco over GM Building," *Wall Street Journal*, February 9, 2002. Bill Hornaday, "Trump Sues Conseco for a Billion," *Indianapolis Star*, February 8, 2002. Eric Herman, "Conseco Threatens to Remove Donald Trump's Name as GM-Building Feud Continues," *New York Daily News*, February 9, 2002.

Page 4 *In the summer* "Arbitration Award," *Carmel Fifth and Conseco v. Donald J. Trump*, American Arbitration Association, New York, New

York. "Trump Ordered to Sell His Share of G.M. Building to Insurance Firm," *New York Times*, June 13, 2003.

Page 4   *An Illinois bankruptcy*   "Order granting application for entry of an order (1) authorizing the employment and retention of Eastdil Reality Company L.L.C. as debtor's real estate agent and (2) approving payment of a professional service fee." *Conseco Inc., et al.*, United States Bankruptcy Court, Northern District of Illinois, Eastern Division.

Page 4   *To make the*   Interview with Charles Cremens.

Page 4   *Cremens told Trump*   Interview with Charles Cremens.

Page 4   *The negotiations were*   Interview with Reed Oslan.

Page 4   *Cremens would later*   Interview with Charles Cremens.

Page 4   *"I wanted them*   Interview with Donald Trump.

Page 4   *"Big sheets"*   Interview with Reed Oslan.

Page 4   *"I was sad*   Interview with Donald Trump.

Page 4   *Over at Eastdil*   Interviews with Charles Cremens and Wayne Maggin.

Page 4   *Reed Oslan has*   Interviews with Chuck Cremens and Reed Oslan.

Page 4   *Mary Anne Tighe*   Interviews with Charles Cremens and Mary Anne Tighe.

Page 4   *Cremens was baffled*   Interviews with Reed Oslan and Charles Cremens.

Page 4   *A month later*   Interview with Charles Cremens.

Page 5   *And just like that*   "Trump Ordered to Sell His Share of G.M. Building to Insurance Firm," *New York Times*, June 13, 2003.

Page 5   *They all felt*   Interviews with Charles Cremens, Benjamin Lambert, Wayne Maggin, and Roy March.

Page 5   *Cremens noted*   Interview with Charles Cremens.

Page 5   *"I thought*   Interview with Harry Macklowe.

Page 5   *On June 6, 2003*   Deposition of Charles Cremens, *Sheldon H. Solow vs. Conseco Inc.*, U.S. District Court, Southern District of New York, March 6, 2008.

Page 5   *No one considered*   Interviews with Robert Horowitz, Benjamin Lambert, and Wayne Maggin.

Page 5   *Macklowe didn't have*   Interviews with Douglas Harmon, Rob Horowitz, Benjamin Lambert, and Wayne Maggin.

Page 5   *Maggin knew there*   Interview with Wayne Maggin.

Page 5   *Ben Lambert, Eastdil's*   Interview with Benjamin Lambert.

Page 6   *Thought his charm*   Author's observation.

Page 6   *"He can be*   Interview with Douglas Harmon.

Page 6   *Macklowe has always*   Author's observation.

Page 6   *"He is quite*   Interview with Douglas Harmon.

Page 6   *He'd love to*   Interview with Harry Macklowe.

Page 6   *"His lines … the*   Ibid.

Page 6   *"Very clever"*   Ibid.

Page 6   *Accumulated a "massive"*   Ibid.

Page 6   *Collection that includes*   Interview with art world professional.

Page 7   *"There are layers*   Interview with Douglas Harmon.

Page 7   *"SRO debacle"*   Ibid.

Page 7   *As Macklowe and*   Interviews with Harry Macklowe and a friend of Linda Macklowe.

Page 7   *SRO stands for*   Interview with Joseph Forstadt.

Page 7   *In 1984 Macklowe*   Martin Gottlieb, "City Is Planning Action to Block Razing of Hotels," *New York Times*, January 12, 1985. Josh Barbanel, "City Sues for $10 Million in Demolition on 44th St.," *New York Times*, January 15, 1985. Interview with Joseph Forstadt.

Page 7   *The city government*   Sydney H. Schanberg, "Gold on 44th Street," *New York Times*, January 12, 1985. Editorial desk, "White-Collar Vandalism on 44th St.," *New York Times*, January 12, 1985. Alan Finder, "Supreme Court Won't Review S.R.O. Ruling," *New York Times*, November 28, 1989. Interview with Joseph Forstadt.

Page 7   *Macklowe needed to*   Interview with Harry Macklowe.

Page 7   *On January 7*   *The People of the State of New York vs. John Tassi*, Supreme Court of the State of New York, County of New York. Martin Gottlieb, "Nighttime Demolition Leaves 44th St. Mystery," *New York Times*, January 10, 1985. Sydney H. Schanberg, "Gold on 44th Street," *New York Times*, January 12, 1985.

Page 7   *A crane was*   Martin Gottlieb, "Nighttime Demolition Leaves 44th St. Mystery," *New York Times*, January 10, 1985. Editorial Desk, "White-Collar Vandalism on 44th St.," *New York Times*, January 12, 1985. Sydney H. Schanberg, "New York; Gold on 44th Street," *New York Times*, January 12, 1985.

Page 7   *"In hand,"*   Interview with Harry Macklowe.

Page 7   *The gas had*   Martin Gottlieb, "Nighttime Demolition Leaves 44th St. Mystery," *New York Times*, January 10, 1985. Sydney H. Schanberg, "Gold on 44th Street," *New York Times*, January 12, 1985.

Page 7   *The Real Estate*   Sam Roberts, "Hotel Is Macklowe's Bid for a Shinier Image," *New York Times*, August 4, 1990.

Page 8   *Macklowe waived immunity*   Martin Gottlieb, "Developer Told Jury He Ordered Illegal Demolition," *New York Times*, December 19, 1985. Martin Gottlieb, "Liability for Demolition," *New York Times*, December 27, 1985.

Page 8   *His vice president*   Marcia Chambers, "Guilty Pleas Entered in Demolition in Times Square," *New York Times*, May 8, 1985. Martin Gottlieb, "Macklowe Demolition Man Is Given a No-Jail Sentence," *New York Times*, February 12, 1986. Martin Gottlieb, "Liability for Demolition," *New York Times*, December 27, 1985.

Page 8   *Garofolo would later*   Donatella Lorch, "Mob-Linked Businessman Slain Outside His Home," *New York Times*, August 10, 1990.

Page 8   *Macklowe was not*   Martin Gottlieb, "Liability for Demolition," *New York Times*, December 27, 1985.

Page 8   *The foreman of*   Martin Gottlieb, "Macklowe Demolition Man Is Given a No-Jail Sentence," *New York Times*, February 12, 1986.

Page 8   *District Attorney Robert Morgenthau*   Martin Gottlieb, "Liability for Demolition," *New York Times*, December 27, 1985.

Page 8   *The city sued*   "City Sues for $10 Million in Demolition on 44th St.," *New York Times*, January 15, 1985. Editorial Desk, "A Bargain Justice for a Bulldozer," *New York Times*, May 9, 1985. Martin Gottlieb, "Liability for Demolition," *New York Times*, December 27, 1985.

Page 8   *"We have sent*   Marcia Chambers, "Guilty Pleas Entered in Demolition in Times Square," *New York Times*, May 8, 1985.

Page 8   *Just two years later*   "Harry Macklowe Real Estate," *Wall Street Journal*, April 26, 1988. Shawn Kennedy, "A Mixed-Use Tower Rising off Times Sq.," *New York Times*, August 10, 1988. Alan Finder, "Ban Disappears, and a New Hotel Appears," *New York Times*, January 14, 1989.

Page 8   *The New York Times*   "The Macklowe Mess: Still a Mess," *New York Times*, January 25, 1989. Alan Finder, "How the City Council Changed the Law Behind its own Back," *New York Times*, January 22, 1989.

Page 8   *"Very, very brilliant*   Interview with Harry Macklowe.

Page 8   *In a rather*   Alan Finder, "Koch Clarifies Comment on S.R.O. Law," *New York Times*, January 20, 1989. Alan Finder, "How the City Council Changed the Law behind Its Own Back," *New York Times*, January 22, 1989. Alan Finder, "Goldin Requests Inquiry on Shift in S.R.O. Law," *New York Times*, January 25, 1989.

Page 8   *"What a privilege*   Interview with Harry Macklowe.

Page 9   *He bought buildings*   Peter Grant, "Notorious Developer Makes a Comeback," *New York Daily News*, April 27, 1997. "Macklowe Lands 300 Park Ave., Seeks Loan," *Commercial Mortgage Alert*, September 26, 2003. Linda Barr, "Macklowe Spree Continues with $378m Park Ave Buy," *Real Estate Weekly*, October 15, 2003.

Page 9   *He lost them*   Hui-yong Yu and David M. Levitt, "Macklowe Loses Manhattan Office Tower Stake to Otera," Bloomberg, April 22, 2009. Iliana Jonas, "Macklowe to Lose Another N.Y. Building in Auction," Reuters, April 21, 2009. Jennifer S. Forsyth, "Real-Estate Credit Crisis Squeezes Macklowe," *Wall Street Journal*, February 1, 2008.

Page 9   *He fought with*   Rick Murphy, "In a Nasty Neighborly Dispute, It's Power versus Power," *New York Times*, January 26, 1996. Charles V. Bagli, "Man with Past Speculates on Future," *New York Times*, March 11, 1998. Linda Sandler, "To Harry Macklowe, Winning Is All: New York Tycoon Now Is Battling Lenders over His Empire," *Wall Street Journal*, January 6, 1999. Devin Leonard, "A $300 Million Dispute: Bank Sues Harry Macklowe over Grand Skyscraper Plan," *New York Observer*, March 1, 1999. "Developer Is Sued by Former Deputy," *New York Times*, October 21, 1999.

Page 9   *He defaulted on*   Peter Grant, "Macklowe Defaults on Debt," *Crain's New York Business*, December 20, 1993. David Henry, "Macklowe's Finances May Be Crumbling," *Newsday*, December 23, 1993.

Page 9   *In 1995 he*   Complaint, *Harry Macklowe and Linda Macklowe v. Travertine Corporation and Martha Stewart*, Supreme Court of the State of New York, County of Suffolk, June 14, 1996. Mitchell Freedman, "Long-Simmering Beef/Stewart Spars with Neighbor over Land," *Newsday*, April 14, 1996. Bob Morris, "Let the Games Begin," *New York Times*, July 14, 1996. Stefan Fatsis, "Love Thy Neighbor, Sue Thy Neighbor," *Wall Street Journal*, August 2, 1996.

Page 9   *In 1997, as*   "Law Could Let Macklowe Bulldoze 13 Regulated Tenants," Associated Press Newswires, June 23, 1997. Randy Kennedy, "In Final Deal, the Hidden Power of a Paragraph," *New York Times*, June 29, 1997.

Page 9   *Later that year*   David Chen, "Blocks Still Closed After Wall Peels Off," *New York Times*, December 9, 1997. Charles V. Bagli, "Shoddy Bricklaying Cited in Madison Ave Hazard," *New York Times*, December 16, 1997. Editorial Desk, "Looking Upward, with Anxiety," *New York Times*, December 17, 1997. Bill Hutchinson, "Brick Risk Owner'll Pay Up," *New York Daily News*, December 17, 1997.

Page 9   *The son of*   Interview with Harry Macklowe.

Page 9   *He used leverage*   Interview with real estate executive.

Page 9   *A college dropout*   Interview with Harry Macklowe.

Page 9   *By the late*   Interview with Robert Horowitz.

Page 9   *"I just … love*   Interview with Harry Macklowe.

Page 9   *"There's a German*   Interview with friend of Harry Macklowe.

Page 10   *He believed he*   Interview with Harry Macklowe.

Page 10   *"A very clever*   Ibid.

Chapter 2 Alpha Males

Page 11   *The two advisers*   Interviews with Robert Horowitz and Robert Sorin.

Page 11   *He and Macklowe*   Interview with Robert Sorin.

Page 11   *That was a*   Interview with Robert Horowitz.

Page 12   *A 3.43-acre*   Charles V. Bagli, "A Deal Is Struck for Coliseum Site," *New York Times*, July 28, 1998.

Page 12   *Whose $455 million*   Alan Finder with Shawn G. Kennedy, "Cutting the Losses: A Special Report; Lessons in the Rubble of the MTA Deal," *New York Times*, July 23, 1994.

Page 12   *Macklowe appreciated Sorin's*   Interview with Harry Macklowe.

Page 12   *Other lawyers, bankers*   Interviews with Chuck Cremens, Robert Horowitz, Benjamin Lambert, Harry Macklowe, Wayne Maggin, Reed Oslan, and Eric Schwartz.

Page 12   *He diplomatically described*   Interview with Robert Sorin.

Page 12 *Who had started working* David Jones, "Billy Macklowe No Longer the Kid," *Real Deal,* June 2, 2009.

Page 12 *When Macklowe told* Interview with Robert Sorin.

Page 12 *Sorin sensed Macklowe* Ibid.

Page 12 *Now the Ritz-Carlton* www.ritzcarlton.com/en/RealEstate/ResidenceDetails/CentralParkSouth.htm.

Page 12 *It was a* Interview with Robert Sorin.

Page 12 *Macklowe told Sorin* Interview with Harry Macklowe.

Page 12 *"I don't give* Ibid.

Page 13 *Sorin understood.* Interview with Robert Sorin.

Page 13 *Had played a* Interview with Robert Horowitz.

Page 13 *"We're buying the* Ibid.

Page 13 *Cooper-Horowitz, the* Interview with Robert Horowitz.

Page 13 *But when Macklowe* Ibid.

Page 13 *Harry Macklowe and* Ibid.

Page 13 *On December 18* Letter from Harry Macklowe to Robert Horowitz.

Page 14 *As Macklowe got* Interview with Robert Horowitz.

Page 14 *Macklowe also trusted* Letter from Harry Macklowe to Donald Trump.

Page 14 *Horowitz had started* Interview with Robert Horowitz.

Page 14 *Trump was very* Ibid.

Page 14 *If Trump received* Correspondence from Donald Trump to Rob Horowitz.

Page 14 *And when Trump's* Interview with Robert Horowitz.

Page 15 *Horowitz liked Trump* Interview with Robert Horowitz.

Page 15 *But the friendship* Author's observation.

Page 15 *Sorin explains the way* Interview with Robert Sorin.

Page 15 *Liked working with* Interview with Eric Schwartz.

Page 15 *But most important* Ibid.

Page 16 *Helicopter co-owner* Interviews with Robert Horowitz and Harry Macklowe.

Page 16 *Nemesis* Interviews with Rob Horowitz and Michael Fascitelli.

Page 16 *With a market capitalization* www.wikinvest.com/stock/Vornado_Realty_Trust_%28VNO%29/Data/Market_Capitalization.

Page 16   *Vornado held a*   Interviews with various former Deutsche bankers.

Page 16   *Who had grown up*   Interview with Michael Fascitelli.

Page 16   *Until 1996 he'd*   Ibid.

Page 16   *They adored him* Interviews with former Deutsche Bank employees.

Page 16   *He still used*   Author's observations.

Page 16   *Roth paid Fascitelli*   Peter Truell, "A Partner at Goldman Leaves for $50 Million," *New York Times*, December 3, 1996. Barry Vinocur, "Deal Maker Leaves Goldman Sachs for Big-Bucks Job at REIT," *Barron's*, December 9, 1996.

Page 16   *Fascitelli kept trying*   Interview with Michael Fascitelli.

Page 17   *Her price was*   Ibid.

Page 17   *Meanwhile Harry Macklowe*   Interview with Robert Horowitz.

Page 17   *Robert "Rob" Verrone*   Interview with Robert Verrone.

Page 17   *This was the*   Ibid.

Page 17   *His eagerness to*   Devin Leonard, "The Ballad of 'Large Loan' Verrone," *Bloomberg Businessweek*, September 9, 2010.

Page 17   *He'd grown up*   Ibid.

Page 17   *They were still*   Interview with Robert Verrone.

Page 17   *The two men*   Interviews with Robert Horowitz and Robert Verrone.

Page 17   *Macklowe told him*   Interview with Robert Verrone.

Page 17   *Verrone had stayed*   Ibid.

Page 17   *Wachovia lent Macklowe*   Interviews with Harry Macklowe, Robert Verrone, and Robert Horowitz.

Page 18   *Soon after, Macklowe*   Interviews with Harry Macklowe and Robert Verrone.

Page 18   *Macklowe (and everyone else)*   Interviews with Benjamin Lambert, Harry Macklowe, Wayne Maggin, Robert Horowitz, and Robert Sorin.

Page 18   *Verrone also had*   Interview with former Deutsche Bank employees.

Page 18   *Verrone offered to*   Interviews with Robert Horowitz, Robert Verrone, and Steven Stuart.

Page 18   *Steve Stuart, the*   Interview with Robert Horowitz.

Page 18   *Verrone felt comfortable*   Interview with Robert Verrone.

Page 18   *This was part*   Author's observation.

Page 18   *Finally, he drew*   Interview with Robert Verrone.

Page 18   *Over at Eastdil's*   Interview with Wayne Maggin.

Page 19   *Cremens trusted Maggin*   Interview with Chuck Cremens.

Page 19   *During the summer*   Interview with Wayne Maggin.

Page 19   *Maggin made a*   "Internal Status Report for GM Building," Eastdil, July 9, 2003.

Page 19   *He and his*   Eastdil Memorandum, Re: The General Motors Building, August 1, 2003.

Page 19   *First bids were*   Wayne Maggin affidavit, *Solow Building Corporation v. Carmel 5th LLC*, the Court of the Chancery of Delaware in or for New Castle County.

Page 19   *Maggin gave a*   Interview with Wayne Maggin.

Page 19   *On August 1*   Memorandum from Wayne Maggin and Jon Schneidman, Eastdil, to Chuck Cremens, Conseco, Re: The General Motors Building, August 1, 2003.

Page 19   *It looked like*   Interview with Wayne Maggin.

Page 19   *On August 11*   Wayne Maggin affidavit, *Solow Building Corporation v. Carmel 5th LLC*, the Court of the Chancery of Delaware in or for New Castle County.

Page 19   *He issued a*   Interview with Wayne Maggin. Wayne Maggin affidavit, *Solow Building Corporation v. Carmel 5th LLC*, the Court of the Chancery of Delaware in or for New Castle County.

Page 19   *Those were: hard*   Interview with Wayne Maggin.

Page 19   *The cash deposit*   Ibid.

Page 20   *"Most of the*   Ibid.

Page 20   *Vornado—just as*   Interview with Michael Fascitelli.

Page 20   *Maggin looked over*   Interview with Wayne Maggin.

Page 20   *His money was*   Wayne Maggin affidavit, *Solow Building Corporation v. Carmel 5th LLC*, the Court of the Chancery of Delaware in or for New Castle County.

Page 20   *But he was*   Wayne Maggin affidavit, *Solow Building Corporation v. Carmel 5th LLC*, the Court of the Chancery of Delaware in or for New Castle County. Deposition of Benjamin Lambert, *Sheldon H. Solow v. Conseco, Inc. and Carmel Fifth, LLC*, United States District Court Southern District of New York, April 9, 2008. Guelda Voien, "Solow's Strategy," *Real Deal*, March 1, 2013. Charles

V. Bagli, "Back at Work and as Contentious as Ever," *New York Times*, June 4, 2010.

Page 20   *This was the*   Interview with Wayne Maggin.

Page 20   *Nor was Ben*   Interview with Benjamin Lambert.

Chapter 3 The Rigged Bid

Page 21   *Wayne Maggin and*   Interviews with Benjamin Lambert and Wayne Maggin.

Page 21   *Maggin noticed that*   Interview with Wayne Maggin.

Page 22   *Maggin was also*   Interview with Wayne Maggin. Wayne Maggin deposition, *Sheldon H. Solow vs. Conseco Inc. and Carmel Fifth LLC*, United States District Court, Southern District of New York, New York, NY, April 9, 2008.

Page 22   *Solow, obliviously, thought*   Deposition of Sheldon Solow, *Sheldon H. Solow, plaintiff, vs. Conseco Inc. and Carmel Fifth LLC*, United States District Court, Southern District of New York, New York, NY, May 13, 2008.

Page 22   *He liked to*   Ibid.

Page 22   *After all, he*   Plaintiff's Motion for Preliminary Injunction: Oral Arguments, *Solow Building Corporation vs. Carmel Fifth, LLC*, New Castle County Courthouse, Wilmington, Delaware, Tuesday, September 3, 2003.

Page 22   *Still, he also*   Interview with Andrew Hayes.

Page 22   *Eastdil's offering letter*   Interview with Andrew Hayes. Affidavit of Wayne L. Maggin, *Solow Building Corporation v. Carmel Fifth, LLC*, in the court of the Chancery in the State of Delaware in and for New Castle County.

Page 22   *So he wanted*   Deposition of Sheldon Solow, *Sheldon H. Solow vs. Conseco Inc. and Carmel Fifth LLC*, United States District Court, Southern District of New York, New York, NY, May 13, 2008.

Page 22   *"I said to*   Ibid.

Page 22   *"You have my word,"*   Ibid.

Page 23   *We informed Solow*   Memorandum from Wayne Maggin to File, re: "Sheldon Solow Meeting re: General Motors Building," August 26, 2003.

Page 23   *Back in the*   Interview with Robert Rayne.

Page 23   *Solow had grown up*   Franklin Whitehouse, "A 'Loner' Is Building on 57th Street," *New York Times*, March 29, 1970. "Forbes 400: #134 Sheldon Solow," *Forbes*, www.forbes.com/profile/sheldon-solow/. Charles V. Bagli, "Towering Vision by Developer Stirs East Side," *New York Times*, November 15, 2007.

Page 23   *The experience molded*   Interview with Andrew Hayes.

Page 23   *Andrew "Andy" Hayes*   Ibid.

Page 23   *The young Solow*   Ibid.

Page 23   *He put together*   Franklin Whitehouse, "A 'Loner' Is Building on 57th Street," *New York Times*, March 29, 1970. "9 West 57th Street Office Tower," SOM, www.som.com/projects/9_west_57th_Street_Office_Tower.

Page 23   *Like the GM Building*   Lance Leighton, "The Top 5 Office Buildings in New York City," Hedge Fund Spaces, May 27, 2012, www.hedgefundspaces.com/2012/05/top-5-hedge-fund-buildings/.

Page 23   *The two buildings*   Ibid. Daniel Edward Rosen, "A Room with a View of Central Park," *New York Observer*, October 25, 2011, http://observer.com/2011/10/a-room-with-a-view-of-central-park/.

Page 23   *In 2000, construction*   "Tyco International Headquarters: New York, NY," Alayo, http://006196c.netsolhost.com/tyco.htm.

Page 23   *The company paid*   Interview with Andrew Hayes.

Page 23   *In 2001 Tyco's*   Ibid.

Page 23   *Solow has filed*   Guelda Voien, "Solow's Strategy," *Real Deal*, March 1, 2013.

Page 24   *"I wanted to*   Interview with Andrew Hayes.

Page 24   *Yet beneath the*   Ibid.

Page 24   *Over the years*   Interview with David Boies.

Page 24   *Dreier would go on*   William K. Rashbaum and Charles V. Bagli, "Man of Contradictions, Accused in a Scheme," *New York Times*, January 3, 2009. Bryan Burrough, "Marc Dreier's Crime of Destiny," *Vanity Fair*, November 2009.

Page 24   *But even after*   Interview with Andrew Hayes and David Boies.

Page 24   *Solow told Boies*   Interview with David Boies.

Page 24   *Solow would say*   Deposition of Sheldon Solow, *Sheldon H. Solow, plaintiff, vs. Conseco Inc. and Carmel Fifth LLC*, United States District Court, Southern District of New York, New York, NY, May 13, 2008.

Page 24   *He didn't see*   Interviews with Benjamin Lambert and Wayne Maggin.

Page 24   *The day after*   Interview with Andrew Hayes, transcribed June 4, 2013. Declaration of Steven Cherniak, *Sheldon H. Solow v. Conseco Inc. and Carmel Fifth LLC*, United States District Court, Southern District of New York.

Page 24   *He didn't offer*   Interview with Andrew Hayes.

Page 24   *Harry Macklowe, meanwhile*   Interview with Harry Macklowe.

Page 24   *The architect he had*   Interview with Daniel Shannon.

Page 25   *He drew a big*   Interview with Harry Macklowe.

Page 25   *So Macklowe scaled*   Interviews with Harry Macklowe and Daniel Shannon.

Page 25   *"Harry knew that*   Interview with Daniel Shannon.

Page 25   *Macklowe called George*   Interview with Harry Macklowe.

Page 25   *Macklowe had limited*   Interview with Harry Macklowe.

Page 25   *Blankenship told Macklowe*   Ibid.

Page 25   *Macklowe says, "He*   Ibid.

Page 25   *In the midst*   Interview with Robert Horowitz.

Page 25   *The Macklowes always*   Interview with Harry Macklowe.

Page 26   *So he got*   Ibid.

Page 26   *Macklowe looked at*   Interview with Harry Macklowe.

Page 26   *After exiting the*   Ibid.

Page 26   *"Do you by*   Interview with Roy March.

Page 26   *"Yeah," he replied*   Ibid.

Page 26   *Macklowe knew he'd*   Interview with Harry Macklowe.

Page 26   *Macklowe grinned and*   Interview with Roy March.

Page 26   *March told the*   Interview with Harry Macklowe.

Page 27   *Where the disgraced*   "Kozlowski Bash Rated XXX: Details Emerge of Lavish Birthday Bash Ex-Tyco CEO Threw with Company Funds," CNN.com, September 17, 2002, http://money.cnn.com/2002/09/17/news/companies/tyco_party/.

Page 27   *Like Macklowe, March*   Interview with Roy March.

Page 27   *His wife Barbara*   Jack Foley, "Barbara Baldieri—From Modeling to Acting to Singing," IndieLondon.com, www.indielondon.co.uk/music/mu_barbara_baldieri_biog.html. Retrieved June 15, 2014.

Page 27   *Whose nude portraits*   Author's observation.

Page 27   *She had grown up*   Jack Foley, "Barbara Baldieri—From Modeling to Acting to Singing," IndieLondon.com, www.indielondon.co.uk/music/mu_barbara_baldieri_biog.html. Retrieved June 15, 2014.

Page 27   *Two nights after*   Interview with Harry Macklowe.

Page 27   *The next day*   Ibid.

Page 27   *The cluster of*   Juliet Chung, "Private Islands and Estate in Italy Ask $263 Million," *Wall Street Journal*, February 18, 2011, http://online.wsj.com/news/articles/SB1000142405274870434340457614 6731065834252. Retrieved June 15, 2014.

Page 27   *Invited them over*   Interview with Harry Macklowe.

Page 27   *A relationship often*   Interview with friend of Linda Macklowe.

Page 27   *"They drive each other*   Ibid.

Page 28   *Linda Burg grew up*   Interview with Harry Macklowe.

Page 28   *In interviews, Harry*   Ibid.

Page 28   *When she met*   Interview with Andrew Fabricant.

Page 28   *He'd dropped out*   Alan Feuer and Charles V. Bagli, "Harry Macklowe Gambles Again," *New York Times*, October 4, 2013.

Page 28   *The Macklowes began*   Interview with Andrew Fabricant.

Page 28   *What started as*   Interview with expert in the art world.

Page 28   *Harry loves [bidding at auction]*   Interview with an art adviser.

Page 28   *He also liked*   Interview with Harry Macklowe. "Past Projects," Macklowe Properties.com, www.mackloweproperties.com/pastProjects/projects-2HammarskjoldPlaza.html. Michael Brenson, "12 Artists Shown in 'Underknown,' at P.S. 1," *New York Times*, October 20, 1984. Michael Brenson, "Sculpture Goes Outdoors for Summer," *New York Times*, July 13, 1984.

Page 29   *"An assistant helps*   Interview with friend of Linda Macklowe.

Page 29   *Liz, their daughter*   Ibid.

Page 29   *Every summer the*   Ibid.

Page 29   *Her friends have*   Ibid.

Page 29   *"She doesn't like*   Interview with Harry Macklowe.

Page 29   *Anything that reminded*   Interviews with friends of Linda Macklowe.

Page 29   *Once they got back*   Interviews with Roy March and Harry Macklowe.

Page 29   *"We had struck*   Interview with Roy March.

Page 29   *March and Macklowe*   Interview with Roy March.

Page 30   *Macklowe reported all*   Interviews with Robert Horowitz, Robert Sorin, and Robert Verrone.

Page 30   *"There are other*   Interview with Robert Horowitz.

Page 30   *Macklowe knew Eastdil*   Interview with Harry Macklowe.

Page 30   *By his name*   Eastdil document, "Final Bids."

Page 30   *He suggested to*   Affidavit of Wayne L. Maggin, *Solow Building Corporation v Carmel Fifth, LLC*, in the court of the Chancery in the State of Delaware in and for New Castle County.

Page 30   *"The meeting wasn't*   Interview with Robert Sorin.

Page 30   *Maggin later testified*   Affidavit of Wayne L. Maggin, *Solow Building Corporation v. Carmel Fifth, LLC*, in the court of the Chancery in the State of Delaware in and for New Castle County.

Page 30   *Macklowe returned to*   Interviews with Harry Macklowe, Robert Verrone, and Robert Sorin.

Page 30   *He picked up*   Interview with Robert Sorin.

Page 30   *Which would be delivered*   Wayne Maggin deposition, *Sheldon H. Solow vs. Conseco Inc. and Carmel Fifth LLC*, United States District Court, Southern District of New York, New York, NY, April 9, 2008.

Page 30   *But he was*   Interview with Robert Sorin.

Page 31   *Sorin says he*   Ibid.

Page 31   *As Macklowe talked*   Interview with Macklowe business associate.

Page 31   *"Shut the fuck up*   Ibid.

Page 31   *He left for*   Interviews with Harry Macklowe and Macklowe business associates.

Page 31   *At around five*   Plaintiff's Motion for Preliminary Injunction: Oral Arguments, *Solow Building Corporation vs. Carmel Fifth, LLC*, New Castle County Courthouse, Wilmington, Delaware, Tuesday, September 3, 2003.

Page 31   *He entered the*   Interview with Wayne Maggin. Plaintiff's Motion for Preliminary Injunction: Oral Arguments, *Solow Building Corporation vs. Carmel Fifth, LLC*, New Castle County Courthouse, Wilmington, Delaware, Tuesday, September 3, 2003. Affidavit of Wayne L. Maggin, *Solow Building Corporation vs. Carmel Fifth, LLC*, in the court of the Chancery in the State of Delaware in and for New Castle County.

Page 31 *"I had advised* Affidavit of Wayne L. Maggin, *Solow Building Corporation vs. Carmel Fifth, LLC,* in the court of the Chancery in the State of Delaware in and for New Castle County.

Page 31 *He knew that* Deposition of Harry Macklowe, *Sheldon H. Solow v. Conseco, Inc. and Carmel Fifth, LLC,* United States District Court, Southern District of New York, New York, NY, May 7, 2008.

Page 31 *Around 7:30 P.M.* Ibid.

Page 31 *Lambert laughed.* Interview with Ben Lambert.

Page 32 *They remained in the office* Interviews with Charles Cremens and Wayne Maggin. Affidavit of Wayne L. Maggin, *Solow Building Corporation vs. Carmel Fifth, LLC,* in the court of the Chancery in the State of Delaware in and for New Castle County.

Page 32 *It was Harry* Interview with Wayne Maggin.

Page 32 *At 9:00 the* Wayne Maggin deposition, *Sheldon H. Solow vs. Conseco Inc. and Carmel Fifth LLC,* United States District Court, Southern District of New York, New York, NY, April 9, 2008. Harry Macklowe deposition, *Sheldon H. Solow vs. Conseco, Inc. and Carmel Fifth, LLC,* United States District Court, Southern District of New York, New York, NY, May 7, 2008.

Page 32 *Maggin told him* Interviews with Harry Macklowe and Wayne Maggin. Wayne Maggin deposition, *Sheldon H. Solow vs. Conseco Inc. and Carmel Fifth LLC,* United States District Court, Southern District of New York, New York, NY, April 9, 2008.

Page 32 *Macklowe was thrilled* Interview with Harry Macklowe.

Page 32 *"I said, 'Hey* Ibid.

Page 32 *By lunchtime, father* Interviews with Harry Macklowe and Rob Horowitz.

Page 32 *Billy, according to* Interview with Harry Macklowe.

Page 32 *The biggest real estate* Charles V. Bagli, "G.M. Building Sells for $1.4 Billion, a Record," *New York Times,* August 30, 2003. Louis Weiss, "GM Building Sold—Macklowe Pays Record $1.4b for Fifth Ave. Tower," *New York Post,* August 30, 2003. James Doran, "US Building Sets Record," *The Times* (London), September 1, 2003.

Page 32 *All they had* Interviews with Robert Horowitz and Robert Sorin.

Page 32　*Sheldon Solow felt*　Interviews with David Boies and Andrew Hayes. Deposition of Sheldon Solow, *Sheldon Solow v. Carmel Fifth*, Court of Chancery for the State of Delaware in and for New Castle County, September 19, 2003.

Page 32　*Wayne Maggin had*　Affidavit of Wayne L. Maggin, *Solow Building Corporation vs. Carmel Fifth, LLC*, in the court of the Chancery in the State of Delaware in and for New Castle County.

Page 32　*He began to*　Deposition of Sheldon Solow, *Sheldon Solow v. Carmel Fifth*, Court of Chancery for the State of Delaware in and for New Castle County, September 19, 2003.

Page 32　*The billionaire phoned*　Interview with Andrew Hayes.

Page 33　*Solow took the tapes*　Ibid.

Page 33　*On Sunday afternoon*　Interview with Andrew Hayes. Plaintiff's Motion for Preliminary Injunction: Oral Arguments, *Solow Building Corporation vs. Carmel Fifth, LLC*, New Castle County Courthouse, Wilmington, Delaware, Tuesday, September 3, 2003.

Page 33　*A few minutes*　Interview with Andrew Hayes. Plaintiff's Motion for Preliminary Injunction: Oral Arguments, *Solow Building Corporation vs. Carmel Fifth, LLC*, New Castle County Courthouse, Wilmington, Delaware, Tuesday, September 3, 2003.

Page 33　*The three men*　Interview with Andrew Hayes.

Page 33　*Solow was "outraged,"*　Ibid.

Page 33　*David Boies would*　Interview with David Boies.

Page 33　*"It's a fix,"*　Interview with Andrew Hayes.

Page 33　*Andy Hayes hunkered*　Ibid.

Page 33　*On September 23*　Court's Ruling on Plaintiff's Motion for Preliminary Injunction, *Solow Building Company vs. Carmel Fifth LLC*, in the Court of the Chancery of the State of Delaware in and for New Castle County, Wilmington, Delaware, September 23, 2003.

Page 33　*And watched the video*　Interview with Reed Oslan.

Page 33　*He denied the injunction*　Court's Ruling on Plaintiff's Motion for Preliminary Injunction, *Solow Building Company vs. Carmel Fifth LLC*, in the Court of the Chancery of the State of Delaware in and for New Castle County, Wilmington, Delaware, September 23, 2003.

Page 33　*Conseco could sell*　Letter from William B. Chandler, Chancellor, Court Chancery of the Court of Delaware, to Jesse A.

Finkelstein, Richards Layton and Finger, and Richard D. Allen, Morris, Nicols Arsht & Tunnell, Re: *Solow Building Corp. v. Carmel Fifth LLC et al.*, civil action no. 20542, September 24, 2003.

Page 33   *Even though, it*   Affidavit of Wayne L. Maggin, *Solow Building Corporation vs. Carmel Fifth, LLC*, in the court of the Chancery in the State of Delaware in and for New Castle County.

Page 33   *He would, years*   Eliot Brown, "Sheldon Solow Sues (Again) over GM Building as Sale Nears," *New York Observer*, March 5, 2008.

Page 34   *David Boies would*   Interview with David Boies.

Page 34   *"Less than two*   Interview with Robert Sorin.

Page 35   *"We all thought*   Interview with Robert Horowitz.

Page 35   *"That whole closing*   Interview with Eric Schwartz.

Page 36   *"Just before*   Interview with Harry Macklowe.

Page 36   *"Deutsche Bank made*   Interview with Michael Fascitelli.

Page 36   *"We had 30 days*   Interview with Robert Verrone.

Chapter 4 Harry's Hero

Page 37   *Harry Macklowe's love*   Interview with Harry Macklowe.

Page 37   The *place to live*   Ibid.

Page 38   *Kennedy also had*   Nellie Bly, *The Kennedy Men: Three Generations of Sex, Scandal and Secrets* (New York: Kensington, 1996).

Page 38   *A McKim, Mead*   "Savoy-Plaza Opens at Special Dinner," *New York Times*, September 30, 1927. "Hostelery," *New Yorker*, October 8, 1927.

Page 38   *Macklowe loved the*   Interview with Harry Macklowe.

Page 38   *Gossip columnists felt*   Lloyd Stuart, "New York's Old Savoy Fading Out," *Star-Telegram*, June 8, 1965.

Page 38   *So-called because*   Gloria Steinem, "The Fate of Zsa Zsa's Bed (and Other New York Landmarks)," *Ladies' Home Journal*, August 1965.

Page 38   *Mayor Jimmy Walker*   Ken Mayer, "Entertainment Loses a Friend as Savoy Plaza Falls to a Wrecker," *Boston Herald*, May 10, 1966.

Page 38   *Many people chose*   Interview with Robert A.M. Stern.

Page 38   *In 1965 Gloria*   Gloria Steinem, "The Fate of Zsa Zsa's Bed (and Other New York Landmarks)," *Ladies' Home Journal*, August 1965.

Page 39   *The actress Zsa Zsa*   Lloyd Stuart, "New York's Old Savoy Fading Out," *Star-Telegram*, June 8, 1965.

Page 39   *She had three*   Gloria Steinem, "The Fate of Zsa Zsa's Bed (and Other New York Landmarks)," *Ladies' Home Journal*, August 1965.

Page 39   *In the late*   "N.Y. Savoy Plaza to Be Demolished for GM Building," *Hotel Herald*, September 1, 1964. Harry Altshuler, "Memories Fill Empty Rooms at the Savoy," *New York World-Telegram and Sun*, June 30, 1965. Robert McDonald, "Final Service at Savoy Plaza Sad Farewell," *Daily News*, July 1, 1965.

Page 39   *It had an*   Harry Altshuler, "Memories Fill Empty Rooms at the Savoy," *New York World-Telegram and Sun*, June 30, 1965. Robert McDonald, "Final Service at Savoy Plaza Sad Farewell," *Daily News*, July 1, 1965.

Page 39   *It had been built*   "Savoy Plaza Corp. Files Plans for Thirty-Three Story Hotel," *New York Times*, January 31, 1926.

Page 39   *Black had come*   Alice Sparberg Alexiou, *The Flatiron: The New York Landmark and the Incomparable City That Arose with It* (New York: St. Martin's Griffin, 2013), 22–29.

Page 39   *After Fuller's death*   Paul Starrett, *Changing the Skyline: An Autobiography* (New York: McGraw-Hill, 1938). Alice Sparberg Alexiou, *The Flatiron: The New York Landmark and the Incomparable City That Arose with It* (New York: St. Martin's Griffin, 2013).

Page 39   *As his success*   Alice Sparberg Alexiou, *The Flatiron: The New York Landmark and the Incomparable City That Arose with It* (New York: St. Martin's Griffin, 2013), 179–193; 203; 254–255.

Page 40   *His suicide was*   Paul Starrett, *Changing the Skyline: An Autobiography* (New York: McGraw-Hill, 1938).

Page 40   *Black once said*   "By-the-Bye in Wall Street," *Wall Street Journal*, July 29, 1931.

Page 40   *Especially lots*   Kenneth D. Ackerman, *Boss Tweed: The Corrupt Pol Who Conceived the Soul of Modern New York* (Falls Church, VA: Viral History Press, 2011).

Page 40   *In 1870*   Christopher Gray, "A Plaza Evolves from Oversight to Landmark," *New York Times*, July 23, 2006.

Page 40   *Within eight years*   Kenneth D. Ackerman, *Boss Tweed: The Corrupt Pol Who Conceived the Soul of Modern New York* (Falls Church, VA: Viral History Press, 2011), 344.

Page 40   *The next Icarus*   "Is Congress a Career or an Incident for a Young Man?" *New York Press*, May 28, 1909.

Page 40   *In 1890 Judge*   "Justice P. H. Dugro Dies in 65th Year," *New York Times*, March 2, 1920.

Page 41   *And in 1957*   "Savoy in Deal," *New York Times*, February 12, 1957.

Page 41   *Ex-wife Zsa Zsa*   Ibid. "Hotels: By Golly!" *Time*, July 19, 1963.

Page 41   *Gabor went on*   Leslie Bennetts, "It's a Mad Mad Zsa Zsa World," *Vanity Fair*, September 6, 2007, www.vanityfair.com/culture/features/2007/10/zsazsa200710.

Page 41   *In 1961, the*   "New Madison Square Garden to Rise above Penn Station," *New York Times*, July 25, 1961. Foster Hailey, "'62 Start Is Set for New Garden: Penn Station to Be Razed to Street Level in Project," *New York Times*, July 27, 1961.

Page 41   *Protests sprang up*   Christopher Gray, "'The Destruction of Penn Station'; A 1960's Protest That Tried to Save a Piece of the Past," *New York Times*, May 20, 2001. Ada Louise Huxtable, "Farewell to Penn Station," *New York Times,* October 30, 1963.

Page 41   *The official Landmarks*   Anthony C. Wood, *Preserving New York: Winning the Right to Protect a City's Landmarks* (New York: Routledge, 2007).

Page 41   *In her best-selling*   Interview with Robert A.M. Stern. Christopher Gray, "A Woman with an Architectural Appetite," *New York Times*, July 5, 2012.

Page 41   *But this was*   Interviews with Robert Rayne and Leonard Lauder.

Page 41   *The man's name*   Interview with Harry Macklowe.

Page 41   *Samuel F. Zell*   Interview with Samuel Zell.

Page 42   *Zeckendorf sometimes hung out*   Interview with Harry Macklowe.

Page 42   *William Zeckendorf was*   Chris Welles, "A Big Man on a Thin Edge: Bill Zeckendorf's Big Plans Gone Blooey," *Life*, February 12, 1965.

Page 42   *Zeckendorf curtailed his*   Ibid.

Page 42   *A hulk of a*   Ibid.

Page 43   *"In the sky,"*   Interview with Robert Rayne.

Page 43   *A round penthouse*   Alden Whitman, "In Zeckendorf's Mind, Ideas Are Spinning," *New York Times*, April 26, 1970. Michael Stern, "William Zeckendorf, Real Estate Developer, 71, Dies," *New York Times*, October 2, 1976.

Page 43   *The lighting would*   Interview with Robert Rayne.

Page 43   *Among Zeckendorf's more*   Michael Stern, "William Zeckendorf, Real Estate Developer, 71, Dies," *New York Times*, October 2, 1976. Chris Welles, "A Big Man on a Thin Edge: Bill Zeckendorf's Big Plans Gone Blooey," *Life*, February 12, 1965.

Page 43   *He flew by*   Chris Welles, "A Big Man on a Thin Edge: Bill Zeckendorf's Big Plans Gone Blooey," *Life*, February 12, 1965.

Page 43   *"He understood that*   Chris Welles, "A Big Man on a Thin Edge: Bill Zeckendorf's Big Plans Gone Blooey," *Life*, February 12, 1965.

Page 43   *In 1953, while*   Ibid.

Page 43   *"He even made*   Interview with Robert Rayne.

Page 43   *From 1949 to 1960*   Chris Welles, "A Big Man on a Thin Edge: Bill Zeckendorf's Big Plans Gone Blooey," *Life*, February 12, 1965.

Page 44   *"He could sell*   Interview with Lester Crown.

Page 44   *The problem, according*   Ibid.

Page 44   *"He got into*   Chris Welles, "A Big Man on a Thin Edge: Bill Zeckendorf's Big Plans Gone Blooey," *Life*, February 12, 1965.

Page 44   *Slowly the debts*   Ibid.

Page 44   *Right to the end*   Chris Welles, "A Big Man on a Thin Edge: Bill Zeckendorf's Big Plans Gone Blooey," *Life*, February 12, 1965. Alden Whitman, "In Zeckendorf's Mind, Ideas Are Spinning," *New York Times*, April 26, 1970. Michael Stern, "William Zeckendorf, Real Estate Developer, 71, Dies," *New York Times*, October 2, 1976.

Page 44   *With a market*   General Motors Annual Report, 1963.

Page 44   *All big businesses*   Interview with Walter Deane. "World's Fair: Wither Bound?" *Variety*, January 5, 1966. Glenn Fowler, "Building

Slump May Be Averted," *New York Times*, January 10, 1965. "No Letup in Office Construction: 20 New Buildings on the Way Here," *Commerce News*, September 1965. Historic Districts Council, "270 Park Avenue: Union Carbide Building," November 7, 2012, http://hdc.org/hdc-across-nyc/manhattan/proposed-east-midtown-rezoning-proposed-individual-landmarks/attachment/270-park-web. "1251 Avenue of the Americas," Emporis.com, www.emporis.com/building/1251-avenue-of-the-americas-new-york-city-ny-usa.

Page 44   *GM was planning*   Dennis Duggan, "40-Story GM Tower to Replace Savoy Plaza Hotel," *Herald Tribune*, August 21, 1964. Foster Hailey, "Savoy Plaza to Be Razed for G.M. Offices," *New York Times*, August 21, 1964. "Associated Architects Set for G.M. Building," *Hackensack Record*, December 18, 1964.

Page 44   *Zeckendorf wrote*   William Zeckendorf and Edward McCreary, *Zeckendorf* (New York: Holt, Rinehart & Winston, 1970).

Page 45   *He thought he*   Ibid.

Page 45   *Zeckendorf then went*   Ibid.

Page 45   *On the final page*   Ibid.

Page 45   *Something Crown's son*   Interview with Lester Crown.

Page 45   *Among the many*   Chris Welles, "A Big Man on a Thin Edge: Bill Zeckendorf's Big Plans Gone Blooey," *Life*, February 12, 1965.

Page 45   *Who was competing*   Clyde H. Farnsworth, "US Real Estate Attracts British," *New York Times*, August 22, 1964. "Developer Acquires Site for a GM Skyscraper in Midtown New York," *Wall Street Journal*, October 29, 1964.

Page 45   *Zeckendorf figured that*   "Developer Acquires Site for a GM Skyscraper in Midtown New York," *Wall Street Journal*, October 29, 1964.

Page 45   *In 1962, Webb*   David Binder, "Zeckendorf Buys the Savoy Hilton," *New York Times*, May 26, 1962. "Savoy Hilton Hotel in $25 Million Deal," *New York Times*, June 22, 1962.

Page 45   *Speculators idly wondered*   Interview with Robert Rayne.

Page 45   *In 1963, his*   Interview with Harry Macklowe.

Page 46   *The way Zeckendorf*   "Developer Acquires Site for a GM Skyscraper in Midtown New York," *Wall Street Journal*, October 29, 1964.

Page 46   *But in 1965*   Michael Stern, "William Zeckendorf, Real
Estate Developer, 71, Dies," *New York Times*, October 2, 1976. William
Zeckendorf and Edward McCreary, *Zeckendorf* (New York: Holt,
Rinehart & Winston, 1970).

Page 46   *He went to*   William Zeckendorf and Edward McCreary,
Zeckendorf (New York: Holt, Rinehart & Winston, 1970).

Page 46   *Her plane never*   "Mrs. Zeckendorf One of 63 Dead in Jetliner
Crash in Guadeloupe," *New York Times*, March 7, 1968. William Zeck-
endorf and Edward McCreary, *Zeckendorf* (New York: Holt, Rinehart
& Winston, 1970).

Page 46   *Just as he had*   William Zeckendorf and Edward McCreary,
Zeckendorf (New York: Holt, Rinehart & Winston, 1970).

Page 46   *He would suffer*   Michael Stern, "William Zeckendorf, Real Estate Developer, 71, Dies," *New York Times*, October 2,
1976.

Page 46   *"He was a genius."*   Interview with Harry Macklowe.

Page 47   *William Zeckendorf Jr. died*   Douglas Martin, "William Zeckendorf Jr., 84, Dies; Developer Put Stamp on Skyline," *New York Times*,
February 13, 2014.

Page 47   *William and Arthur Zeckendorf*   Paul Goldberger, "The King
of Central Park West," *Vanity Fair*, September 2008. Michael Gross,
"Inside the Walls of Swanky 15 Central Park West," *New York Post*,
March 9, 2014.

Chapter 5 The Odd Couple: The English Lord and the Housewife Tycoon

Page 49   *In 1960, Max Rayne*   Interview with Robert Rayne.

Page 50   *In 1962, Zeckendorf*   Ibid.

Page 50   *Then [Zeckendorf] got*   Ibid.

Page 50   *"During that period*   Ibid.

Page 50   *"The deal of the year."*   David English, "Housewife Tycoon,"
Daily Express, August 26, 1964.

Page 50   *He was hailed*   "More Than Meets the Eye in GM Skyscraper,"
Fortune, February 1965.

Page 50   *But there was*   Interview with Robert Rayne.

Page 50   *Penn Station had*   Christopher Gray, "The Destruction of Penn Station; A 1960's Protest That Tried to Save a Piece of the Past," *New York Times*, May 20, 2001. Ada Louise Huxtable, "Farewell to Penn Station," *New York Times,* October 30, 1963.

Page 50   *Protesters led a*   Thomas W. Ennis, "Coming Demise of Savoy Plaza Mourned by Student Marchers," *New York Times*, October 3, 1964. "Students Stage Funeral for Doomed Hotel," *Los Angeles Herald Examiner*, October 3, 1964. "Students Mourn Hotel's Razing," *New Bern Sun-Journal*, October 3, 1964. "Mock Funeral," *New Virginian*, October 3, 1964. "Funeral March Staged as Protest," *Tuscaloosa News*, October 4, 1964. "Faculty Students Stage Mock Funeral," *Hays Kansas News*, October 4, 1964.

Page 50   *Typically—and sensibly*   Interview with Robert Rayne. Nicolas Barker, "Lord Rayne: Property Developer and Philanthropist," *The Independent*, October 13, 2003.

Page 50   *He was just*   Stanley Burch, "John Bull Rules the New York Skyline," *London Daily News*, October 21, 1964. "More Than Meets the Eye in GM Skyscraper," *Fortune*, February 1965.

Page 50   *He holidayed in*   John London, "Mr. Rayne Keeps in Touch," *Evening News and Star,* August 21, 1964.

Page 50   *He had an important*   "Lord Rayne—Obituary," *Daily Telegraph*, October 11, 2003.

Page 50   *His second wife*   Suzy Knickerbocker, "Lady Jane Eyes Altar," *Philadelphia Inquirer,* June 1963. "Lord Rayne—Obituary," *Daily Telegraph*, October 11, 2003.

Page 50   *She'd held the*   "Lord Rayne—Obituary," *Daily Telegraph*, October 11, 2003.

Page 50   *And was later*   "The Maids of Honour Sixty Years On and Still Stylish," *Mail Online*, June 4, 2013, www.dailymail.co.uk/femail/article-2335684/Hats-girls-The-Duchess-Cambridge-leads-stylish-display-headgear-Queens-coronation-celebrations.html.

Page 50   *He was the son*   Nicolas Barker, "Lord Rayne: Property Developer and Philanthropist," *The Independent*, October 13, 2003.

Page 50   *He was so*   "Conglomerator Who Won the Trust of Great Estates," *Financial Times*, October 18, 2003. Nicolas Barker, "Lord

Rayne: Property Developer and Philanthropist," *The Independent*, October 13, 2003.

Page 50 *He became one* Interview with Robert Rayne. "Lord Rayne Obituary," *The Times* (London), October 11, 2003. Oliver Marriott, *The Property Boom* (London: H. Hamilton, 1967), 48.

Page 51 *In 1957 he* "Obituary of Lord Rayne Businessman and Patron of the Arts Who Dispensed Millions of Pounds," *Daily Telegraph*, October 11, 2003. Nicolas Barker, "Obituary—Lord Rayne," *The Independent*, October 13, 2003. "Lord Rayne—Obituary," *The Times* (London), October 11, 2003.

Page 51 *In 1969 he* "Lord Rayne—Obituary," *Daily Telegraph*, October 11, 2003.

Page 51 *The press reports* Glenn Fowler, "Fifth Avenue, City's Grande Dame, Graciously Suffers Change," *New York Times*, August 5, 1965. George W. Cornwell, "Gotham Loses Famed Hotel," Associated Press, July 2, 1965. "Old and New Architecture," *Industrial Design*, January 1965. Russell Kirk, "We Erect Glass Towers and Destroy the Past," *Times* (Atlanta, GA), January 6, 1965.

Page 51 *This was not* Interview with Robert Rayne.

Page 51 *"It wasn't so* Ibid.

Page 51 *"Truly remarkable"* Interview with Ira Millstein.

Page 51 *Wolff was a* Ibid.

Page 51 *"He was a* Interview with Ira Millstein.

Page 51 *Wolff was considered* Ibid.

Page 51 *Among his prominent* Interview with Ira Millstein.

Page 51 *The latter a* "Walter Bareiss," MoMA Archives Oral History, September 25, 1991, www.moma.org/momaorg/shared/pdfs/docs/learn/archives/transcript_bareiss.pdf. Retrieved June 20, 2014.

Page 51 *Bareiss was the* Interview with Ira Millstein.

Page 52 *"A long process* Ibid.

Page 52 *It was to be* Ibid.

Page 52 *That person was* Interview with Geoffrey Wharton.

Page 52 *But she didn't* Interviews with Simon Benattar, Ira Millstein, Harvey Miller, Geoffrey Wharton, and Robert Rayne.

Page 52 *She was a* David English, "Housewife Tycoon," *Daily Express*, August 26, 1964. Kenneth Smith, "The Little Lady Who Will Knock Your Block Off," *Globe and Mail*, March 30, 1966.

Page 52   *She spoke with*   "She Doesn't Cry in Business," *Life*, October 1, 1965.

Page 52   *She had won*   David English, "Housewife Tycoon," *Daily Express*, August 26, 1964. Rita Reif, "British Builder Alters Course," *New York Times*, July 13, 1975.

Page 52   *She met Rayne*   Interviews with Robert Rayne and Simon Benattar.

Page 52   *She would later*   Lotta Dempsey, "Private Line," *Toronto Daily Star* [date unknown].

Page 52   *Rayne wasn't threatened*   Interview with Robert Rayne.

Page 52   *While Max Rayne*   Ibid.

Page 53   *Max Rayne suspected*   Ibid.

Page 53   *"He said, 'You*   Ibid.

Page 53   *In 1957, Benattar*   Interviews with Robert Rayne, Simon Benattar, and Geoffrey Wharton.

Page 53   *She was working*   Interviews with Simon Benattar and Robert Rayne.

Page 53   *"'I'm going to*   Interview with Harvey Miller.

Page 53   *Benattar's first priority*   Interview with Ira Millstein.

Page 53   *Jesse Wolff died*   "Jesse Wolff Obituary," *New York Times* (paid death notice), July 10, 2011.

Page 53   *Cecilia would even*   Interview with Simon Benattar.

Page 53   *She knew she*   Interviews with Ira Millstein, Simon Benattar, and Geoffrey Wharton.

Page 53   *Next she had*   Ibid.

Page 53   *"It wasn't obvious,"*   Interview with Robert Rayne.

Page 54   *She also had*   Interviews with Ira Millstein, Simon Benattar, and Geoffrey Wharton.

Page 54   *"She went to*   Interview with Geoffrey Wharton.

Page 54   *"I had nothing*   Interview with Simon Benattar and Geoffrey Wharton.

Page 54   *Benattar was able*   Interview with Robert Rayne.

Page 54   *"GM's lease was*   Ibid.

Page 54   *In August 1964 the deal*   Dennis Duggan, "40-Story GM Tower to Replace Savoy Plaza Hotel," *Herald Tribune*, August 21, 1964. Foster Hailey, "Savoy Plaza to Be Razed for G.M. Offices," *New York Times*, August 21, 1964.

Page 55   *There was a* "Developer Acquires Site for a GM Sky-scraper in Midtown New York," *Wall Street Journal*, October 29, 1964. David English, "Housewife Tycoon," *Daily Express*, August 26, 1964. "Demolition! Old-Timers' Tragedy," *Star Journal*, October 15, 1964. "Another Pan Am?" *Progressive Architecture*, October 1964.

Page 55   *In August 1964 he wrote*   David English, "Housewife Tycoon," *Daily Express,* August 26, 1964.

Page 55   *"When the last*   Ibid.

Page 55   *In September 1964*   "Old and New Architecture," *Industrial Design,* January 1965.

Page 55   *In December 1964*   Ibid.

Page 55   *Benattar, according to*   Interview with Simon Benattar.

Page 55   *But she could*   Interview with Simon Benattar. Rita Reit, "British Builder Alters Course," *New York Times*, July 13, 1975.

Page 55   *Stone was very*   Glenn Fowler, "48-Story Tower to Rise on Savoy Plaza Site," *New York Times*, December 16, 1964.

Page 55   *In December 1964*   Ada Louise Huxtable, "Nothing Inviolate Here," *New York Times*, December 16, 1964.

Page 55   *Ada Louise Huxtable*   Ibid.

Page 56   *Stone promised the*   Glenn Fowler, "48-Story Tower to Rise on Savoy Plaza Site," *New York Times*, December 16, 1964.

Page 56   *His vision was*   "Sunken Plaza Planned for G.M. Building on 5th Ave.," *New York Times*, August 6, 1965.

Page 56   *The concept was*   "Saving the Landmarks," *Union-Sun and Journal*, February 12, 1965. "Down with the Savoy Plaza," *New York Times*, Monday, August 24, 1964. Ada Louise Huxtable, "More on How to Kill a City," *New York Times*, March 5, 1965. "Staunch Defenders of the Savoy Plaza," *New York Herald Tribune*, February 17, 1965. "An Eye on New York," March 2, 1965. *Tonight Show*, April 9, 1965.

Page 56   *In early 1965*   Thomas W. Ennis, "Women Score GM on Building Plan," *New York Times*, January 20, 1965. "Whoa, GM! High Society Stomping to Save Savoy," *Free Press*, January 21, 1965. "Clients of Famed NY Hotel Plan Economic War on GM," *Providence Journal*, January 21, 1965. Francis Stilley, "Teacup Ladies Dish It Out with GM," *Philadelphia Inquirer*, January 21, 1965. "Saving the Landmarks,"

Union-Sun and Journal, February 12, 1965. "GM Threatened by a 'Womancott," *Los Angeles Herald Examiner,* January 20, 1965.

Page 56   *Famed economist John Kenneth Galbraith*   Martin A. Nolin, "Must We Destroy America's Past?" *Boston Globe,* November 29, 1964.

Page 56   *"I Said I"*   Kenneth Smith, "The Little Lady Who Will Knock Your Block Off," *Globe and Mail,* March 30, 1966.

Page 56   *When told the*   Interview with Simon Benattar.

Page 56   *She decided to*   Gloria Steinem, "The Fate of Zsa Zsa's Bed (and Other New York Landmarks)," *Ladies' Home Journal,* August 1965.

Page 56   *She hired an*   "Special Bargains for Monogram Hunters," *New York Herald Tribune,* July 6, 1965. "The Initial Response Proves Overwhelming," *New York Times,* July 7, 1965. Jerome Zuckosky, "Stomping at the Savoy—For Chairs, Tables and Drapes," *Herald Tribune,* July 4, 1965.

Page 56   *The result? Would-be*   "Special Bargains for Monogram Hunters," *New York Herald Tribune,* July 6, 1965. "The Initial Response Proves Overwhelming," *New York Times,* July 7, 1965. Jerome Zuckosky, "Stomping at the Savoy—For Chairs, Tables and Drapes," *Herald Tribune,* July 4, 1965.

Page 56   *It was the*   Patricia Davis, "Furnishings from the Savoy-Plaza," *Gazette* (Cedar Rapids, Iowa), July 6, 1965. Maggis Daly, "Daly Diary," *American* (Chicago), July 6, 1965. Mel Heimer, "My New York" (Syndicated), July 12, 1965. "They Were Sold on Each Other," *Daily News,* July 17, 1965. "Zsa Zsa's Beds to Be Converted to Dining Booths," *Post Times & Star,* July 8, 1965. "Zsa Zsa Slept Here," *Newark Star-Ledger,* July 25, 1965. "From Zsoup to Nuts," *New York Daily News,* July 30, 1965. Gloria Steinem, "The Fate of Zsa Zsa's Bed (and Other New York Landmarks)," *Ladies' Home Journal,* August 1965.

Page 56   *Benattar earned more*   "Closing a Hotel at a Profit," *BusinessWeek,* July 23, 1966. Frank Farrell, "New York—Day by Day," *New York World-Telegram and Sun,* August 14, 1965.

Page 56   *"It took a*   Gloria Steinem, "The Fate of Zsa Zsa's Bed (and Other New York Landmarks)," *Ladies' Home Journal,* August 1965.

Page 57   *And there was*   Ibid.

Page 57   *She was asking*   Interviews with Ira Millstein, Harvey Miller, and Robert Rayne.

Page 57   *Estée Lauder, the*   "1960: Lauder Goes International," Elcompanies. com, www.elcompanies.com/Pages/Heritage-of-Innovation.aspx. Retrieved June 20, 2014.

Page 57   *Cecilia befriended her*   Interview with Leonard Lauder.

Page 57   *Leonard thought it*   Ibid.

Page 57   *She also didn't*   Interview with Robert Rayne.

Page 57   *They also expanded*   Interview with James Nagy.

Page 57   *She told her*   Interview with Leonard Lauder.

Page 57   *Charles Revson, the*   Ibid.

Page 58   *His successor, Ronald*   Interview with Ira Millstein.

Page 58   *In 1968 Helena Rubenstein*   "News of Realty: Japan Air Lease Helena Rubenstein Building Is Rented for 1.35 Million," *New York Times*, April 29, 1968. Interview with Leonard Lauder.

Page 58   *The building acquired*   Interview with Leonard Lauder.

Page 58   *People like to*   Interview with Walter Deane.

Page 58   *She explained her*   Interview with Geoffrey Wharton.

Page 58   *A young broker*   Interview with Harry Macklowe.

Page 58   *Macklowe introduced the*   Ibid.

Page 58   *They did*   Interview with Mary Wells.

Page 58   *There was a*   Interview with Ira Millstein and Harvey Miller.

Page 59   *She told Wolff*   Interview with Ira Millstein.

Page 59   *"It was not*   Ibid.

Page 59   *At one point*   Ibid.

Page 59   *"Sylvan, you can*   Ibid.

Page 59   *Weil Gotshal would*   Interview with Ira Millstein.

Page 60   *As more and more*   Interview with Simon Benattar.

Page 60   *In 1969, Robbie*   Interview with Robert Rayne.

Page 60   *Benattar did not*   Interviews with Robert Rayne, Simon Benattar, Ira Millstein, and Harvey Miller.

Page 60   *Robbie Rayne had*   Ibid.

Page 60   *Benattar returned to*   Ibid.

Page 60   *Colleagues recall that*   Interviews with James Nagy and Geoffrey Wharton.

Page 60   *She explained in*   Lotta Dempsey, "Private Line," *Toronto Daily Star* [date unknown]. Kenneth Smith, "The Little Lady Who Will Knock Your Block Off," *Globe and Mail*, March 30, 1966.

Page 60   *"I strive to*   David English, "Housewife Tycoon," *Daily Express*, August 26, 1964.

Page 60   *The men around*   Interviews with Ira Millstein, Harvey Miller, James Nagy, Geoffrey Wharton, and Jerry Speyer.

Page 60   *"She always looked*   Interview with James Nagy.

Page 61   *She loved doing*   Interview with Geoffrey Wharton.

Page 61   *She also asked*   Ibid.

Page 61   *As her friend*   Ibid.

Page 61   *Once the building*   Interview with Robert Rayne.

Page 61   *Wolff smelled trouble*   Interviews with Ira Millstein and Geoffrey Wharton.

Page 61   *So she hired*   Interviews with Robert Rayne and Simon Benattar. Rita Reit, "British Builder Alters Course," *New York Times*, July 13, 1975.

Page 61   *Jack Benattar, the*   Interview with Robert Rayne.

Page 61   *Schwartz did his*   Ibid.

Page 61   *Lindsay was running*   Interviews with Simon Benattar and Geoffrey Wharton.

Page 61   *"She felt he*   Interview with Geoffrey Wharton.

Page 61   *Suddenly, she found*   Interview with Robert Rayne.

Page 62   *Max Rayne had*   Ibid.

Page 62   *Max and Cecilia*   Interview with Simon Benattar.

Page 62   *Simon Benattar says*   Ibid.

Page 62   *Of course the Londoners*   Interviews with Simon Benattar and Harry Macklowe.

Page 62   *Max Rayne was*   Interview with Robert Rayne.

Page 62   *"Cecilia was very*   Ibid.

Page 62   *In 1971, Benattar*   Interviews with Simon Benattar and Geoffrey Wharton.

Page 62   *"Of course had*   Interview with Robert Rayne.

Page 62   *She got a*   Interviews with Simon Benattar and Robert Rayne.

Page 62 *Letters from her* Interview with Simon Benattar. Rita Reit, "British Builder Alters Course," *New York Times*, July 13, 1975.

Page 63 *She relocated to* Interviews with Robert Rayne, Simon Benattar, and Harvey Miller.

Page 63 *Benattar was openly* Interview with Harvey Miller.

Page 63 *She was also* Interview with Simon Benattar.

Page 63 *In 1978 she* Ibid.

Page 63 *Across the Atlantic* Interview with Robert Rayne.

Page 63 *But Cecilia Benattar* Interview with Simon Benattar.

Page 63 *Max Rayne also* "Obituary of Lord Rayne Businessman and Patron of the Arts Who Dispensed Millions of Pounds," *Daily Telegraph*, October 11, 2003. "Conglomerator Who Won the Trust of Great Estates," *Financial Times*, October 18, 2003. "Lord Rayne—Obituary," *The Times* (London), October 11, 2003.

Page 63 *"Most people thought* Interview with Harry Macklowe.

Page 63 *"Right after I* Interview with Jerry Speyer.

Page 63 *"The toughest woman* "She Doesn't Cry in Business," *Life*, October 1, 1965.

Chapter 6 The Age of the Wolf

Page 65 *There was a* "GM's 'Engine Charlie' Wilson Learned to Live with a Misquote," *Detroit Free Press*, September 14, 2008. "Generations of GM History: Wilson, Charles E." GM Heritage Center, http://history .gmheritagecenter.com/wiki/index.php/Wilson,_Charles_E.

Page 66 *He might have* "Company: History & Heritage—Revolution 1960–1979," GM.com, www.gm.com/company/historyAndHeritage/ revolution.html. Retrieved June 20, 2014.

Page 66 *It became "dirty* Interviews with Ira Millstein and Harvey Miller.

Page 66 *GM turned to* Ibid.

Page 66 *On January 5* Douglas Martin, "G.M. to Get $500 Million for Edifice," *New York Times*, January 5, 1982.

Page 66 *A report in* Douglas Martin, "G.M. to get $500 Million for Edifice," *New York Times*, January 5, 1982. "Kuwaiti Investors

Have Stake in Refinancing GM Office Tower," *Wall Street Journal*, February 10, 1982.

Page 66   *This was exactly*   Interview with Walter Deane.

Page 66   *His headquarters at*   Interview with Thomas Zacharias.

Page 67   *Roderick "Rod" Johnson*   Interview with Roderick Johnson.

Page 67   *The wolf was*   Charles V. Bagli, "Disque D. Deane, 89, Real Estate Investor," *New York Times*, November 10, 2010.

Page 67   *Disque Deane had*   Interviews with Hans Mautner and Thomas Zacharias.

Page 67   *His father was*   Disque Deane's unpublished diaries.

Page 67   *He was neither*   Ibid.

Page 67   *He was so*   Ibid.

Page 67   *He hired a*   Interview with Hans Mautner.

Page 67   *Colleagues recalled that*   Interviews with Hans Mautner and Thomas Zacharias.

Page 67   *Mautner was worried*   Interview with Hans Mautner.

Page 67   *But Deane took*   Interviews with Hans Mautner and Thomas Zacharias.

Page 68   *Most of Wall Street*   Interview with Hans Mautner.

Page 68   *Meyer, with Deane's*   Interviews with Hans Mautner and Thomas Zacharias.

Page 68   *He loved Deane's*   Disque Deane's unpublished diaries.

Page 68   *When the property*   Ibid.

Page 68   *Meyer also saw*   Interviews with Walter Deane, Hans Mautner, and Thomas Zacharias. Disque Deane's unpublished diaries.

Page 68   *Considered "more elegant"*   Interview with Thomas Zacharias.

Page 68   *"He phrased it*   Interview with Hans Mautner.

Page 68   *Deane was happy*   Interview with Thomas Zacharias.

Page 69   *When Meyer died*   Interview with G. Martin Fell.

Page 69   *In 1972, Meyer*   Carter B. Horsley, "Housing for 24,000 Begun in Brooklyn," *New York Times*, July 16, 1972. "Obituary: Disque Deane," *Boston Globe*, November 11, 2010. Interview with Donald Trump. Charles V. Bagli, "Disque D. Deane, 89, Real Estate Investor," *New York Times*, November 20, 2010.

Page 69   *Despite the fact*   Interview with Donald Trump.

Page 69   *One of Deane's*   Interview with Walter Deane.

Page 69   *Donald Trump came*   Interview with Donald Trump.

Page 70   *In 1991, when*   Ibid.

Page 70   *"He said, 'I have*   Ibid.

Page 70   *Even those with*   Interview with Thomas Zacharias.

Page 70   *Deane had also*   Ibid.

Page 70   *The first was*   Interviews with Thomas Zacharias, Walter Deane, and Kathryn Deane.

Page 70   *Deane had married*   Interview with Walter Deane. Nora Krug, "Marjorie Deane, Authority on Fashion," *New York Times*, November 27, 2003.

Page 70   *His first marriage*   "Anne S. Delafield Bride of Officer," *New York Times*, May 26, 1945.

Page 70   *They'd had a*   Interview with Walter Deane.

Page 70   *Walter Deane would*   Ibid.

Page 70   *Despite the fact*   Interview with William Cohan.

Page 70   *Marjorie Schlesinger Deane*   Interviews with Walter and Kathryn Deane.

Page 70   *Both Kathy and*   Ibid.

Page 71   *Though he would*   Interview with Walter Deane.

Page 71   *His daughter Kathy*   Interview with Kathryn Deane.

Page 71   *He was thrown*   Interviews with Warren Hamer and Thomas Zacharias.

Page 71   *He could be*   Interview with Walter Deane.

Page 71   *Yet he spent*   Interview with Thomas Zacharias.

Page 71   *"He believed that*   Ibid.

Page 71   *Deane had started*   Ibid.

Page 71   *He once flew*   Interviews with Thomas Zacharias and Warren Hamer.

Page 71   *One memorable Christmas*   Interviews with Walter and Kathryn Deane.

Page 71   *It was Koz*   Ibid.

Page 71   *He installed a*   Interview with Thomas Zacharias.

Page 72   *Finding tax exemptions*   Interview with Warren Hamer.

Page 72   *But in 1982*   Interviews with Walter Deane and G. Martin Fell.

Page 72   *"It was not*   Interview with G. Martin Fell.

Page 72   *Deane believed firmly*   Interview with Walter Deane.

Page 72 *He was so* Interview with Hans Mautner.

Page 72 *Most of it* Interview with Thomas Zacharias.

Page 72 *"We bought the* Interview with Thomas Zacharias. "Kuwaiti Investors Have Stake in Refinancing GM Office Tower," *Wall Street Journal*, February 10, 1982.

Page 72 *The Kuwaitis* Interview with Hans Mautner.

Page 72 *The KIA signed* Interview with Hans Mautner.

Page 73 *Deane kept a* Interview with Walter Deane.

Page 73 *The only successful* Interview with Roderick Johnson.

Page 73 *Everything else, including* Interviews with Roderick Johnson and Walter Deane.

Page 73 *And the plaza* Interview with Walter Deane.

Page 73 *Disque Deane held* Interview with Hans Mautner.

Page 73 *Johnson suggested raising* Interviews with Hans Maunter and Walter Deane.

Page 73 *In 1991, after* Richard D. Hylton, "Real Estate Group Buys G.M. Building," *New York Times*, February 15, 1991. Interviews with Ira Millstein and Harvey Miller.

Page 73 *Rod Johnson, the* Interview with Roderick Johnson.

Page 73 *His son Walter* Interview with Walter Deane.

Page 73 *But the tranquility* Ibid.

Page 73 *This was a* Randall Smith and Mitchell Pacelle, "REIT Success Draws Investors but Doubts and Pitfalls Abound," *Wall Street Journal*, August 25, 1993. Interview with Walter Deane.

Page 73 *Months before, when* Interview with Hans Mautner.

Page 73 *But the board* Interviews with Walter Deane, Hans Mautner, and Thomas Zacharias.

Page 74 *Inside he was* Interview with Walter Deane.

Page 74 *As part of* Ibid.

Page 74 *Deane watched from* Ibid.

Page 74 *In 1998 Hans* Interview with Hans Mautner.

Page 74 *A young Midwesterner* Interview with David Simon.

Page 74 *The shopping center* Greg Andrews, "Simon Boosts Stock Yield to Pull Off Huge Offering," *Indianapolis Business Journal*, December 20, 1993.

Page 74 *Simon didn't know* Interviews with David Simon and Joseph Perella.

Page 74   *"David said, 'Hey*   Interview with Joseph Perella.

Page 74   *Mike Fascitelli and*   Interview with Michael Fascitelli.

Page 75   *CPI preferred Simon's*   Interview with Hans Mautner. "Simon Says: Buy More Malls," *CNN Money*, February 19, 1998. Steven Morris, "Takeover Cements Power in Malls," *Chicago Tribune* (*Bloomberg News*), February 20, 1998.

Page 75   *Mautner would later*   Interview with Hans Mautner.

Page 75   *David Simon never*   Interview with David Simon.

Page 75   *He had gotten*   Interviews with Thomas Zacharias and Walter and Kathryn Deane.

Page 75   *According to Tom*   Interview with Thomas Zacharias.

Page 75   *Within days of*   Interview with Walter Deane.

Page 75   *In 1991, she*   Ibid.

Page 75   *Right before Carol*   Interviews with Thomas Zacharias, Walter Deane, and Kathryn Deane.

Page 75   *"What happened to*   Interview with Kathryn Deane.

Page 76   *Disque and Carol*   Charles V. Bagli, "Disque D. Deane, 89, Real Estate Investor," *New York Times*, November 20, 2010.

Page 76   *Once his second*   Interview with Thomas Zacharias.

Page 76   *He and Carol*   Interviews with Walter Deane and Thomas Zacharias. Disque Deane's unpublished diaries.

Page 76   *He donated $20 million*   Jerry E. Bishop, "Philanthropist Aims to Help Scientists at Duke Spend More Time on Research," *Wall Street Journal*, November 9, 1995.

Page 76   *But, in rather*   Susan Kauffman, "Once-Spurned Duke Benefactor Returns with Gift," *News & Observer Raleigh*, November 11, 1995.

Page 76   *There was a*   Ibid.

Page 76   *Deane suffered a*   Interview with G. Martin Fell.

Page 76   *In 2006 and*   "Schumer to New Starrett Owners: Keep It Affordable or Else," *New York Observer*, February 12, 2007. Rich Calder, "Block Starrett Sale: Schumer," *New York Post*, February 16, 2007. Charles V. Bagli, "Schumer and State Legislators Seek to Block Starrett City Sale," *New York Times*, April 14, 2007.

Page 76   *The Deanes were*   Charles V. Bagli, "Disque D. Deane, 89, Real Estate Investor," *New York Times*, November 20, 2010, "Decision and Order," *Harvey Rudman and Harold Kuplesky v. Carol Gram Deane, the estate of Disque D. Deane*, Supreme Court of the State of New York, County of New York: Part 54.

Page 76   *After their father's*   Interviews with Walter and Kathryn Deane.

Page 77   *On November 8*   Interview with Walter Deane.

Page 77   *On November 19*   "Obituary, Disque Deane," *Boston Globe*, November 11, 2010.

Page 77   *Hare, his unrecognized son*   Interview with Walter Deane.

Page 77   *According to Tom*   Interview with Thomas Zacharias.

Page 77   *D.D. ended*   Ibid.

Chapter 7 Donald Trump's Bag Man

Page 79   *David Simon knew*   Interview with David Simon.

Page 80   *In February 1998*   Ibid.

Page 80   *He soon realized*   Ibid.

Page 80   *There was one*   Ibid.

Page 80   *His casino business*   Dan Collins, "Should Trump Be Fired?" CBSNews.com, November 22, 2004, www.cbsnews.com/news/should-donald-trump-be-fired-22-11-2004/. Retrieved June 20, 2014.

Page 80   *Simon remembers that*   Ibid.

Page 80   *Jenrette was infamous*   Ariel Levy, "The Renovation," *New Yorker*, November 28, 2011.

Page 80   *Recently the inspiration*   Richard Leiby, "To the Players in Abscam, the Real-Life 'American Hustle,' the Bribes Now Seem Quaint," *Washington Post*, December 26, 2013.

Page 80   *After he was*   Albin Krebs and Robert McG. Thomas Jr., "Notes on People: Rita Jenrette Granted Divorce," *New York Times*, July 23, 1981.

Page 81   *She later posed*   Ariel Levy, "The Renovation," *New Yorker*, November 28, 2011.

Page 81   *"I wanted to*   Interview with Principessa Rita Boncompagni Ludovisi.

Page 81   *She saw a*   Ibid.

Page 81   *Jenrette humorously*   Ibid.

Page 81   *"Wouldn't you want*   Ibid.

Page 81　*He recalls telling*　Interview with Abraham Wallach.

Page 81　*Wallach also received*　Ibid.

Page 81　*Wallach spun out*　Ibid.

Page 81　*When Trump landed*　Interviews with Donald Trump and David Simon.

Page 82　*Hilbert did*　Ibid.

Page 82　*Jenrette phoned and*　Interviews with Principessa Rita Boncompagni-Ludovisi and Abraham Wallach.

Page 82　*"We didn't need*　Interview with Abraham Wallach.

Page 82　*As it happened*　Interview with Steve Hilbert.

Page 82　*The Simons owned*　Carleen Hawn, "In the First Place," *Forbes* (online), October 12, 1998, www.forbes.com/global/1998/1012/0114008a.html. Hank Lowenkron, "Pacers Reach Naming Rights Deal," Associated Press, May 22, 1998.

Page 82　*Hilbert loved the idea*　Interview with Steve Hilbert.

Page 82　*Hilbert was the*　Interviews with Reed Oslan and Charles Cremens. Will Higgins, "Conseco Execs and Hilbert Era of Gilded Excess." *Indianapolis Star*, April 13, 2001. Dann Denny, "Lifestyles of the Rich and Famous: A Monet over the Mantle, His-and-Hers Harleys, an Indoor Basketball Court: How Insurance Mogul Steve Hilbert Spends Indy's Biggest Paycheck," *Indianapolis Monthly*, November 1995.

Page 82　*There was a*　Interviews with David Simon and Steve Hilbert.

Page 82　*He met with*　Interview with David Simon.

Page 83　*The Simons trusted*　Ibid.

Page 83　*Abe Wallach was, as usual*　Interview with Abraham Wallach.

Page 83　*Cuneo was widely respected*　Interview with Charles Schoenherr.

Page 83　*Even so, Wallach*　Interview with Abraham Wallach.

Page 83　*Next Wallach raced*　Ibid.

Page 84　*It was imperative*　Interviews with Stephen Hilbert, Charles Schoenherr, David Simon, and Abraham Wallach.

Page 84　*Fascitelli recalls the*　Interview with Michael Fascitelli.

Page 84　*Trump played like*　Ibid.

Page 84　*Wallach told Hilbert*　Interview with Abraham Wallach.

Page 84   *Fascitelli didn't know*   Interview with Michael Fascitelli.

Page 84   *Their point person*   Interview with Charles Schoenherr.

Page 84   *Schoenherr, Horowitz, and*   Interviews with Robert Horowitz, Charles Schoenherr, and Abraham Wallach.

Page 85   *The final terms*   Interview with Charles Schoenherr.

Page 85   *Trump pushed them*   Ibid.

Page 85   *Trump was concerned*   Interview with Donald Trump.

Page 85   *On the last*   Ibid.

Page 85   *"I fixed up*   Ibid.

Page 85   *Steve Hilbert was*   Interview with Stephen Hilbert.

Page 86   *Trump also raised*   Interview with Donald Trump.

Page 86   *Then, in a*   Interview with Donald Trump. Don Kaplan, "What the Neighbors Think about Bryant—CBS Breakfast Show Moves into Fancy New Digs," *New York Post*, May 5, 1999, http://nypost.com/1999/05/05/what-the-neighbors-think-about-bryant-cbs-breakfast-show-moves-into-fancy-new-digs/. Retrieved June 20, 2014.

Page 86   *Next, Trump drew*   Interview with Donald Trump.

Page 86   *Abe Wallach worried*   Interview with Abraham Wallach.

Page 87   *But, regardless, Wallach*   Interviews with Donald Trump and Abraham Wallach.

Page 87   *Wallach was gay*   Interview with Abraham Wallach.

Page 87   *"I called the*   Abraham Wallach's unpublished memoirs.

Page 88   *Wallach had headed*   Abraham Wallach, "How to Get Hired by Donald Trump," YouTube.com, uploaded January 4, 2012, www.youtube.com/watch?v=KlwCXgZwSCc. Retrieved June 21, 2014.

Page 88   *"On the show*   Interview with Abraham Wallach.

Page 88   *Then he dropped*   Ibid.

Page 89   *"When he first*   Ibid.

Page 89   *Wallach was genuinely*   Interview with Abraham Wallach.

Page 89   *"I started to*   Ibid.

Page 89   *When he was*   Interviews with Donald Trump and Abraham Wallach.

Page 89   *"You can't stop*   Interview with Abraham Wallach.

Page 89   *Trump reflected*   Interview with Donald Trump.

Chapter 8 The Money Hunters and the Salesman from Indianapolis

Page 91   *Hilbert was forced*   "Next for Conseco," *Indianapolis Star*, April 29, 2000. Jonathan Berke, "Conseco's Hilbert Resigns," *Daily Deal*, April 28, 2000. Shawn Tully, "A Deal Too Far," *Fortune*, November 8, 1999. Floyd Norris and Alex Berenson, "Conseco Files for Bankruptcy Protection," *New York Times*, December 19, 2002. Leslie Eaton, "Conseco and Green Tree, an Improbable Merger," *New York Times*, April 8, 1998. James P. Miller, "Conseco to Unload Former Green Tree; Expects $350 Million After-Tax Charge," *Wall Street Journal*, April 3, 2000, http://online.wsj.com/news/articles/ SB954508013416539212. Retrieved June 20, 2014. Debra Sparks, "Conseco's Morning After," *BusinessWeek*, June 4, 2000.

Page 91   *It fell from*   Debra Sparks, "Conseco's Morning After," *BusinessWeek*, June 4, 2000.

Page 92   *This was largely*   "Next for Conseco," *Indianapolis Star*, April 29, 2000. Jonathan Berke, "Conseco's Hilbert Resigns," *Daily Deal*, April 28, 2000. Shawn Tully, "A Deal Too Far," *Fortune*, November 8, 1999.

Page 92   *It booked its*   Interview with Reed Oslan. James P. Miller, "Conseco to Unload Former Greentree; Expects $350 Million After-Tax Charge," *Wall Street Journal*, April 3, 2000, http://online.wsj.com/ news/articles/SB954508013416539212. Retrieved June 20, 2014.

Page 92   *But it would*   "In the Matter of Rollin Dick, CPA, Respondent. Order Instituting Administrative Proceedings Pursuant to Rule 102(e) of the Commission's Rules of Practice, Making Findings, and Imposing Remedial Sanctions." Administrative Proceedings, United States of America before the Securities and Exchange Commission, July 25, 2006.

Page 92   *Conseco borrowed more*   Shawn Tully, "A Deal Too Far," *Fortune*, November 8, 1999.

Page 92   *For which it*   Interview with Charles Cremens.

Page 92   *And 10 other*   Interview with Reed Oslan. Stephen Taub, "Conesco Settles with Former CFO," CFO.com. Mark Jewell, "Conseco Barred from Freezing Ex-CEO Assets," Associated Press, November 12, 2003.

Page 92   *Hilbert owed $218 million*   Ibid. Joseph T. Hallinan and Mitchell Pacelle, "Turn of Fortune: In Collection Battle, Conseco Ex-CEO Is Fighting Back," *Wall Street Journal*, December 5, 2003.

Page 92   *Class action lawsuits*   Debra Sparks, "Conseco's Morning After," *BusinessWeek,* June 4, 2000. Mark Tatge and Evan Hessel, "It's Not Over," *Forbes*, December 12, 2003, www.forbes.com/forbes/2003/1222/060a.html. Retrieved June 20, 2014. Joseph T. Hallinan and Mitchell Pacelle, "Turn of Fortune: In Collection Battle, Conseco Ex-CEO Is Fighting Back," *Wall Street Journal*, December 5, 2003.

Page 92   *But he felt*   Interview with Donald Trump.

Page 92   *"They [Conseco] spent*   Interview with Donald Trump.

Page 92   *Hilbert had felt*   Shawn Tully, "A Deal Too Far," *Fortune*, November 8, 1999.

Page 93   *The Boston leveraged*   Debra Sparks, "Conseco's Morning After," *BusinessWeek*, June 4, 2000. Floyd Norris and Alex Berenson, "Conseco Files for Bankruptcy Protection," *New York Times*, December 19, 2002.

Page 93   *"The worst investment*   Interview with Thomas H. Lee.

Page 93   *Conseco's board of directors insisted*   Floyd Norris, "Founder Resigns Conseco Post, under Pressure of Falling Profits," *New York Times*, April 29, 2000. Deborah Lohse, "Conseco Board Forces CEO and Finance Chief to Resign," *Wall Street Journal*, May 1, 2000.

Page 93   *He was given*   Interview with Chuck Cremens. "Hilbert Gets Cash, Jet Privileges," Associated Press, May 2, 2000.

Page 93   *Gary C. Wendt, the*   Floyd Norris, "Conseco Chief Got Big Bonus for Signing On," *New York Times*, July 11, 2002.

Page 93   *This isn't quite*   Interview with Stephen Hilbert.

Page 93   *The son of*   Shawn Tully, "A Deal Too Far," *Fortune*, November 8, 1999. Thomas Wyman, "Making of a Mogul," *Indianapolis Star*, April 29, 2000. United States Census Bureau: Terra Haute, Indiana.

Page 93   *Population 60,000*   United States Census Bureau: Terra Haute, Indiana. http://quickfacts.census.gov/qfd/states/18/1875428.html.

Page 93   *Someone who didn't*   Interview with Hilbert associate.

Page 93   *Hilbert dropped out*   Shawn Tully, "A Deal Too Far," *Fortune*, November 8, 1999. Thomas Wyman, "Making of a Mogul," *Indianapolis Star*, April 29, 2000.

Page 93   *By the mid-1970s*   Thomas Wyman, "Making of a Mogul," *Indianapolis Star*, April 29, 2000.

Page 93   *His father loaned*   Interview with Stephen Hilbert. Shawn Tully, "A Deal Too Far," *Fortune*, November 8, 1999. Thomas Wyman, "Making of a Mogul," *Indianapolis Star*, April 29, 2000.

Page 93   *And he charmed*   Shawn Tully, "A Deal Too Far," *Fortune*, November 8, 1999. Thomas Wyman, "Making of a Mogul," *Indianapolis Star*, April 29, 2000.

Page 93   *In 1979, Conseco*   Shawn Tully, "A Deal Too Far," *Fortune*, November 8, 1999. Thomas Wyman, "Making of a Mogul," *Indianapolis Star*, April 29, 2000.

Page 93   *From there it*   Thomas Wyman, "Making of a Mogul," *Indianapolis Star*, April 29, 2000.

Page 93   *Hilbert bought more than*   Thomas Wyman, "Making of a Mogul," *Indianapolis Star*, April 29, 2000. Debra Sparks, "Conseco's Morning After," *Business Week*, June 4, 2000. Greg Andrews, "Conseco Pouring Millions into Entertainment Ventures," *Indianapolis Business Journal*, October 24, 1993.

Page 94   *At one stage*   "The Prize," *Forbes*, May 19, 1997, www .forbes.com/forbes/1997/0519/5910166a.html. Retrieved June 20, 2014.

Page 94   *There were always*   Floyd Norris, "Steve Hilbert Made $172 Million, and Ran Out of Cash," *New York Times*, May 26, 2000.

Page 94   *His 23,000-square-foot*   Mark Tatge with Evan Hessel, "It's Not Over," *Forbes*, December 22, 2003. Dann Denny, "Lifestyles of the Rich and Famous: A Monet over the Mantle, His-and-Hers Harleys, an Indoor Basketball Court: How Insurance Mogul Steve Hilbert Spends Indy's Biggest Paycheck," *Indianapolis Monthly*, November 1995.

Page 94   *Indiana is a*   Interview with Reed Oslan.

Page 94   *In the foyer*   Susan Guyett, "'H' Marked Hilberts' Spot," *Indianapolis Star*, February 16, 2005.

Page 94   *Lou Harry, the*   Ibid.

Page 94   *There were a*   Ibid.

Page 94   *The estate had*   Dann Denny, "Lifestyles of the Rich and Famous: A Monet over the Mantle, His-and-Hers Harleys, an Indoor Basketball Court: How Insurance Mogul Steve Hilbert Spends Indy's Biggest Paycheck," *Indianapolis Monthly*, November 1995. Joseph Hallinan and Mitchell Pacelle, "Turn of Fortune: In Collection Battle, Conseco Ex-CEO Is Fighting Back—Mr. Hilbert Borrowed Millions to Buy Company Stock; Then, It Went Under—His Wife's Holdings Grow," *Wall Street Journal*, December 5, 2003.

Page 94   *"A phenomenal body"*   Interview with associate of Stephen Hilbert.

Page 94   *lept out of*   Interviews with Reed Oslan and Chuck Cremens. Wallace Matthews, "Derby Forecast Is Fair and Wild," *New York Post*, May 1, 1999. Thomas Wyman, "Making of a Mogul," *Indianapolis Star*, April 29, 2000.

Page 94   *Two weeks later*   Interviews with Reed Oslan and Chuck Cremens.

Page 94   *Hilbert married Tomisue*   Joseph Hallinan and Mitchell Pacelle, "Turn of Fortune: In Collection Battle, Conseco Ex-CEO Is Fighting Back," *Wall Street Journal*, December 5, 2003.

Page 94   *He "respected" the fact*   Shawn Tully, "A Deal Too Far," *Fortune*, November 8, 1999.

Page 95   *The couple acquired*   Joseph T. Hallinan and Mitchell Pacelle, "In Collection Battle, Conseco Ex-CEO Is Fighting Back," *Wall Street Journal*, December 5, 2003.

Page 95   *Designed by Tomisue*   Interview with Charles Cremens.

Page 95   *And a place*   Dann Denny, "Lifestyles of the Rich and Famous: A Monet over the Mantle, His-and-Hers Harleys, an Indoor Basketball Court: How Insurance Mogul Steve Hilbert Spends Indy's Biggest Paycheck," *Indianapolis Monthly*, November 1995. Joseph T. Hallinan and Mitchell Pacelle, "In Collection Battle, Conseco Ex-CEO Is Fighting Back," *Wall Street Journal*, December 5, 2003.

Page 95   *They owned a*   "Hilbert's Horse Comes in Second," Associated Press, May 2, 1997.

Page 95   *The duo was*   Thomas Wyman, "Making of a Mogul," *Indianapolis Star*, April 29, 2000. Debra Stark, "Conseco's Morning After," *Business Week*, June 4, 2000.

Page 95   *The Hilberts attended*   Thomas Wyman, "Making of a Mogul," *Indianapolis Star*, April 29, 2000. John Fritze, "Woes Limit Reach of Charitable Arm; Endowment's Annual Contributions Shrank from $3 Million to $860,000 in a Year," *Indianapolis Star*, August 10, 2002. Jeff Swiatek, "Health of Hospital Is in Doctor's Hands," *Indianapolis Star*, September 29, 2002.

Page 95   *The SEC reported*   "In the Matter of Rollin Dick, CPA, Respondent. Order Instituting Administrative Proceedings Pursuant to Rule 102(e) of the Commission's Rules of Practice, Making Findings, and Imposing Remedial Sanctions." Administrative Proceedings, United States of America before the Securities and Exchange Commission, July 25, 2006.

Page 95   *Gary Wendt saved*   Floyd Norris and Alex Berenson, "Policyholders Won't Be Harmed, Conseco, Regulators Say," *New York Times*, December 19, 2002.

Page 95   *But that left*   Joseph T. Hallinan, "Wendt Fails to Deliver Conseco's Turnaround," *Wall Street Journal*, August 8, 2002.

Page 95   *In October 2002*   Floyd Norris and Alex Berenson, "Policyholders Won't Be Harmed, Conseco, Regulators Say," *New York Times*, December 19, 2002.

Page 95   *And was replaced*   Interview with Charles Cremens.

Page 95   *A "firefighter"*   Interview with Reed Oslan.

Page 95   *He'd worked with*   Interviews with Charles Cremens, Wayne Maggin, and Reed Oslan.

Page 96   *Charles "Chuck" Cremens*   Ibid.

Page 96   *When he heard*   Author's observation.

Page 96   *Shea summoned Cremens*   Interview with Charles Cremens.

Page 96   *Somehow—he never*   Ibid.

Page 96   *All these situations*   Interviews with Charles Cremens and Reed Oslan.

Page 96   *"Chuck is a*   Interview with Reed Oslan.

Page 97   *"It was like*   Ibid.

Page 97   *In 2003 Steve Hilbert*   Joseph Hallinan and Mitchell Pacelle, "Turn of Fortune: In Collection Battle, Conseco Ex-CEO Is Fighting Back," *Wall Street Journal*, December 5, 2003.

Page 97   *Cremens and Oslan*   Interviews with Charles Cremens and Reed Oslan. Joann S. Lublin, "Dunning the Deposed Boss," *Wall Street Journal*, July 9, 2004.

Page 97   *But Cremens and*   Interview with Reed Oslan.

Page 97   *With the help*   Interviews with Charles Cremens and Reed Oslan.

Page 97   *Rollin Dick—who*   Ibid. Greg Andrews, "Dicks' Trust under Attack," *Indianapolis Business Journal*, February 7, 2005. Steven Taub, "Conseco Settles with Former CFO," CFO.com, March 14, 2005.

Page 97   *"They have the*   Interview with Reed Oslan.

Page 97   *Much to the*   Interviews with Chuck Cremens and Reed Oslan.

Page 97   *The discovery caused*   Interview with Chuck Cremens.

Page 98   *And then there*   Interviews with Chuck Cremens and Reed Oslan.

Page 98   *The two had*   Jessica Burke, "Insurer Sells House Received in Settlement with Former Exec," *Broward Daily Business Review*, September 29, 2006. Joseph T. Hallinan, "Playing Hide & Seek with Cash: More Firms, like Conseco, Find It's No Game Trying to Reclaim Bad Loans to Former Executives," *Wall Street Journal*, February 9, 2005.

Page 98   *Oslan knew that*   Interview with Reed Oslan.

Page 98   *Immediately Oslan obtained*   Ibid.

Page 98   *It was intriguing*   Joseph T. Hallinan, "Playing Hide & Seek with Cash: More Firms, like Conseco, Find It's No Game Trying to Reclaim Bad Loans to Former Executives," *Wall Street Journal*, February 9, 2005. Bill W. Hornaday, "Ex-Conseco Official and Husband Defend Move," *Indianapolis News/Indianapolis Star*, June 30, 2004.

Page 98   *The Cuneos were*   Jessica Burke, "Insurer Sells House Received in Settlement with Former Exec," *Broward Daily Business Review*, September 29, 2006.

Page 98   *By 2005 most*   Interview with Reed Oslan.

Page 98   *There was still*   Ibid.

Page 98   *The young Mrs. Hilbert*   Ibid.

Page 98   *Cremens had never*   Interview with Charles Cremens.

Page 98   *Neither he nor*   Interviews with Charles Cremens and Reed Oslan.

Page 99   *One of Hilbert's*   "Former Conseco Head Says He Is Broke," Associated Press Newswires, November 16, 2004. Joseph Hallinan and Mitchell Pacelle, "Turn of Fortune: In Collection

Battle, Conseco Ex-CEO Is Fighting Back," *Wall Street Journal*, December 5, 2003. Joann S. Lublin, "Dunning the Deposed Boss," *Wall Street Journal*, July 9, 2004. Joseph T. Hallinan, "Where Did the CEO's Money Go?" *Globe and Mail* (Canada), February 9, 2005.

Page 99 *Oslan cried foul* Interview with Reed Oslan.

Page 99 *Tomisue Hilbert rebutted* "Former Conseco Head Says He Is Broke," Associated Press Newswires, November 16, 2004.

Page 99 *In 2006 Tomisue* Interview with Reed Oslan.

Page 99 *He told the court* Ken MacFadyen, "Suit Targets Hilbert's Private Equity Profits," *Investment Dealers Digest*, October 23, 2006.

Page 99 *Meanwhile, the Hilberts* Interviews with Charles Cremens and Reed Oslan.

Page 99 *"The lap pool"* Interview with Reed Oslan.

Page 99 *Finally, on December 7* J. K. Wall, "'It's All Over Now,'" *Indianapolis Star*, December 7, 2006.

Page 99 *Which would eventually* Shira Ovide, "The Twisted History of Conseco's Opulent Indiana Mansion," *Wall Street Journal* (Deal Journal blog), October 7, 2010, http://blogs.wsj.com/deals/2010/10/07/the-twisted-history-of-consecos-opulent-indiana-mansion/. Retrieved June 20, 2014.

Page 99 *But they held on to* J. K. Wall, "'It's All Over Now,'" *Indianapolis Star*, December 7, 2006.

Page 99 *Both sides declared* Ibid.

Page 99 *The couple moved* Interview with Reed Oslan.

Page 100 *The Hilberts mailed* Susan Guyett, "Greetings from Our Family," *Indianapolis Star*, December 25, 2005.

Page 100 *Reed Oslan would* Interview with Reed Oslan.

Page 100 *"Tomisue never sank* Interview with Stephen Hilbert.

Page 100 *In 2008, the* Leslie Scism and Mark Maremont, "Life, Death and Insurance: Indiana's $15 Million Mystery," *Wall Street Journal*, April 12, 2010.

Page 100 *Suzy Tomlinson was* Ibid.

Page 100 *AIG sued for* "Insurance Dispute Takes Odd Turn; Case C over $15M Life Policy for Hilbert's Mother-in-Law Sparks a Probe, Fight for Cash," *Indianapolis Business Journal*, July 13, 2009.

Page 100   *The Hilberts also*   Ibid. Leslie Scism and Mark Maremont, "Family Sues AIG over Policy on Mom's Life," *Wall Street Journal Online*, July 23, 2010. Leslie Scism and Mark Maremont, "Judge Allows 'Death Bet' Case," *Wall Street Journal Online*, October 5, 2010.

Page 100   *The case was*   "Tomisue Hilbert Settles Suit over $15M Policy," *Indianapolis Business Journal*, June 27, 2011.

Page 100   *An investigation ultimately*   "Tomisue Hilbert Investigates Mother's Death, $15M Policy," *Indianapolis Business Journal*, April 17, 2010.

Page 100   *Just as things*   "Menard Ousts Hilbert from Investment Firm; Hardware King Says Private Equity Bets Fueled Big Losses," *Indianapolis Business Journal*, March 11, 2013.

Page 100   *Menard claimed that*   J. K. Wall, "Hilbert Says Menard Has 'Picked on the Wrong People,'" *Indianapolis Business Journal*, November 13, 2013. "Menard Ousts Hilbert from Investment Firm; Hardware King Says Private Equity Bets Fueled Big Losses," *Indianapolis Business Journal*, March 11, 2013.

Page 101   *Three months later*   "Sparks Fly in Lawsuit Dismissal; Tomisue Accuses Menard of Sexual Harassment," *Indianapolis Business Journal*, June 17, 2013.

Page 101   *Also embroiled in*   IBJ Staff, "Trump Wins Court Battle with Menard over Skin-Care Products Deal," *Indianapolis Business Journal*, November 26, 2013. Erin Carlyle, "Lawsuit Alleges Hardware Billionaire John Menard Pressured Former Business Partner's Wife for Sex," *Forbes*, June 20, 2013. Sadie Whitlock, "'It Really Damaged My Brand': Melania Trump Seeks $50 Million in Damages After Beauty Firm 'Failed to Promote' Her Skincare Line," *Mail Online*, November 28, 2013.

Page 101   *Chuck Cremens and*   Interview with Reed Oslan.

Page 101   *That Tomisue wore*   Susan Guyett, "Hilberts Attend Trumps' Nuptials," *Indianapolis Star*, January 28, 2005.

Page 101   *Reports show that*   "Donald Trump Buys Estate in Caribbean," *World Property Channel*, October 11, 2013.

Page 101   *The purchase was*   J. K. Wall, "Hilbert Says Menard Has 'Picked on the Wrong People,'" *Indianapolis Business Journal*, November 13, 2013.

Page 101   *Hilbert believed that Trump*   Interview with Stephen Hilbert.

Page 101   *Reed Oslan remembered*   Interview with Reed Oslan.

Page 101   *Oslan couldn't help*   Ibid.

Page 101   *plus a letter*   Interviews with Reed Oslan and Charles Cremens. "Arbitration Award," *Carmel Fifth LLC and Conseco v. Donald J. Trump 767 Manager and Trump 767 Management LLC*, American Arbitration Association, New York, New York.

Page 102   *Gary Wendt allegedly*   Interviews with Reed Oslan and Chuck Cremens.

Page 102   *"He should've*   Interview with Reed Oslan.

Chapter 9 Donald's "Force Majeure"

Page 103   *Pardon me if*   Direct examination of Donald Trum, *Donald J. Trump v. Carmel Fifth, LLC*, State Supreme Court of New York, Country of New York.

Page 103   *In March 2001*   Deposition of Andrew Hubregsen, *Donald J. Trump v. Carmel Fifth, LLC*, State Supreme Court of New York, County of New York. Interviews with Chuck Cremens and Andrew Hubregsen.

Page 103   *He could buy*   "Agreement," Conseco Inc. and Donald Trump, July 3, 2001.

Page 104   *He could even*   Ibid.

Page 104   *Conseco just wanted*   Deposition of Andrew Hubregsen, *Donald J. Trump v. Carmel Fifth, LLC*, State Supreme Court of New York, County of New York.

Page 104   *Andrew Hubregsen, Conseco's*   Deposition of Andrew Hubregsen, *Donald J. Trump v. Carmel Fifth, LLC*, State Supreme Court of New York, County of New York. "Arbitration Award," *Carmel Fifth LLC and Conseco v. Donald J. Trump 767 Manager and Trump 767 Management LLC*, American Arbitration Association, New York, New York.

Page 104   *Trump had clearly*   Deposition of Andrew Hubregsen, *Donald J. Trump v. Carmel Fifth, LLC*, State Supreme Court of New York, County of New York.

Page 104   *Though Trump's office*   "Arbitration Award," *Carmel Fifth LLC and Conseco v. Donald J. Trump 767 Manager and Trump 767 Management LLC*, American Arbitration Association, New York, New York.

Page 104   *But at Conseco*   Deposition of Andrew Hubregsen, *Donald J. Trump v. Carmel Fifth, LLC*, Supreme Court of the State of New York, County of New York.

Page 104   *People close to*   Interview with Robert Horowitz.

Page 104   *On July 3*   "Petition to Vacate Award of Arbitration," *Donald J. Trump v. Carmel Fifth, LLC*, State Supreme Court of New York, County of New York (undated). *Carmel Fifth LLC v. Donald J. Trump*, American Arbitration Association, case number 13115 00829 02.

Page 104   *If Conseco hadn't*   Deposition of Andrew Hubregsen, *Donald J. Trump v. Carmel Fifth, LLC*, Supreme Court of the State of New York, County of New York.

Page 104   *"Foot-dragging"*   "Arbitration Award" *Carmel Fifth LLC and Conseco v. Donald J. Trump 767 Manager and Trump 769 Management LLC*, American Arbitration Association, New York, New York.

Page 104   *When asked about*   Interview with Donald Trump.

Page 104   *In 2000 he had*   Interviews with Benjamin Lambert and Roy March.

Page 105   *Trump also had*   Interview with Samuel Zell.

Page 105   *Trump interpreted this*   Interview with Donald Trump.

Page 105   *Zell was indeed thinking*   Interview with Samual Zell.

Page 105   *The* New York Times   Diana B. Henriques, "Trump Sues Pritzker as a Feud Goes Public," *New York Times*, July 29, 1993.

Page 105   *It was eventually*   Charles V. Bagli, "Trump Sells Hyatt Share to Pritzkers," *New York Times*, October 8, 1996.

Page 105   *By summer 2001*   "Proposed findings of facts and conclusions of law," *Carmel Fifth v. 767 Manager and Donald J. Trump*, American Arbitration Association, New York, New York, case number 13115 00829 02.

Page 105   *On August 6*   *Carmel Fifth LLC v. Donald J. Trump*, American Arbitration Association, case number 13115 00829 02.

Page 105   *At the bottom*   "Arbitration Award," *Carmel Fifth LLC and Conseco v. Donald J. Trump 767 Manager and Trump 767 Management LLC*, American Arbitration Association, New York, New York.

Page 105   *Conseco officially rejected*   Ibid.

Page 105   *"Tempers flared,"*   Ibid.

Page 105   *The bank was unable*   "Petition to Vacate Award of Arbitration," *Donald J. Trump v. Carmel Fifth, LLC*, Supreme Court of the State of New York, County of New York (undated).

Page 105   *Trump had to*   Interview with Donald Trump.

Page 105   *On October 4*   "Complaint," *Donald J. Trump v. Conseco Inc, Carmel Fifth LLC and 767 LLC.*

Page 106   *In December 2001*   Interview with Charles Cremens.

Page 106   *On January 14*   "Petition to Vacate Award of Arbitration," *Donald J. Trump v. Carmel Fifth, LLC*, Supreme Court of the State of New York, County of New York (undated).

Page 106   *Trump had 60 days*   "Arbitration Award," *Carmel Fifth LLC and Conseco v. Donald J. Trump 767 Manager and Trump 767 Management LLC*, American Arbitration Association, New York, New York.

Page 106   *On March 13*   "Petition to Vacate Award of Arbitration," *Donald J. Trump v. Carmel Fifth, LLC*, Supreme Court of the State of New York, County of New York (undated). Deposition of Andrew Hubregsen, *Donald J. Trump v. Carmel Fifth, LLC*, Supreme Court of the State of New York, County of New York.

Page 106   *He claimed Conseco*   "Arbitration Award," *Carmel Fifth LLC and Conseco v. Donald J. Trump 767 Manager and Trump 767 Management LLC*, American Arbitration Association, New York, New York.

Page 106   *Trump later said*   Interview with Donald Trump.

Page 106   *The case went*   Interview with Reed Oslan.

Page 106   *The hearing dragged*   Ibid.

Page 106   *The whole process*   Ibid.

Page 106   *In January 2003*   Wayne Maggin affidavit, *Solow Building Corporation v. Carmel 5th LLC*, Court of the Chancery of Delaware in or for New Castle County.

Page 106   *Maggin told his*   Interview with Benjamin Lambert.

Page 106   *"I felt it*   Interview with Donald Trump.

Page 106   *Lambert's view was*   Interview with Benjamin Lambert.

Page 106   *Within 24 hours*   Interview with Roy March.

Page 107   *In March 2003*   "Application for entry of an order (1) authorizing the employment and retention of Eastdil Realty Company, L.L.C. as debtor's real estate agent and (2) approving payment of a professional service fee," *Conseco, Inc. et al. debtors*, in the United States Bankruptcy Court for the Northern District of Illinois, Eastern Division, March 6, 2003.

Page 107   *Trump tried to*   Interview with Donald Trump.

Page 107   *Lambert heard this*   Interview with Benjamin Lambert.

Page 107   *The court ruled*   "Affidavit and disclosure in support of application for entry of an order (1) authorizing the employment and retention of Eastdil Realty Company L.L.C. as debtor's real estate agent and (2) approving payment of a professional service fee," *Conseco, Inc. et al. debtors*, in the United States Bankruptcy Court for the Northern District of Illinois, Eastern Division, March 17, 2003.

Page 107   *In May, the*   Interview with Reed Oslan.

Page 107   *Trump sounded furious*   Direct examination of Donald Trump, *Donald J. Trump v. Carmel Fifth, LLC*, Supreme Court of the State of New York, County of New York.

Page 107   *On May 28*   *Carmel Fifth LLC v. Donald J. Trump*, American Arbitration Association, case number 13115 00829 02.

Page 107   *Trump declared the*   Interview with Donald Trump.

Page 107   *And when it*   Ibid.

Page 107   *He's not one*   Interview with Abraham Wallach.

Chapter 10 Paradise, Briefly

Page 109   *Harry Macklow knew*   Interview with Harry Macklowe.

Page 109   *Macklowe pestered George*   Ibid.

Page 109   *Dan Shannon accompanied*   Interviews with Harry Macklowe, Daniel Shannon, and Peter Bohlin.

Page 109   *Macklowe recalled*   Ibid.

Page 110   *"Smallest skyscraper"*   Interview with Peter Bohlin.

Page 110   *The answer, according*   Interviews with Harry Macklowe, Dan Shannon, Karl Backus, and Peter Bohlin.

Page 110   *"The point of*   Interview with Daniel Shannon.

Page 110   *Said Macklowe: "[Jobs]*   Interview with Harry Macklowe.

Page 110   *Macklowe knew that*   Interviews with Harry Macklowe and Dan Shannon.

Page 110   *Around two in*   Ibid.

Page 111   *Now Macklowe had*   Interview with Harry Macklowe.

Page 111 *Jobs phoned* Interviews with Harry Macklowe and Dan Shannon.

Page 111 *Macklowe felt that* Interview with Harry Macklowe.

Page 111 *For Macklowe to* Ibid.

Page 111 *"None of these* Interview with Robert Sorin.

Page 111 *"I did them* Interview with Harry Macklowe.

Page 111 *Macklowe also got* Ibid.

Page 111 *On May 19, 2006* Steve Lohr, "Apple, a Success at Stores, Bets Big on Fifth Avenue," *New York Times*, May 19, 2006. Steven Matarzzaro, "Apple Store Fifth Avenue Grand Opening," YouTube.com, www.youtube.com/watch?v=eQjFPTQUU5g. Uploaded May 21, 2006.

Page 112 *It was such* Interview with Robert Sorin.

Page 112 *The store attracted* Jerry Unseem, "How Apple Became the Best Retailer in America," *Fortune*, March 8, 2007.

Page 112 *Though still known* Author's observation.

Page 112 *At the opening* Interview with friend of Linda Macklowe.

Page 112 *With the retail* Interview with Harry Macklowe.

Page 112 *Thomas "Tommy" H. Lee* Ibid.

Page 112 *He put aside* "Company Overview of Thomas H. Lee Capital Management LLC," Businessweek.com, http://investing .businessweek.com/research/stocks/private/snapshot.asp?privcapId= 25953500.

Page 113 *Macklowe phoned him* Interview with Harry Macklowe.

Page 113 *Macklowe had an* Ibid.

Page 113 *Weill now has* Interview with Ira Millstein.

Page 113 *Joseph "Joe" Perella* Interview with Joseph Perella.

Page 113 *Macklowe approached Perella* Ibid.

Page 113 *Perella created a* Ibid.

Page 113 *Perella told Macklowe* Ibid.

Page 113 *Leases in the* 767 Fifth Avenue: August 2006 Rent Roll.

Page 113 *Fisher wouldn't be* Interview with Joseph Perella.

Page 114 *The building soon* Lance Leighton, "The Best Office Buildings in Midtown Manhattan," Hedge Fund Spaces, March 11, 2014, www.hedgefundspaces.com/tag/gm-building/. Retrieved June 20, 2014. Lance Leighton, "New Availability at the GM Building—767 Fifth Avenue," Hedge Fund Spaces, February 26,

2014, www.hedgefundspaces.com/2014/02/new-availability-at-the-gm-building-767-fifth-avenue/. Retrieved June 20, 2014.

Page 114   *This concerned the*   Interview with Ira Millstein.

Page 114   *Carl Icahn, who*   Ibid.

Page 114   *In November 2006*   Deposition of Harry Macklowe, *Meadow Star LLC v. Harry Macklowe and WH Rome Partners LLC*, Supreme Court of the State of New York, County of New York, October 29, 2009.

Page 114   *SL Green Realty was*   "Memorandum of Law in Support of Defendant's Motion for Summary Judgment," *Meadow Star LLC v. Harry Macklowe and WH Rome Partners LLC*, Supreme Court of the State of New York, County of New York.

Page 114   *The initial offer*   "Plaintiff's Memorandum of Law in Opposition to Defendant's Motion for Summary Judgment," Herbert Beigel & Associates and Storch Amini & Munves PC. Deposition of Carl Icahn, *Meadow Star LLC v. Harry Macklowe and WH Rome Partners LLC*, Supreme Court of the State of New York, County of New York, October 21, 2009.

Page 114   *Time, though, was*   Deposition of Carl Icahn, *Meadow Star LLC v. Harry Macklowe and WH Rome Partners LLC*, Supreme Court of the State of New York, County of New York, October 21, 2009.

Page 114   *They had to*   "Memorandum of Law in Support of Defendant's Motion for Summary Judgment," *Meadow Star LLC v. Harry Macklowe and WH Rome Partners LLC*, Supreme Court of the State of New York, County of New York.

Page 114   *On November 15*   Memorandum of Law in Support of Defendant's Motion for Summary Judgment," *Meadow Star LLC v. Harry Macklowe and WH Rome Partners LLC*, Supreme Court of the State of New York, County of New York.

Page 114   *Billy Macklowe later*   Deposition of William Macklowe, *Meadow Star LLC v. Harry Macklowe and WH Rome Partners LLC,* Supreme Court of the State of New York, County of New York, October 29, 2009.

Page 114   *Advising the Macklowes*   Interview with Andrew Bednar.

Page 115   *By late November*   Deposition of Carl Icahn, *Meadow Star LLC v. Harry Macklowe and WH Rome Partners LLC*, Supreme Court of the State of New York, County of New York, October 21, 2009.

Page 115   *They were scrambling*   Interviews with Robert Horowitz and Deutsche Bank executive. "Plaintiff's Memorandum of Law in Opposition to Defendant's Motion for Summary Judgment," Herbert Beigel & Associates and Storch Amini & Munves PC.

Page 115   *Fortress promised to*   Interviews with Robert Horowitz, Steven Stuart, and Eric Schwartz.

Page 115   *This was not*   Deposition of Carl Icahn, *Meadow Star LLC v. Harry Macklowe and WH Rome Partners LLC*, Supreme Court of the State of New York, County of New York, October 21, 2009.

Page 115   *Macklowe was cooling*   Interviews with Robert Horowitz, Steven Stuart, and Eric Schwartz and former Deutsche Bank executives.

Page 115   *"He gave Fortress*   Interview with Robert Horowitz.

Page 115   *Icahn went ahead*   "Memorandum of Law in Support of Defendant's Motion for Summary Judgment," *Meadow Star LLC v. Harry Macklowe and WH Rome Partners LLC*, Supreme Court of the State of New York, County of New York. Terry Pristin, "Icahn Tries a Solo Bid for Reckson but Is Rejected," *New York Times*, December 5, 2006.

Page 115   *He later sued*   "Complaint," *Meadow Star LLC v. Harry Macklowe and WH Rome Partners LLC*, Supreme Court of the State of New York, County of New York.

Page 115   *The case was*   "Judgment on Jury Verdict," *Meadow Star LLC v. Harry Macklowe and WH Rome Partners LLC*, Supreme Court of the State of New York, County of New York.

Chapter 11 Mr. Toad's Wild Ride

Page 117   *By the end*   Interview with Robert Horowitz.

Page 118   *Rob Horowitz wrote*   Ibid.

Page 118   *Horowitz documented the*   Notes of Robert Horowitz.

Page 118   *He drove to*   Interview with Harry Macklowe.

Page 118   *He bought a*   Michael Calderone, "Macklowe's Mansion," *New York Observer*, March 20, 2006. Steve Cuozzo, "Macklowe's March—Plans Hotel/Condos for Midtown Corner," *New York Post*, March 7, 2006.

Page 118   *And in early*   Braden Keil, "Gimme Shelter," *New York Post*, January 28, 2006.

Page 118   *The Drake was*   Jessica Dailey, "Remembering NYC's Grandest Forgotten Hotels, in Pictures," Curbed.com, June 26, 2013, http://ny.curbed.com/archives/2013/06/26/remembering_nycs_grandest_forgotten_hotels_in_photos.php. Retrieved June 20, 2014.

Page 118   *Deutsche Bank provided*   Interview with Robert Horowitz.

Post 118   *Harry planned to*   Steve Cuozzo, "Holdouts Give Macklowe Fits," *New York Post*, April 25, 2006.

Page 118   *He encountered opposition*   Ibid.

Page 118   *Those who really*   Interviews with Robert Horowitz and Robert Sorin.

Page 118   *"As good as*   Interview with Samuel Zell.

Page 118   *Doug Harmon described*   Interview with Douglas Harmon.

Page 119   *He was understated*   Author's observation. David Carey and John E. Morris, *King of Capital: The Remarkable Rise, Fall, and Rise Again of Steve Schwartzman and Blackstone* (New York: Crown Business, 2010), 242.

Page 119   *He had earned*   Interview with Jonathan Gray.

Page 119   *Under his watch*   Ibid.

Page 119   *Worth about $41 billion*   David Roeder, "Equity Office Party," *Chicago Sun-Times*, February 6, 2007.

Page 119   *EOP had 662*   David Carey and John E. Morris, *King of Capital: The Remarkable Rise, Fall, and Rise Again of Steve Schwartzman and Blackstone* (New York: Crown Business, 2010), 240.

Page 119   *EOP was owned*   Jennifer Forsyth, "Vornado CEO Covets Equity Office," *Wall Street Journal*, January 22, 2007. Michael Oneal and Steve Mills, "Zell's Big Gamble," *Chicago Tribune*, January 2013.

Page 119   *"Prices of office*   Michael Stoler, "Leaders Forecast Broken Records for Office Space," *New York Sun,* May 11, 2006.

Page 119   *Even so, Zell*   Interview with Samuel Zell.

Page 119   *The process began*   Interview with Jonathan Gray. David Carey and John E. Morris, *King of Capital: The Remarkable Rise, Fall, and Rise Again of Steve Schwartzman and Blackstone* (New York: Crown Business, 2010), 239.

Page 119   *"We saw we*   Interview with Jonathan Gray.

Page 120   *By November he*   Interview with Jonathan Gray. David Carey and John E. Morris, *King of Capital: The Remarkable Rise, Fall, and Rise Again of Steve Schwartzman and Blackstone* (New York: Crown Business, 2010), 251.

Page 120   *Gray couldn't afford*   Ibid.

Page 120   *"The key," he*   Interview with Samuel Zell.

Page 120   *Initially it was*   Ibid. David Carey and John E. Morris, *King of Capital: The Remarkable Rise, Fall, and Rise Again of Steve Schwartzman and Blackstone* (New York: Crown Business, 2010), 245–246.

Page 120   *What Zell wanted*   David Carey and John E. Morris, *King of Capital: The Remarkable Rise, Fall, and Rise Again of Steve Schwartzman and Blackstone* (New York: Crown Business, 2010), 247.

Page 120   *He wanted* Godfather   Interview with Samuel Zell.

Page 120   *Gray knew the*   Interview with Jonathan Gray.

Page 120   *This was, after all*   David Carey and John E. Morris, *King of Capital: The Remarkable Rise, Fall, and Rise Again of Steve Schwartzman and Blackstone* (New York: Crown Business, 2010), 246.

Page 120   *What he was*   Interview with Jonathan Gray.

Page 120   *He was already*   Ibid.

Page 120   *To Sam Zell's*   David Carey and John E. Morris, *King of Capital: The Remarkable Rise, Fall, and Rise Again of Steve Schwartzman and Blackstone* (New York: Crown Business, 2010), 248.

Page 120   *Finally, on January 15*   Ibid.

Page 120   *He received a reply*   Ibid.

Page 121   *On January 22*   David Carey and John E. Morris, *King of Capital: The Remarkable Rise, Fall, and Rise Again of Steve Schwartzman and Blackstone* (New York: Crown Business, 2010), 250.

Page 121   *Gray knew there*   Interview with Jonathan Gray.

Page 121   *So Gray asked*   Interview with Jonathan Gray. David Carey and John E. Morris, *King of Capital: The Remarkable Rise, Fall, and Rise Again of Steve Schwartzman and Blackstone* (New York: Crown Business, 2010), 250.

Page 121   *Harry Macklowe first*   Interviews with Jonathan Gray, Roy March, and Anthony Myers.

Page 121   *Roy March had*   Interviews with Jonathan Gray and Roy March.

Page 121   *Gray knew Macklowe*   Interview with Jonathan Gray.

Page 121   *"Seven million square feet*   Ibid.

Page 121   *From Gray's perspective*   Ibid.

Page 122   *Harry told Gray*   Interviews with Jonathan Gray and Anthony Myers.

Page 122   *There was only*   Interview with Roy March.

Page 122   *Myers, for one*   Ibid.

Page 122   *They agreed on*   Interviews with Roy March and Anthony Myers.

Page 122   *Macklowe asked Roy March*   Ibid.

Page 122   *Rob Horowitz called*   Interviews with Rob Horowitz and Eric Schwartz.

Page 122   *The next two*   Interview with Roy March.

Page 122   *Roy March came*   Ibid.

Page 122   *March promised Gray*   Interviews with Jonathan Gray and Roy March.

Page 123   *What Gray and*   Interview with Anthony Myers.

Page 123   *Gray soon found*   Interview with Jonathan Gray.

Page 123   *"I would never*   Interview with Richard Kincaid.

Page 123   *On Sunday, February 4*   Interview with Jonathan Gray. David Carey and John E. Morris, *King of Capital: The Remarkable Rise, Fall, and Rise Again of Steve Schwartzman and Blackstone* (New York: Crown Business, 2010), 252.

Page 123   *Gray saw his*   Interview with Jonathan Gray. David Carey and John E. Morris, *King of Capital: The Remarkable Rise, Fall, and Rise Again of Steve Schwartzman and Blackstone* (New York: Crown Business, 2010), 253.

Page 123   *He knew Zell*   Interview with Jonathan Gray.

Page 123   *Gray called Macklowe*   Interviews with Jonathan Gray, Robert Horowitz, and Robert Sorin.

Page 123   *Sorin recalls his*   Interview with Robert Sorin.

Page 124   *Sorin felt it*   Ibid.

Page 124   *"He was very*   Interview with Macklowe business associate.

Page 124   *"The biggest, trickiest*   Ibid.

Page 124   *By Tuesday, Eric*   Interview with Robert Horowitz.

Page 124   *Stuart presented a*   Ibid.

Page 124   *But—and it*   Interview with Robert Horowitz.

Page 124 *Stuart took this* Interviews with Peter Briger and Steven Stuart.

Page 124 *Stuart showed him* Interview with Steven Stuart.

Page 124 *Briger agreed to* Interviews with Peter Briger and Steven Stuart.

Page 125 *Rob Sorin watched* Interview with Robert Sorin.

Page 125 *Even Rob Horowitz* Interview with Robert Horowitz.

Page 125 *The team at* Interview with Jonathan Gray.

Page 125 *Mike Fascitelli heard* Interview with Michael Fascitelli.

Page 125 *Macklowe went on* Interviews with Jonathan Gray, Roy March, and Anthony Myers.

Page 125 *He now says* Interview with Harry Macklowe.

Page 125 *Once Harry had* Interview with Anthony Myers.

Page 125 *He left the bulk* Ibid.

Page 125 *Billy Macklowe was* Interviews with Macklowe associates.

Page 125 *Every day* Interview with Anthony Myers.

Page 126 *The Macklowes were* Interview with Roy March.

Page 126 *For a reason* Interview with Anthony Myers.

Page 126 *But he went* Ibid.

Page 126 *The legal papers* Ibid.

Page 126 *Billy Macklowe looked* Interview with Macklowe associate.

Page 126 *"Billy was tense* Ibid.

Page 126 *A new page* Interview with Anthony Myers.

Page 127 *Back at Blackstone's* Ibid.

Page 127 *Forty-or-so* Ibid.

Page 127 *Jonathan Gray burst* Ibid.

Chapter 12 Tick Tock—A Year on the Clock

Page 129 *They had a* Interviews with Robert Sorin and Robert Horowitz.

Page 130 *Rob Sorin reflected* Interview with Robert Sorin.

Page 130 *The next day* Interview with Robert Horowitz.

Page 130 *On February 13* John Koblin, "Macklowes Stomping Back with Big Buy," *New York Observer*, February 26, 2007.

Page 130   *The Macklowe plan*   Interviews with Robert Sorin, Robert Horowitz, and Eric Schwartz.

Page 131   *A source on*   Interview with Deutsche Bank team member.

Page 131   *The general perception*   Interviews with Macklowe associates.

Page 131   *A* Fortune *magazine*   Devin Leonard, "Reckoning for a Real Estate Mogul," *Fortune*, February 15, 2008.

Page 131   *Linda was also*   Interview with friend of Linda Macklowe.

Page 131   *She told Rob*   Interview with Robert Horowitz.

Page 131   *Harry seemed uncharacteristically*   Interviews with Robert Horowitz and Eric Schwartz.

Page 131   *It was very*   Interview with Macklowe adviser.

Page 131   *Mike Fascitelli believed*   Interview with Michael Fascitelli.

Page 131   *Joe Perella saw*   Interview with Joseph Perella.

Page 131   *Perella recalled: "[Harry]*   Ibid.

Page 132   *But there was*   Interviews with Andrew Bednar, Joseph Perella, Robert Horowitz, and Eric Schwartz.

Page 132   *The problem with*   Ibid.

Page 132   *Eric Schwartz had*   Interview with Eric Schwartz.

Page 132   *And Perella never*   Interview with Joseph Perella.

Page 133   *Deutsche Bank told*   Interviews with Robert Horowitz and Eric Schwartz.

Page 133   *Perella Weinberg had*   Interviews with Andrew Bednar, Robert Horowitz, Joseph Perella, and Eric Schwartz.

Page 133   *Even Schwartz would*   Interview with Eric Schwartz.

Page 133   *So late that*   Interview with Robert Horowitz.

Page 133   *But Harry had*   Interview with Joseph Perella.

Page 133   *In September, Andrew*   Interview with Andrew Bednar.

Page 133   *Joe Perella was*   Interview with Joseph Perella.

Page 133   *He and Linda*   Joey Arak, "Mack Daddy Sinking Large Fortune in the Plaza," Curbed.com, June 7, 2008, http://ny.curbed.com/archives/2007/06/07/mack_daddy_sinking_large_fortune_into_plaza.php. Retrieved June 20, 2014. Matt Woosley, "The Biggest Real Estate Deals of 2007," ABCNews.com, December 7, 2007, http://abcnews.go.com/Business/IndustryInfo/story?id=3970611. Retrieved June 20, 2014.

Page 133   *He would later*   Interview with Harry Macklowe.

Page 134   *He invited a*   Interview with Macklowe associate.

Page 134   *Schwartz's team was*   Interview with Eric Schwartz.

Page 134   *On August 14*   Interview with Joseph Perella.

Page 134   *In October the*   Interview with Robert Sorin.

Page 135   *Harry didn't want*   Ibid.

Page 135   *But Eric Schwartz*   Interviews with Robert Horowitz, Eric Schwartz, and Robert Sorin.

Page 135   *So, reluctantly—and*   Interviews with Harry Macklowe and Robert Sorin.

Page 135   *"I was investing*   Interview with Harry Macklowe.

Page 135   *Rob Sorin was*   Interview with Robert Sorin.

Page 135   *In Sorin's mind*   Ibid.

Page 135   *On Sorin's advice*   Ibid.

Page 135   *Harry Macklowe now*   Interview with Robert Horowitz.

Page 135   *Horowitz believed he*   Ibid.

Page 136   *On November 10*   Electronic mail from Robert Horowitz to Harry and William Macklowe, November 10, 2007.

Page 136   *On November 12*   Electronic mail from Robert Horowitz to Harry and William Macklowe, November 12, 2007.

Page 136   *As we discussed*   Ibid.

Page 136   *Horowitz also mentioned*   Interview with Robert Horowitz.

Page 136   *On Saturday, November 17*   Electronic mail from Robert Horowitz to Harry and William Macklowe, November 17, 2007.

Page 136   *"No."*   Electronic mail from William Macklowe to Robert Horowitz, November 17, 2007.

Page 136   *Rob Sorin would*   Interview with Robert Horowitz.

Page 137   *"Believe me, if*   Ibid.

Page 137   *Horowitz, in turn*   Ibid.

Page 137   *Unlike Horowitz, Sorin*   Interview with Robert Sorin.

Page 137   *Increasingly, Horowitz found*   Interview with Robert Horowitz.

Page 137   *By January 2008*   Ibid.

Page 137   *As the new*   Interview with Robert Sorin.

Page 137   *On February 9*   Jennifer Forsyth, "Macklowe Gets Default Notice as Talks Stall with Lenders," *Wall Street Journal*, February 12,

2008. "Developer Harry Macklowe Served Notice of Default," Dow Jones Newswire, February 12, 2008.

Page 138   *The bank wanted to*   Interviews with Robert Sorin and Eric Schwartz. Jennifer S. Forsyth, "Real-Estate Credit Crisis Squeezes Macklowe," *Wall Street Journal*, February 1, 2008.

Page 138   *By the end*   Jennifer S. Forsyth, "Real-Estate Credit Crisis Squeezes Macklowe," *Wall Street Journal*, February 1, 2008. Daniel Geiger, "Macklowe to Hand EOP Portfolio Over to Bank," *Real Estate Weekly*, February 6, 2008.

Page 138   *Pete Briger gave*   Interview with Peter Briger.

Page 138   *Harry listed the*   Jennifer S. Forsyth, "Deutsche Bank Borrower Seeks to Sell Landmark," *Wall Street Journal*, January 16, 2008. Peter Slatin, "GM Building Sale Shows REIT Resilience," *Forbes*, May 27, 2008.

Page 138   *Harry was still so*   Interview with Robert Sorin and Roy March.

Page 138   *Billy, meanwhile, was*   Interviews with Paul Ingrassia, Jonathan Mechanic, Andrew Trickett, and Robert Sorin.

Page 138   *While Omers would*   Ibid.

Page 138   *Omers said it*   Interview with Andrew Trickett.

Page 138   *Still, the talks*   Ibid.

Page 138   *He pointed at*   Interview with Peter Briger and Andrew Trickett.

Page 138   *He was deliberately*   Ibid.

Page 138   *Billy Macklowe was*   Interviews with executives involved in negotiations.

Page 139   *Briger stayed for*   Interviews with Peter Briger and Andrew Trickett.

Page 139   *But six weeks*   Interview with Andrew Trickett.

Page 139   *Suddenly the Macklowes*   Ibid.

Page 139   *The Omers people were surprised*   Ibid.

Page 139   *Citigroup explained that*   Ibid.

Page 139   *There are all*   Interview with real estate accountants.

Page 139   *Omers was not*   Ibid.

Page 140   *In April and*   Interviews with Michael Fascitelli and Robert Sorin.

Page 140   *Once again, Fascitelli*   Interview with Michael Fascitelli.

Page 140   *For three weeks*   Ibid.

Page 140   *Jonathan Mechanic, a*   Interview with Jonathan Mechanic.

Page 140   *The drama of*   Interview with Michael Fascitelli.

Page 141   *But his family*   Ibid.

Page 141   *They were yelling*   Ibid.

Page 141   *"He [Harry] wanted*   Ibid.

Page 141   *Someone else was*   Ibid.

Page 141   *Linda Macklowe, in*   Ibid.

Page 142   *Harry was going*   Interviews with Michael Fascitelli and Robert Sorin.

Page 142   *Fascitelli found it*   Interview with Michael Fascitelli.

Page 142   *On May 24*   Michelle Coffey, "Macklowe to Sell GM Building to Boston Properties," Market Watch, May 24, 2008.

Page 142   *The GM Building*   Charles V. Bagli, "Macklowes Sell GM Building for $2.9 Billion," *New York Times*, May 25, 2008.

Page 142   *In return, public*   Records documenting Mortimer Zuckerman's purchase of the General Motors Building.

Page 142   *He paid off all*   Interview with Robert Sorin.

Page 142   *Rob Sorin figured*   Ibid.

Page 143   *But even Sorin*   Interview with Robert Sorin.

Page 143   *Harry walked into*   Interview with Robert Sorin.

Page 143   *Sorin recalled*   Ibid.

Chapter 13 The Fall That Wasn't

Page 145   *To this day*   Author's observation.

Page 145   *And there is*   Theresa Agovino, "It's Splitsville; Harry and Billy Macklowe Go Separate Ways as Father-Son Property Empire Sinks," *Crain's New York Business*, May 17, 2010.

Page 146   *In 2008, right*   Alex Frangos and Jennifer S. Forsyth, "Son Poised to Rise at Macklowe," *Wall Street Journal*, May 27, 2008.

Page 146   *Harry Macklowe's friends*   Interviews with Michael Fascitelli, Benjamin Lambert, Robert Horowitz, and Robert Sorin.

Page 146   *Rob Horowitz called*   Interview with Robert Horowitz.

Page 146   *Ben Lambert offered*   Interview with Benjamin Lambert.

Page 146   *Even Rob Sorin*   Interview with Robert Sorin.

Page 146   *On June 12*   "Harry Macklowe Steps Down as Head of Firm," Reuters, June 12, 2008.

Page 146   *On May 17*   Theresa Agovino, "It's Splitsville; Harry and Billy Macklowe Go Separate Ways as Father-Son Property Empire Sinks," *Crain's New York Business*, May 17, 2010.

Page 146   *One was his*   Julie Creswell, "With Fortune Falling, a 1 Percent Divorce," *New York Times*, February 1, 2004. Dareh Gregorian, "Living in a Dupe-Plex Big Realtor and Wife Take Legal Swings," *New York Daily News*, May 5, 2013. Julia March, "Macklowe Wins Big in Family Feud," *New York Post*, July 10, 2013. Dareh Gregorian, "Titans' Cash Clash," *New York Daily News*, March 15, 2013. Dareh Gregorian, "Estranged Wife of Real Estate Big Sues for Punitive Damages over $12.5 Million Loan," *New York Daily News*, May 5, 2013.

Page 146   *"Divorce is so*   Interview with Harry Macklowe.

Page 146   *And then there*   Interview with Harry Macklowe.

Page 146   *Harry Macklowe no longer*   Ibid.

Page 146   *"You've had an interesting*   Ibid.

Page 146   *Initially it was*   Charles V. Bagli, "Macklowes Sell GM Building for $2.9 Billion," *New York Times*, May 25, 2008.

Page 147   *The* Wall Street Journal   Jennifer Forsyth, "Zuckerman Takes Manhattan: Boston Properties Assumes Some Risk with GM Building," *Wall Street Journal*, June 11, 2008.

Page 147   *Was he "an*   Adam Piore, "Mort Zuckerman Gets Last Laugh; Mort Zuckerman and His Boston Properties," *Real Deal*, September 1, 2008.

Page 147   *Weil Gotshal*   Jennifer Forsyth, "Zuckerman Takes Manhattan: Boston Properties Assumes Some Risk with GM Building," *Wall Street Journal*, June 11, 2008. "767 Fifth Ave: August 2006 Rent Roll," August 10, 2006.

Page 147   *The building yielded*   Interview with Mortimer Zuckerman.

Page 147   *Boston Properties had*   Jennifer Forsyth, "Zuckerman Takes Manhattan: Boston Properties Assumes Some Risk with GM Building," *Wall Street Journal*, June 11, 2008. Charles V. Bagli, "Macklowes Sell GM Building for $2.9 Billion," *New York Times*, May 25, 2008.

Page 147   *He invests in*   Boston Properties, www.bostonproperties.com/.

Page 147 *The constrictions, he said* Interview with Mortimer Zuckerman.

Page 148 *In 2013 it* Gus Delaporte, "GM Building Stake Sold to International Buyers," *Commercial Observer*, May 3, 2013, http://commercialobserver.com/tag/m-safra-and-co-inc/. Retrieved June 20, 2014. Hui-yong-Yu, "GM Building Stake Said to Sell to Zhang, Safra Families," *Bloomberg Online*, June 2, 2103, www.bloomberg.com/news/2013-06-02/gm-building-stake-said-to-sell-to-zhang-safra-families.html. Retrieved June 20, 2014.

Page 148 *As of 2014* Interview with Robert Rayne.

Page 148 *It was worth more* Patrick McGeehan, "Chinese Developer Gets Minority Stake in GM Building," *New York Times*, June 3, 2013.

Page 148 *Brazil's Safra family* Anjli Raval, "Foreign Investors Buy GM Building Stake," *Financial Times,* June 3, 2013.

Page 148 *Most famously, one* Dominick Dunne, "Death in Monaco," *Vanity Fair*, December 2000.

Page 148 *In December 2002* Ian Sparks, "Ten Years for Firebug Who Killed Billionaire," *Daily Mail*, www.dailymail.co.uk/news/article-149929/Ten-years-firebug-killed-billionaire.html. Retrieved June 20, 2014.

Page 148 *A cloud of* Dominick Dunne, "Death in Monaco," *Vanity Fair*, December 2000.

Page 148 *The Safras joined* Ilaina Jonas, "Two Big Manhattan Property Deals Signal Recovery, China Interest," *Reuters News*, June 2, 2013. "Sky High Prices," *Wall Street Journal Online*, June 10, 2013, http://online.wsj.com/news/articles/SB10001424127887323495604578537681598857840#2. Retrieved June 22, 2014. "SOHO China Falls as It Denies Money Laundering: Hong Kong Mover," *Bloomberg News* (online), February 5, 2013, www.bloomberg.com/news/2013-02-06/soho-china-falls-as-it-denies-money-laundering-hong-kong-mover.html. Retrieved June 20, 2014.

Page 149 *She was born* Jianying Zha, "The Turtles: Letter from Bejing," *New Yorker*, July 11, 2005.

Page 149 *Zhang bought the* "SOHO China Falls as It Denies Money Laundering: Hong Kong Mover," *Bloomberg News* (online), February 5, 2013, www.bloomberg.com/news/2013-02-06/

soho-china-falls-as-it-denies-money-laundering-hong-kong-mover
.html. Retrieved June 20, 2014. Amy Li, "SOHO China CEO Denies
Money Laundering Scandal," *South China Morning Post*, February 8,
2013, www.scmp.com/news/china/article/1145921/soho-china-ceo-
denies-money-laundering-accusations. Retrieved June 20, 2014.
Yvonne Liu and Amy Li, "Soho China Hit by Gong Scandal," *South
China Morning Post*, February 9, 2013. Fu Tao, "The Link between
SOHO's Slumping Shares and China's Unwritten Rules," CaixinOn-
line, February 7, 2013.

Page 149   *With a net worth*   "Power Women: Zhang Xin & Family," *Forbes* (online), www.forbes.com/profile/zhang-xin/. Retrieved
June 22, 2014.

Page 149   *In November 2013*   Michael Cole, "SOHO China's
Zhang Xin Beats Out Brad Pitt to Buy NY Townhouse," Mingti-
andi: Chinese Real Estate Intelligence, November 11, 2013. www
.mingtiandi.com/real-estate/outbound-investment/soho-chinas-
zhang-xin-beats-out-brad-pitt-to-buy-ny-townhouse/.

Page 149   *"They are solid*   Interview with Mortimer Zuckerman.

Page 149   *"Is there another*   Interview with Jonathan Gray.

Page 149   *They never publicly*   Author's observation.

Page 149   *Billy Macklowe bought*   Daniel Geiger, "Vanilla-Flavored
Billy Macklowe Offers a Taste of What's to Come," *Real Estate Weekly*,
April 20, 2011.

Page 149   *He tried to*   Lauren Elkies, "Billy Macklowe," *Real Deal*,
http://therealdeal.com/closings/the-closing-billy-macklowe/. Retrieved
June 20, 2014. Daniel Geiger, "Vanilla-Flavored Billy Macklowe
Offers a Taste of What's to Come," *Real Estate Weekly*, April 20,
2011.

Page 149   *His wife Julie*   vbeauté advertisement, *Vogue*, May 2014.

Page 149   *Harry and Linda*   Interview with anonymous friend of the
Macklowe family.

Page 150   *Dealers noticed one*   Interview with anonymous art professional.

Page 150   *The Drake, or*   Eliot Brown and Craig Karmin, "Details
Revealed for Super-Tall Tower in New York," *Wall Street Journal*,
May 29, 2012. Guelda Volin, "DOB Issues Permit for City's Tall-
est Residential Tower," *Real Deal*, May 18, 2012. Theresa Agovino,

"Harry Macklowe's Second Coming," *Crain's New York Business*, September 25, 2011.

Page 150   *In October 2013*   Alan Feuer and Charles Bagli, "Harry Macklowe Gambles Again," *New York Times*, October 4, 2013.

Page 150   *It was part*   Ibid.

Page 150   *Macklowe was delighted*   Interview with Harry Macklowe.

Page 151   *To coincide with*   Author's observation.

Page 151   *That he sold*   Lily Rothman, "Rothko Fetches $75 Million at Record-Setting Sotheby's Sale," *Time*, November 14, 2012.

Page 151   *There was a*   Author's observation.

Page 151   *As he got*   Jeremiah Budin, "Harry Macklowe Buys One Wall Street, May Take It Residential," Curbed.com, May 22, 2014, http://ny.curbed.com/archives/2014/05/22/harry_macklowe_buys_one_wall_street_may_take_it_residential.php. Retrieved June 20, 2014. Eliot Brown and Keiko Morris, "Bank of Bank of New York to Sell Tower to Investor Harry Macklowe," *Wall Street Journal*, May 21, 2014.

Page 151   *"Was there any way*   Interview with Harry Macklowe.

Chapter 14 Aftermath

Page 153   *"Will he go*   Interview with Jonathan Gray.

Page 154   *And even though*   Ibid.

Page 154   *Donald Trump still*   Interview with Donald Trump.

Page 154   *At EOP's offices*   Interviews with Benjamin Lambert and Roy March.

Page 154   *And Macklowe didn't*   Interview with Benjamin Lambert.

Page 154   *In 2012 Doug*   Interview with Doug Harmon.

Page 154   *He would tell*   Interview with Michael Fascitelli.

Page 155   *Pete Briger would*   Interview with Peter Briger.

Page 155   *Rob Sorin continued*   Interview with Robert Sorin.

Page 155   *Eric Schwartz left*   Interview with Eric Schwartz.

Page 155   *He met Harry*   Interview with Robert Horowitz.

Page 155   *Rob Verrone left*   Interview with Robert Verrone.

Page 155   *Stephen Hilbert was*   Interview with Stephen Hilbert.

Page 155   *Chuck Cremens was*   Interview with Charles Cremens.

Page 155 *Rita Jenrette was* Interview with Principessa Rita Boncompagni Ludovisi.

Page 155 *She had met her new* Ariel Levy, "The Renovation," *New Yorker*, November 28, 2011.

Page 155 *Abe Wallach settled* Interview with Abraham Wallach.

Page 155 *Sheldon Solow took* Eliot Brown, "Sheldon Solow Sues (Again) over GM Building as Sale Nears," *New York Observer*, March 5, 2008.

Page 155 *The Simon Group* Carisa Chappell, "Simon Added to S&P 100," REIT.com, March 12, 2012, www.reit.com/news/articles/simon-added-sp-100. Retrieved June 20, 2014. "Simon Names Spinoff Washington Prime Group, Picks CEO," *Indianapolis Business Journal*, February 25, 2014. Eric Hawthorn, "Top 10 U.S. REITs with the Highest Regional Mall Exposure," Llenrock.com, June 20, 2012, http://llenrock.com/blog/top-10-u-s-reits-with-the-highest-regional-mall-exposure. Retrieved June 20, 2014.

Page 156 *Disque Deane faded* Interviews with Kathryn and Walter Deane.

Page 156 *Simon Benattar ran* Interview with Simon Benattar.

Page 156 *Robbie Rayne runs* Interview with Robert Rayne.

Page 156 *Sam Zell still* Interview with Samuel Zell.

Page 156 *Ira Millstein remains* Interview with Ira Millstein.

Bibliography

Ackerman, Kenneth D. *Boss Tweed: The Corrupt Pol Who Conceived the Soul of Modern New York*. Falls Church, VA: Viral History Press, 2011.

Ahamed, Liaquat. *Lords of Finance: The Bankers Who Broke the World*. New York: Penguin Press, 2009.

Alexiou, Alice Sparberg. *The Flatiron: The New York Landmark and the Incomparable City That Arose with It*. New York: Thomas Dunne Books/St. Martin's Press, 2010.

Bagli, Charles V. *Other People's Money: Inside the Housing Crisis and the Demise of the Greatest Real Estate Deal Ever Made*. New York: Dutton, 2013.

Bergsman, Steve. *Maverick Real Estate Investing: The Art of Buying and Selling Properties Like Trump, Zell, Simon and the World's Greatest Land Owners*. Hoboken, NJ: John Wiley & Sons, 2004.

Bohlin, Cywinski Jackson. *The Nature of Circumstance*. New York: Rizzoli, 2010.

Broderick, Mosette. *Triumvirate McKim, Mead & White: Art, Architecture, Scandal, and Class in America's Gilded Age*. New York: Alfred A. Knopf, 2011.

Burns, Ric (director). *New York*. Steeplechase Films, 1999.

Carey, David, and John E. Morris. *King of Capital: The Remarkable Rise, Fall, and Rise Again of Steven Schwarzman and Blackstone*. New York: Crown Business, 2010.

Cohan, William D. *The Last Tycoons: The Secret History of Lazard Frères & Co*. New York: Doubleday, 2007.

Gray, Christopher. *New York Streetscapes: Tales of Manhattan's Significant Buildings and Landmarks*. New York: Harry N. Abrams, 2003.

Gross, Michael. *740 Park: The Story of the World's Richest Apartment Building*. New York: Broadway Books, 2005.

Hunting, Mary Anne. *Edward Durrell Stone: Modernism's Populist Architect*. New York: W.W. Norton & Company, 2013.

Jaffe, Steven H., and Jessica Lautin. *Capital of Capital: Money, Banking & Power in New York City 1874–2012*. New York: Columbia University Press, 2014.

Johnson, Ben. *Money Talks, Bullshit Walks: Inside the Contrarian Mind of Billionaire Sam Zell*. New York: Penguin Books, 2009.

Lambert, Phyllis. *Building Seagram*. New Haven, CT: Yale University Press, 2013.

Lawrence, Mary Wells. *A Big Life (in Advertising)*. New York: Touchstone, 2002.

Marriott, Oliver. *The Property Boom*. London: Hamish Hamilton, 1967.

O'Brien, Timothy L. *Trump Nation: The Art of Being Donald*. New York: Warner Business Books, 2005.

Okrent, Daniel. *Great Fortune: The Epic of Rockefeller Center*. New York: Viking, 2003.

Patterson, Jerry E. *Fifth Avenue: The Best Address*. New York: Rizzoli, 1998.

Reich, Cary. *Financier: The Biography of André Meyer; A Story of Money, Power, and the Reshaping of American Business*. New York: John Wiley & Sons, 1983.

Rosenzweig, Roy, and Elizabeth Blackmar. *The Park and the People: A History of Central Park*. Ithaca, NY: Cornell University Press, 1992.

Shachtman, Tom. *Skyscraper Dreams: The Great Real Estate Dynasties of New York*. Lincoln, NE: iUniverse.com; an Author's Guild Backinprint.com edition, 2000.

Starrett, Paul. *Changing the Skyline*. New York: McGraw-Hill, 1938.

Stern, Robert A.M., Gregory Gilmartin, and Thomas Mellins. *New York 1930: Architecture and Urbanism between the Two World Wars*. New York: Rizzoli, 1987.

Stone, Hicks. *Edward Durrell Stone: A Son's Untold Story of a Legendary Architect*. New York: Rizzoli, 2011.

Trump, Donald J. *Time to Get Tough: Making America #1 Again*. Washington, DC: Regnery, 2011.

Wiseman, Carter. *I. M. Pei: A Profile in American Architecture*. New York: Harry N. Abrams, 1990.

Zeckendorf, William, and Edward McCreary. *Zeckendorf: The Autobiography of William Zeckendorf*. New York: Holt, Rinehart & Winston, 1970.

About the Author

Vicky Ward is a British-born author and investigative journalist. She is the author of the *New York Times* best seller *The Devil's Casino: Friendship, Betrayal, and the High-Stakes Games Played Inside Lehman Brothers* (John Wiley & Sons, 2010). A former contributing editor to *Vanity Fair* for 11 years, she is also the former executive editor of *Talk* magazine and features editor and news features editor of the *New York Post*. Her work has appeared in the *Financial Times*, the *Times* (London), the *New York Times*, and the *Daily Telegraph*. She holds a master's degree in English literature from Trinity Hall, Cambridge University, and has lived in New York City since 1997.

Index